Instant Messaging
in Java

Instant Messaging
in Java

The Jabber Protocols

IAIN SHIGEOKA

MANNING

Greenwich
(74° w. long.)

For electronic information and ordering of this and other Manning books,
go to www.manning.com. The publisher offers discounts on this book
when ordered in quantity. For more information, please contact:

Special Sales Department
Manning Publications Co.
209 Bruce Park Avenue   Fax: (203) 661-9018
Greenwich, CT 06830   email: orders@manning.com

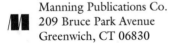

Manning Publications Co.   Copyeditor: Lois Patterson
209 Bruce Park Avenue   Typesetter: Shan Young
Greenwich, CT 06830   Cover designer: Leslie Haimes

ISBN 1-930110-46-4

Printed in the United States of America

1 2 3 4 5 6 7 8 9 10 - VHG 05 04 03 02

This book is dedicated to the Jabber community:
innovation, insight and fun. Who could ask for anything more?

contents

preface

My original background is in robotics and computer-integrated manufacturing. In both, my interests centered on solving communication problems in mission-critical systems. At the beginning, that meant assembly and C programming as well as direct participation in the lowest levels of networking protocols. Forget TCP/IP and Ethernet—we were generating packets by hand on ArcNET networks.

Networks quickly evolved and the problem shifted to an increasing need to integrate the computerized factory floor into large-scale enterprise systems. Unfortunately, manufacturing systems are horribly heterogeneous, with each machine running completely proprietary software (often with one of a kind operating systems and programming languages). In addition, it is common for manufacturing machines to be kept in service for 20–30 years or longer. Long equipment life-spans result in a surprising number of shops still using tape drives, punch cards, and other ancient computer technology.

On systems where you have a full Java 2 Standard Edition (J2SE) or better environment, Java Jini (http://www.jini.org) provides a perfect framework for gluing the various bits together. In addition, it provides a common integration environment (Java) and elegant, distributed computing facilities, such as self-healing properties and distributed transactions. As J2SE begins to find its way onto more and more devices, Jini becomes an increasingly attractive technology for system integration and coordination.

Unfortunately, J2SE isn't everywhere. The J2SE requirement for Java Jini proves to be a significant obstacle on proprietary or limited platforms. We needed a lightweight, flexible communication system to extend into these environments.

Jabber first came to my attention in late 2000. Peer-to-peer frameworks like Gnutella and JXTA were hot but lacked the robustness and predictability needed. Instant Messaging (IM) seemed like a much more promising solution.

Despite strong developer interest in IM technologies, there really wasn't much out there.[1] The largest IM systems are highly proprietary and unusable for systems where you may need to implement, extend, or control the servers. After some searching, it looked like a dead end. It appeared simpler and less expensive to create our own lightweight communication protocol from scratch.

Then I came across Jabber. It is open source, and exploits the very best features of XML, another hot technology. I was familiar with XML and understood the fundamental benefits driving its hype but had yet to see a compelling reason to use XML in my software. Jabber appeared to be that application.

Digging deeper into Jabber revealed a design that was simple and flexible. I'm a firm believer in the KISS philosophy[2] so the appeal only grew. I decided to start playing with the technology.

What finally converted me into a Jabber evangelist was the active and enthusiastic Jabber development community. Jabber is a young technology being shaped on a daily basis by corporate, student, and hobbyist contributors. Although the core of Jabber is relatively stable, many important related technologies such as Jabber security are still under active development.

You have the opportunity to make crucial decisions that shape the future of Jabber IM technology even while Fortune 500 companies are using Jabber today for critical services. In addition, the Microsoft-driven hype behind SOAP and other XML-related technologies has ignited interest from various parties in using Jabber as a way to plug into the web services world without having to become Microsoft shops. Developers like you and me are making decisions today that will determine how Jabber grows to meet tomorrow's challenges. These challenges and their potential rewards are truly exciting. Come and join us!

---

[1] Today there still aren't many IM options available to developers. Jabber remains the strongest option for people who wish to have complete access to the software and protocols, as well as control over deployment.

[2] Keep It Simple Silly. Of course, there are more colorful words that are often used for that last 'S'!

about this book

This book leads the reader in building an IM system using the Java programming language. I believe that the best way of showing how something like instant messaging is done in general is to illustrate how it is done with a particular example. Our IM system uses the Jabber protocols and architecture and we'll cover both in depth as we build our software. Once you understand how the Jabber protocols work to create an IM system, I hope that you will be able to extrapolate your experience to build other IM systems based on Jabber or other protocols if necessary.

I am also a firm believer in code as a method of communication. You can describe an algorithm to people and there will as many different interpretations of that algorithm as there are people. However, a well-written, compliable, executable piece of code removes all doubt. As a consequence, this book contains a great deal of Java source code to explain concepts with detail and rigor not included in the text discussion.

Who should read this book

This book is targeted primarily at intermediate developers, Jabber enthusiasts, and technical managers. Non-technical people who need to know about IM in general or Jabber in particular will gain the most insight from the first part of the book. The latter parts of the book contain many technical details and Java source code that you may find of lesser use if you are not a programmer.

The code examples contained within this book were written assuming an intermediate programming skill level. Server and network software require some intermediate Java programming features such as threading and sockets that may be unfamiliar to beginning programmers. These issues have been de-emphasized in the book but remain potential stumbling blocks to the unprepared.

In addition, I use several design patterns within the code examples. If you're familiar with design patterns, these examples will be easy, allowing you to understand the basic solution and concentrate on the Jabber-specific aspects of the solution. If you are not familiar with design patterns, many code examples will simply appear more complex and require more work to understand. I highly suggest that developers familiarize themselves with design patterns starting with the seminal book on the topic: *Design Patterns: Elements of Reusable Object-Oriented Software*, by Erich Gamma, Richard Helm, Ralph Johnson, and John Vlissides (Addison-Wesley, 1994).

You don't necessarily need to know Java in order to understand the code examples in this book. Java is a simple language similar enough to many other languages that even those unfamiliar with it can read the code and understand the basic operations being undertaken. However, Java developers will gain the most from the code examples.

Contents of this book

This book is split into three parts. Part 1 introduces IM and Jabber technologies and describes the basic architecture of all Jabber-based systems. In part 2, we dig into the gritty details of the core Jabber protocols and develop Java server and client software. Finally, in appendix A, I've included a condensed reference to the Jabber protocols as they stand at the time of this writing. The Jabber protocols are continuing to evolve so you should check the Jabber website (www.jabber.org) for announcements and the book's website (www.manning.com/shigeoka) for updated versions of the reference section.

Part 1—Overview

Chapter 1—Introduction to IM concepts. A non-technical introduction to IM and Jabber technologies. This is a general overview that helps us to establish a common vocabulary and introduce basic concepts. If you're familiar with Jabber IM you can skip this section.

Chapter 2—Jabber technical fundamentals. A technical overview of the Jabber architecture and protocols. We also examine the raw communication stream between the Jabber server and client to illustrate what "raw" Jabber looks like.

Part 2—Building Jabber

Chapter 3—IM concepts and Jabber protocols Examines the details of Jabber streams and packets. In addition, we write the basic Jabber server that we'll expand throughout the book. This chapter is essential for understanding the software we build in the book.

Chapter 4—The Jabber message protocols. Covers the Jabber message protocol and implements support for basic messaging in the server. In addition, we develop a "test Jabber client" to test our evolving Jabber server.

Chapter 5—The presence protocols. Covers the Jabber presence protocols and shows how they are used in the Jabber groupchat messaging protocol. We implement a groupchat manager as part of the Jabber server and expand the test client.

Chapter 6—Info/query and client registration. Covers the final core Jabber protocol, info/query, used for all protocols not covered by messaging and presence. In this chapter, we examine its use in the account registration process.

Chapter 7—Client authentication. Covers the Jabber authentication info/query protocols. The discussion and software cover all aspects of standard Jabber authentication including the proposed zero-knowledge authentication protocol.

Chapter 8—Roster and user presence. With user accounts firmly established in chapters 6 and 7, we're ready to discuss the roster info/query protocol and the user presence protocols. A user's roster stores the "buddy list" of subscribers interested in their presence status. The user presence protocols update the user's presence and subscribe users to other users' rosters.

Chapter 9—Creating a complete Jabber system. Ties up the loose ends for part 2. There is no way to complete a fully featured or "production ready" server or client within the book. This chapter describes what remains to be done and suggests ways to tackle each problem.

Chapter 10—Enterprise Jabber. We end part 2 with a look at advanced forms of Jabber systems. This includes Jabber as enterprise middleware and how Jabber fits into the "alphabet soup" of J2EE, JMS, SOAP and .NET. We'll also look at some examples of advanced Jabber applications and alternatives to Jabber technology.

Appendix—Jabber reference

We end the book with the Jabber reference. The reference does not attempt to document every aspect of any particular protocol. Instead, I provide a condensed reference that will let you quickly look up the most important information about a protocol without wading through each standard. For example, you can use the reference to look up error codes for the `<error>` packet, or the suggested sub-packets in a "normal" `<message>`.

How to use this book

I would suggest that you read chapters 1–3 in order to get a firm grasp of Jabber and the software that we build throughout the book. Chapters 4–8 build upon each other. If you are completely unfamiliar with the Jabber protocols it may be a good idea to read through them in the order presented. If you only want to learn the protocols, you can read the first section of each of those chapters as source code is presented at the end of the chapter.

If you want to know what you need to do to create a production-ready Jabber server or client, you may want to skip ahead to chapter 9. Considering that you are creating a significant server application, I don't think the remaining tasks are exceptionally difficult. However, you may wish to judge for yourself before getting too deep into the book's source code.

Finally, I imagine that many developers will like to skip ahead to chapter 10 for inspiration. I placed it at the end of the book so that you'd have the technical background to understand what would be involved in creating each system. However, you may want to skim it first to let the big ideas sink in. You can then learn about Jabber in more detail by reading chapters 3–9, and return to chapter 10 to fully appreciate the potential of the technology.

Conventions

The following typographical conventions appear throughout the book:

- Technical terms are introduced in *italic* font.
- Code examples and fragments appear in a `fixed-width` font.
- Method names are followed by two parentheses "()" to differentiate them from member variables.
- XML namespaces and attributes, as well as literal values for attributes, also appear in a `fixed-width` font.

- XML elements are surrounded by angle brackets "<>".
- Sections of code that are of special significance appear in a **`bold fixed-width`** font. Typically, these sections highlight changes made to code when compared with a previous example.
- Many sections of code have annotations which appear in the right margin.
- Some advanced topics are discussed that will not be of interest to beginning programmers. These advanced discussions have a gray background and a black diamond in the margin. Beginners can skip these sections.

The source code

I have presented most but not all of the Java source code needed to build the Java server and client covered in this book. Most of the omitted source code represents simple modifications of software covered earlier in the book. In addition, to make the source easier to read, I have omitted much of the error checking and prevention code that I would normally include in software. Keep this in mind when reviewing the code. If you decide to try and put this code into production, you'll need to add the error checking code.

Getting the source code

The full source code for this book is available online from the Manning website at www.manning.com/shigeoka. The source is contained in a zip archive that includes instructions on building and running the included software. All of the source code is released under a modified Apache (BSD) license. This means that you're free to do almost anything with the code, including selling it or building proprietary applications without any obligations.[3]

The online source differs slightly from the source shown in the book. The most visible difference is that the online source contains a logging class called Log and I have placed logging statements throughout the code to make it easier to follow what it is doing. To save space I have omitted these logging statements from the book. You can change the logging level of the Log class by changing the logging level constant set in the Log class (see source for more information).

Tools: a Java development environment

Building the Java software covered in this book requires four tools. I've tried to keep the requirements to a minimum. The following table shows you what tools

---

[3] Technically, you do have some obligations. You can't hold me responsible for anything the software does or doesn't do, or use my name to advertise the product. See the license.html file in the distribution for exact details.

you need and where to obtain them. You can learn more about each of these tools from their respective websites.

The required development tools.

Tool	Source	Description
JDK 1.3.1	http://java.sun.com or 3rd party vendor	The Java Development Kit
Ant 1.4.1	http://jakarta.apache.org	A Java build tool
JUnit 3.7	http://www.junit.org	A Java testing tool
Xerces2 2.0.0	Included with Ant	A Java XML parsing library

To set up your development environment, first obtain and install the JDK. There should be several examples included with your JDK and you should compile and run some of them to ensure that the JDK is properly installed.

The second step is to obtain the Ant build tool from the Jakarta Apache website. Unpack and install the Ant tool according to the Ant installation documentation provided both on the Ant website and in the Ant binary distribution. Make sure to also obtain the extra Ant task jar (`optional.jar`) provided as an optional part of the Ant distribution. My source code uses JUnit tests driven by an Ant task included in that jar file. Ant includes the Xerces XML parsing library

Finally, download and install the JUnit test tool. You will need to modify your Ant batch file or shell script to include the JUnit jar file in the Ant classpath. JUnit tests will be run as part of the Ant build process to ensure the software is built properly.

Building the source in this book

All of the source examples can be built using the appropriate Ant build file. To build a particular example:

- Unpack the book's source code (available at www.manning.com/shigeoka)
- Open up a terminal window or console window
- Change to the chapter directory
- Type "ant" (If your Ant batch file or shell script is not your executable path you may need to specify its full name including path. See your Ant documentation.)

The completed jar files will be created in the out/dist directory.

author online

Free access to a private Internet forum, Author Online, is included with the purchase of this book. Visit the website for detailed rules about the forum, to subscribe to and access the forum, to retrieve the code for each chapter and section, and to view updates and corrections to the material in the book. Make comments, good or bad, about the book; ask technical questions, and receive help from the author and other Jabber programmers. The forum is available at the book's website at www.manning.com/shigeoka.

Instant messaging, Java, and the Jabber protocols cover a lot of ground and I can't claim expertise in too much of it. In addition, I am certainly a student when it comes to writing technical books. In order for me to continue to learn and grow I need your feedback! In addition to comments and criticisms, I would love to hear about your experience with the software and technology and how you're using it. Or simply drop by to chat about Jabber, Java, IM, or just about anything else.

Manning's commitment to readers is to provide a venue where a meaningful dialog among individual readers and among readers and the author can take place. It is not a commitment to any specific amount of participation on the part of the author, whose contribution remains voluntary (and unpaid).

I can also be contacted directly at iainshigeoka@yahoo.com or through my website at www.metamech.com.

acknowledgments

I'd like to first thank my parents, Clifford and Blanche, who have been extremely supportive in the production of this book. From room and board to pats on the back, they've been essential to the book's completion. In addition, my brother Orin and sister Cassie have made sure to "encourage" me in their own unique ways. Thanks guys.

I'd also like to thank the Manning crew for their unflagging assistance and advice on this book. The schedule was tight but things went unexpectedly smoothly thanks to Susan Capparelle, Alex Garret, Ted Kennedy, Elizabeth Martin, Dottie Marsico, Mary Piergies, and Shan Young. I'd like to extend an especially warm thanks to Marjan Bace who was willing to take a chance on yet another book and who responded so enthusiastically to this one. In addition, Lois Patterson deserves special thanks for her help in turning my spotty writing into a professional quality manuscript and doing so under incredible time pressures.

The book also benefited from the reviews of several technical experts. Many of the best, most accurate, and most insightful bits are due to these reviewers. The remaining errors are entirely my fault. Thanks to Bill Abbas, Chris Chen, Ryan Eatmon, David Falck, Harold Gottschalk, Gregory Graham, Julian Missig, Jim Schultz, Max Metral, and Thomas Muldowney.

Finally, I'd like to thank the Jabber community for creating and fueling this exciting Jabber phenomenon. It's been a great ride so far and the future looks bright indeed.

about the cover illustration

The figure on the cover of this book is a "Gobenador de la Abisinia," the governor of Abyssinia, today called Ethiopia. While the exact meaning of his office and responsibilities is for us lost in historical fog, there is no doubt that we are facing a man of authority and power. The illustration is taken from a Spanish compendium of regional dress customs first published in Madrid in 1799. The book's title page states:

> *Coleccion general de los Trages que usan actualmente todas las Nacionas del Mundo desubierto, dibujados y grabados con la mayor exactitud por R.M.V.A.R. Obra muy util y en special para los que tienen la del viajero universal*

Which we translate, as literally as possible, thus:

> *General collection of costumes currently used in the nations of the known world, designed and printed with great exactitude by R.M.V.A.R. This work is very useful especially for those who hold themselves to be universal travelers*

Although nothing is known of the designers, engravers, and workers who colored this illustration by hand, the "exactitude" of their execution is evident in this drawing. The "Gobenador de la Abisinia" is just one of many figures in this colorful collection. Their diversity speaks vividly of the uniqueness and individuality of the world's towns and regions just 200 years ago. This was a time when the dress codes of two regions separated by a few dozen miles identified people uniquely as belonging to one or the other. The collection brings to life a sense of isolation and distance of that period and of every other historic period except our own hyperkinetic present.

Dress codes have changed since then and the diversity by region, so rich at the time, has faded away. It is now often hard to tell the inhabitant of one continent from another. Perhaps, trying to view it optimistically, we have traded a cultural and visual diversity for a more varied personal life. Or a more varied and interesting intellectual and technical life.

We at Manning celebrate the inventiveness, the initiative, and the fun of the computer business with book covers based on the rich diversity of regional life of two centuries ago brought back to life by the pictures from this collection.

Part I

Instant messaging primer

Chapters 1 and 2 present an overview of instant messaging using the Jabber protocols from a general and technical perspective. When you've read these two chapters, you should know the basics of how Java instant messaging using the Jabber protocols works. We will also explore the potential of Java IM systems and the problems facing us in building them. This introduction will get us ready to dive into the technical details of the Jabber protocols in part II.

Introduction to IM concepts

1

In this chapter

- The benefits of instant messaging technology for Java developers
- How the Jabber instant messaging protocols work
- The core concepts of instant messaging in Jabber
- The benefits and drawbacks of the Jabber protocols

Instant messaging (IM) systems using the Java programming language are poised to become a major part of both consumer and enterprise networking, and will play a core communication role similar to email.

Messaging of course has always been a core feature of the Internet. For example, one of the first and still most pervasive Internet technologies is email. It remains an Internet killer app. However, we all know that Internet communication can be even more interesting and powerful than "plain old email." We should be able to better exploit it as an inexpensive medium for transferring data almost instantaneously. And that is the aim of this book.

Most of the examples and IM issues discussed here are from the point of view of an enterprise developer interested in creating systems for medium or large businesses. This is primarily a bias on my part, as my projects tend to fall into this category. However, the same issues that face enterprises also will be important to any other developer who wants to create reliable, secure systems.

To make the discussion concrete, we'll implement an IM system in Java that complies with the Jabber protocols (which you can find at www.jabber.org). By examining the Jabber protocols in particular, we'll get a real sense for what makes a working IM system tick and why I think they may very well be the best ones to implement in the fragmented field of IM. Finally, the Jabber protocols have suffered from a lack of documentation that I hope this book begins to address.

In this chapter, we'll examine IM systems in general and Jabber in particular. The discussion will be largely nontechnical so we can concentrate on why and where we need IM. Discussion of the technical aspects of the Jabber protocols will occupy the remainder of the book and explain the *how* of Jabber. We will develop a basic Jabber server and client in Java throughout chapters 3–8 to help make the concepts concrete. The chapter closes with a look at the benefits and drawbacks associated with Jabber IM.

1.1   *Background on messaging*

The idea of instant messaging has been around for a long time. All of the visible IM features like one-on-one chat and group chats existed in other Internet applications long before IM entered the scene. For example, the classic Unix `talk` application allowed users to chat over the network years before IM ever appeared, and group chats have been carried out on Internet Relay Chat (IRC) systems almost as long as `talk` has been around.

The innovation in today's IM systems is the packaging of these separate systems into a managed messaging platform. Jabber takes this further and establishes a *universal messaging address* and the concept of *presence* that can be applied to that address for an even simpler communication experience. A common address and presence are relatively simple technologies that have existed in other forms. However, it's the packaging of the concepts into a single, easy to use, cohesive messaging system that has really caught on. The need for ease of use has increased as more people (many of whom have less technical knowledge or inclination than earlier Internet users) join the network community.

IM addresses are an extension of the well-established email addresses almost everyone has today. However, your email address can be used only to receive email. In contrast, IM ties many message types together using a single IM address (figure 1.1). In an IM system, you can receive a message, chat, or groupchat[1] with a person using one IM address.

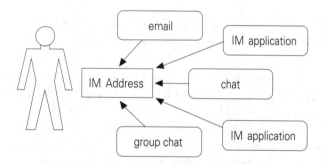

Figure 1.1 IM addresses serve as universal communication destinations. They aggregate many different messaging sources into a single user message endpoint.

Chat and group chat are conversational, and require you to be online at the same time as the person you are chatting with. To make the online rendezvous simple, your IM presence will constantly inform other users when you are online and available for chatting (figure 1.2). IM presence makes communication through IM

---

[1] IM messages are like memos or emails and tend to be complete like a letter. Chat and groupchat allows you to quickly exchange short text messages in a conversation. Each individual chat or groupchat message is like a sentence taken out of a telephone conversation; it doesn't make sense unless you know what has been said before. The difference between chat and groupchat is that chat is a one-on-one conversation while groupchat is a chat among more than two people.

systems similar to striking up conversations around the water cooler. You can easily see who is available to talk, and casually start conversations.

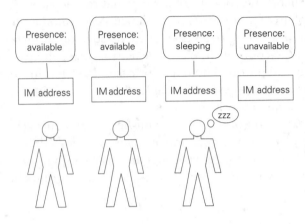

Figure 1.2
Presence shows at a glance who you can communicate with, and the best type of messaging to use (chat, messages, etc).

Older chat systems like Unix `talk` work similarly to the phone system in the sense that they lack presence. When attempting to chat, you have to make blind calls to the person with whom you want to converse, hoping he or she is available to answer the call. Unlike the phone system, though, most people are not available to talk online as much as they are with the phone so the chance of finding someone "at home" online is greatly reduced.

The simplicity and integration of IM systems first caught on with the consumer market. The most successful of these consumer systems is AIM (AOL Instant Messenger) that introduced IM to the mainstream consumer and encouraged its large membership to embrace the technology. The consumer market for IM continues to grow and many opportunities exist for the enterprising developer.

Despite the large consumer market for IM, most of the development community is interested in the opportunities for applying IM technologies in the enterprise (table 1.1). First, enterprises live or die by their ability to communicate within the company and with partners and customers. IM provides new communication channels that are well-suited to many messaging tasks.

Table 1.1   An IDC report's projections for IM usage in the enterprise and consumer markets.[2]

Year	Enterprise IM (messages/year)	Consumer IM (messages/year)
2001	145	262
2003	626	409
2005	1.2B	800

One of the most promising applications of IM in the enterprise is in the area of customer relationship management (CRM) or customer service. First, IM provides yet another way for a company to communicate with its customers. In addition, IM allows you to plug in to the customer's experience to provide better support.

Imagine a computer customer whose software application has just crashed. They start the Help utility that came with the application. The utility is actually a customized IM client. The client joins a chat group dedicated to users of the application. The user can ask anyone online for help. If there is no one available, the client contacts an automated chatbot[3] on the IM system. The chatbot can ask basic questions about the problem and use that information to route the user to the best technical support expert at the company.

Notice how the customer is instantly connected to support resources once a problem emerges. In addition, IM allows you to provide guided assistance starting with free online user groups. Automated chatbots can monitor the customer's progress, make suggestions, and eventually lead them to a company employee that can help. The filtering of simple problems by the free user group can eliminate many customer service incidents that drain profits and reduce customer satisfaction. Since IM is worldwide, your user community has a global reach that is very handy when customers want help outside of your business hours.

In addition to the added communication capabilities, IM provides an enterprise. It provides cost savings. Jabber Inc., a commercial vendor of Jabber software and services, reports significant savings when an IM system is properly integrated into the enterprise.[4]

---

[2] Jennifer DiSabatino, "Win XP to Include Instant Messaging," *Computer World,* June 11, 2001.

[3] Chatbots are special IM client applications that are completely automated. They typically provide services to IM users such as logging conversations, telling you the time, or providing online help. We'll investigate the full spectrum what you can do with chatbots in chapter 10.

[4] See Jabber.com Inc. promotional materials available at www.jabber.com/downloads.

Messaging between individuals is not the only benefit IM can provide to an enterprise. Businesses must also allow computers to communicate with each other. This is true whether the computers are internal to the company such as when accounting applications access customer service databases, or when the computer communication is between business partners in business-to-business (B2B) exchanges (figure 1.3).

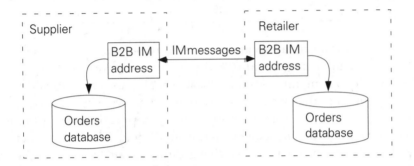

Figure 1.3   IM systems are being used for B2B data exchange including the heavily hyped web services initiatives such as Microsoft .NET.

Using messaging frameworks for computer communication is not a new idea. Products like IBM MQSeries, Micosoft MSMQ, TIBCO Rendezvous, Open Horizon Ambrosia, and Modulus InterAgent have been in enterprise use for years. The benefits of messaging in the enterprise have been well-demonstrated.

In fact, the Java 2 Enterprise Edition (J2EE) includes the Java Message Service (JMS) standard libraries to provide a standard Java interface to messaging systems for enterprise computing. The power and flexibility of Java and enterprise messaging-oriented middleware (MOM) have made the adoption of JMS happen quickly. Most enterprise messaging system vendors support JMS.

For example, imagine you are a telecom company providing local telephone services to residences. You want to create a computer system that will help you handle service problems. Let's consider the scenario where a telephone line has been cut. An IM-based system can log the problem as an IM message and route it to a trouble desk. The trouble desk operator receives the message and knows that she must dispatch a work crew to the site. She can check the IM presence of the work crews, find one that's available, and send a trouble ticket to repair the line.

We can also add expert system functionality to the system by modifying an existing expert system so that it acts as an IM client and receives copies of incoming trouble desk IM messages. It recognizes that a "line down" problem activates several service level agreement (SLA) contracts. In addition, there are several alternate phone lines that service the same area, and traffic can be switched to these if the problem will last longer than a few hours. The expert system sends more trouble tickets to the trouble desk operator alerting her to other actions she needs to take and offering suggestions on solutions. In most cases, the suggestions are routine and she can simply approve the expert system's suggestions allowing it to follow proper procedures.

This example is not far-fetched. Telecom companies spend millions every year developing and maintaining systems with these capabilities. A few innovative companies are experimenting with messaging technologies as the basis for next-generation versions of these systems that are more capable, and less expensive to create and maintain.

If the industry's predictions for the growth of IM in the enterprise prove true, it is obvious that IM systems will become a fundamental part of any enterprise system, just as web, database, and email servers are today. There are many opportunities for IM systems to expand out of simple messaging to meet enterprise needs, perhaps filling in the roles currently filled by JMS systems. Alternatively, existing enterprise messaging systems may wish to expand their capabilities to include IM. The question facing organizations that need to meet the IM needs of today and in the future is: What IM system should they use?

Jabber is a compelling IM solution that is well-suited to meet today's and tomorrow's IM needs. Jabber is not a particular piece of software. Instead, it is an open, freely available set of protocols for building IM systems. Existing messaging systems can implement the Jabber protocols to add IM to their list of features. Alternatively, new systems are being built from the ground up to support the Jabber protocols and prepare for the rapidly expanding responsibilities being assigned to IM systems.

Alternatively, you can use the existing Jabber network supported by standard Jabber servers as a foundation on which you can build specialized applications (figure 1.4). Jabber takes care of the details of messaging, leaving you free to concentrate on your application. An excellent example of this is the next generation of file-sharing applications[5] and games being built on top of existing IM systems.

---

[5] One of the most popular, next-generation file sharing systems is Madster (www.madster.com) which operates on top of AIM. You may be more familiar with its previous name: Aimster. These IM-based systems are picking up where Napster left off.

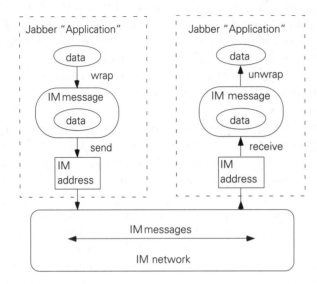

Figure 1.4
Jabber IM systems
can serve as a
generic messaging
network
for distributed or
collaborative
applications.

For example, imagine creating a massive online game where thousands of people participate in a single game universe. Ordinarily, you would create both game clients and a game server. The game server would be hosted on an online game hosting service. All communications between the clients and the game server would be proprietary and would require you to design and implement the various parts from the ground up.

However, if you use an IM system, your game clients can create proprietary data, but wrap them inside normal IM messages. The game can send these messages over existing IM networks like Jabber, to other players. Your game network can host an almost unlimited number of players because it is being hosted by the almost unlimited capacity of the underlying IM network. In addition, your game network avoids the expense and hassle of creating and maintaining custom game servers.

Your server is now another special IM client called a chatbot that maintains the state of the game universe. You don't have to worry about inventing a messaging or routing system, nor does your server have to do anything to support the massive number of connections that IM systems give you for free. You can concentrate on writing your game, leaving the network issues to the IM system.

Sound like something you're interested in? With all of the power that IM systems give you, it may be hard to believe that Jabber is a free, open system, whose inventors want you to use it for your own purposes. Let's take a look at how Jabber became the system it is today.

1.1.1 *A brief history of Jabber*

The Jabber project began in early 1998 as the brainchild of Jeremie Miller. The project quickly grew and evolved. It garnered wide public attention when it was discussed on the popular developer discussion website Slashdot (www.Slashdot.org) in January 1999.

The core Jabber protocols matured and the 1.0 release of the open source reference Jabber server was released in May 2000. The core Jabber protocols that were implemented in the 1.0 release of the reference server have remained relatively unchanged to this day.

From its beginnings, the Jabber development community has tried to create IM standards and encourage interoperability between IM systems. These cooperative efforts are in direct contrast to the behavior of other popular IM providers that actively work to keep their systems proprietary and isolated from other IM networks.

As part of the Jabber IM standards effort, in June 2000 the Jabber community submitted the Jabber protocols as a Request for Comments (RFC) to the Internet Engineering Task Force (IETF)[6] as part of its Instant Messaging and Presence Protocol (IMPP) standard. The IETF maintains some of the most important Internet standards including those for email and Internet addresses. Unfortunately, the IMPP effort bogged down and as of this writing appears to be going nowhere fast. Jabber has also tried to participate in other standardization efforts like IMUnified (www.imunified.org) and the Presence and Availability Management Forum (www.pamforum.org) with varying degrees of success.[7]

In May 2001 the Jabber community (www.jabber.org) and Jabber Inc. (www.jabber.com) created the Jabber Software Foundation (foundation.jabber.org).[8] The Jabber Software Foundation is an organization similar to the successful Apache Foundation. Its charter clearly shows the Jabber community's dedication to open standards and interoperability.

---

[6] The IETF website is at www.ietf.org.

[7] Jabber's success at creating Internet standards for IM have mirrored that of the IM community in general, which is to say its success has been "zero." I'm not sure if this is an indication of the immaturity and proprietary nature of IM today or a factor inherent to the IM community or its technology. I would hazard a guess that it's the former, but a cynic would claim the latter. In any case, standards are desperately needed and work continues within the Jabber community to promote and push for standardization.

> **JABBER SOFTWARE FOUNDATION CHARTER**
> The Jabber Software Foundation shall provide direct organizational assistance
> and indirect technical assistance to the Jabber Community in carrying out its mis-
> sion. Direct organizational assistance will include brand management, logistical
> support, legal assistance, press relations, and communication facilities. Indirect
> technical assistance will include project management, protocol specification,
> standards activities, documentation support, and site development. The Jabber
> Software Foundation will not make technical decisions for Jabber but will help
> the Jabber Community to make technical decisions more effectively. All activities
> and proceedings will be openly accessible and published. Jabber Software Foun-
> dation Announcement: http://jabber.org/?oid=1309.

The Jabber Software Foundation is still in its infancy but I have great expectations
for it. I'm particularly interested in using the Foundation to clarify and formalize
the existing Jabber standards into a form that will allow Jabber technology to be
rapidly adopted by the wider development community. This book is an effort
toward that goal. This book at least begins to address the need for better documentation.

As Jabber moves forward, much work remains to be done. Further standardization work is still under way. In addition, new standards are being proposed to
extend the Jabber protocols beyond simple IM to meet the wider needs for electronic messaging of all forms. These changes include better security, and support for enterprise requirements such as transactions, quality of service, and
delivery guarantees.

1.1.2 *Goals of the Jabber project*

In many ways, the Jabber project's goal is simply to build a better IM system supporting real-time presence and messaging. From my discussions with other Jabber
developers, the underlying goals seem to really be about defining what "better"
means. For most Jabber developers, better means:

---

[8] There is a tight link between the Jabber community and Jabber Inc. (usually called Jabber.com or jc).
Jabber Inc. employs most of the "core" members of the Jabber community and developers including
Jeremie Miller, the creator of Jabber. However Jabber Inc. has been earnest in its efforts to keep the
Jabber community and Jabber standards open. The Foundation is primarily an effort to formalize Jabber Inc.'s commitment to open Jabber standards and provide a legal entity to represent the Jabber community's interests (especially when they don't necessarily match that of Jabber Inc.). Many of the board
members of the Foundation are Jabber Inc. employees; however there are enough outsiders on the
board to keep Jabber commercial interests balanced against that of the community.

- *A completely open system and standards*—Unlike other systems, Jabber will be completely open, thus allowing anyone to create Jabber implementations at no cost and with no strings attached.

- *Open, XML-based technology*—Extensible Markup Language (XML is an enabling technology with many benefits with respect to flexibility, availability, and ease of use. The use of XML helps to "future proof" the Jabber protocols. At the same time, XML is a well-known technology that people are interested in using. There is also an extremely wide selection of tools for modeling, analyzing, programming, and authoring XML.

- *Interoperability with other* IM *systems*—The value of a communication system increases with the number of people with whom you can communicate. Optimally, a user of an IM system should be able to IM with any other user regardless of the underlying IM system. Jabber will maximize its value by working with as many other IM systems as possible.

- *Simple protocols*—Simple protocols are easier to design and implement. In addition, for most Jabber developers, simple things have an inherent appeal that we strive for constantly.

- *Simplifying the responsibilities of clients whenever possible*—There will be many clients and few servers in any Jabber system. It makes sense to design the Jabber system so that writing clients is as simple as possible. In addition, clients may run on resource-constrained systems so reducing their needs increases the possible types of clients.

- *Control over the system*—No organization, group, or service provider should be able to control the system. Jabber's design allows anyone to create a Jabber server and run their own Jabber network as they see fit.

These unwritten goals seem to be commonly held among Jabber community members. They represent an open, self-reliant community that sees the benefits in sharing technology and knowledge whether you are an open-source or commercial developer. From these basic goals, the Jabber community has produced a feature-rich IM framework.

1.2 What is Jabber?

Jabber IM means different things to different people. End users typically associate Jabber with the Jabber IM system as a whole, just as they consider the Web to mean the entire web system including web servers, web clients and the protocols and data structures that power the World Wide Web. Developers often confuse the Jabber open source reference implementation of a Jabber server called jabberd[9] for the Jabber protocols that it supports. For the purposes of this book, we'll restrict the discussion of Jabber IM to the Jabber protocols and messaging model.

One of Jabber's most discussed advantages is its truly open nature. The Jabber protocols and data formats are all documented either directly in the Jabber standards documents or as source code in the freely available Jabber reference server. This is in stark contrast to all other major IM systems that use proprietary standards.

Jabber's advantages don't end there. Its use of XML-based data formats exploits the popularity and extensibility of XML. In addition, Jabber uses a simple, distributed client/server architecture. The combination of the simplicity of the basic client/server communication model with the scalability of distributed servers makes it well-suited to the dynamic environments that IM systems will be used in the future.

Let's break down Jabber technology to get an overview of how it works.

1.2.1 *Jabber's XML-based data formats*

If Jabber's open standards are its primary political and business advantage, its use of XML as its standard data format is its crucial technical advantage. XML is a World Wide Web Consortium (W3C) standard that defines a standard, generic data format for documents. Its primary technical advantages are its simplicity, extensibility, and a compromise between easy human and machine readability.

All Jabber communications involve the exchange of Jabber packets, each being a well-formed XML fragment. These XML fragments can be considered XML subdocuments within the Jabber communication stream. For example, to send a message to iain@shigeoka.com, you would send a Jabber packet that looks like this:

```
<message to='iain@shigeoka.com'>
 <subject>How are you today?</subject>
 <body>Just thought I'd drop a line and see what you're up to.</body>
</message>
```

Even if you don't know anything about XML you can probably figure out what each part of this XML fragment does.[10] If you are XML-savvy, Jabber defines all its packets in standard XML Document Type Definitions (DTD) and uses XML namespaces extensively to define both its own standard packets, and provide

---

[9] The `Jabberd` reference server development is continuing along two separate paths. `Jabberd` will continue to improve and expand for the foreseeable future. It provides the definitive reference implementation of the current Jabber protocols that we'll cover in this book. A revised set of Jabber protocols, referred to as Jabber Next Generation (JNG), is in development. A new reference server named `Jabberd` will be written to implement these protocols when they are settled upon.

mechanisms for you to easily extend Jabber to accommodate your own custom packets while staying Jabber-compliant.

XML NAMESPACES AND JABBER

◆ XML *namespaces* are designed to isolate XML document tag definitions. As the name implies, a namespace defines a separate space where names are unique. Thus, I can create two namespaces like baking and money that use the same tag <bread>.[11] The tag <bread> means different things within the two XML namespaces but there is no confusion between the reuse of the name because each is defined in the context of its namespace. You can fully qualify a particular name by prefixing the normal local tag name with the namespace. So we might use <money:bread> to buy <baking:bread>.

In the hierarchical XML data model, you can create default namespaces that apply to all child elements by using the xmlns attribute. An XML document for our bread example may look like the following:

```
<MyStuff>
 <item xmlns='money'>
  <bread>10</bread>
  <currency>dollar</currency>
 </item>
 <item xmlns='baking'>
  <bread>rye</bread>
  <size>loaf</size>
 </item>
</MyStuff>
```

As it is being parsed, the document creates a stream of data that can be loosely translated as:

- You've got some stuff.
- In your stuff, you've got an "item" entity. All its children will be in the money namespace.
- You have a "bread" entity. Its value is 10. Done with "currency."
- You've got a "currency" entity and its value is "dollar."
- Done with "item." You have left the money namespace.

---

[10] If you aren't familiar with XML, I highly recommend getting a basic understanding of it. You don't need to know anything about XML in particular to program Jabber clients or servers. However, knowledge of XML and its basic vocabulary will make it easier to understand discussions of the Jabber packet formats. A good place to start is *XML Family of Specifications* by Danny Vint (Manning) or *Java & XML* by Brett McLaughlin (O'Reilly).

[11] Bread is a slang term for money.

- You've got another "item" entity. Its children will be in the "baking" namespace.
- You have a "bread" entity. Its value is "rye." Done with "bread."
- You have a "size" entity and its value is "loaf." Done with "size."
- Done with "item."
- That's all the stuff you have.

Notice how namespaces avoid confusion between the uses of the `<bread>` tag. In addition, you can define the data format for `<mystuff>` as simply containing zero or more `<item>` entities. You don't need to know anything about the item namespaces or what they will contain.

Jabber cleverly plays with namespaces to create an extremely flexible protocol. It defines the basics of the Jabber protocol in three namespaces (`stream`, `jabber:client`, and `jabber:server`) containing only a handful of standard entities. However each of the core entities are extended by defining new namespaces. This lets the foundations of the Jabber protocols remain stable and well-defined, yet allows the community to constantly add new namespace extensions including custom namespaces that don't break the Jabber protocols.

In our example, we might define a "my stuff" standard that allows you to send me a list of your stuff. It will always start with `<mystuff>` and contain one or more `<item>` packets. I know about the money and baking namespaces so I can understand what is inside of those items. However, we may decide to add a `playstation2games` namespace in the future. If I get such a packet and don't know about the `playstation2games` namespace I just ignore whatever is inside of the `<item>` packet; nothing breaks. I know it is an `<item>`, but I don't know what it is (other than it's a `playstation2games`). However I can still properly handle it like an `<item>`.

This feature is especially important for Jabber servers who may relay packets with contents they don't understand. Clients are free to invent their own protocols, protect them with custom namespaces, and still send them over generic Jabber networks. XML namespaces also provide freedom to the Jabber community to improve the Jabber protocols while preserving the integrity of the Jabber network.

Unless you've been sleeping for the past year or two, I'm sure I don't need to tell you that XML is one of the current hot technologies. It is a core web standard and is being adopted by enterprise programmers as the lingua franca of corporate data exchange. As with all hot technologies, XML is heavily buzzword-compliant.

In the case of XML, the most touted XML buzzwords are:

- *Open*—As a W3C standard, XML is on track to replace HTML on the web and will be used extensively in future web standards such as messaging (SOAP—Simple Object Access Protocol), and graphics (SVG—Scalable Vector Graphics). The open XML standard meshes well with the open design and philosophy of Jabber.

- *Simple*—One of XML's primary design goals is to maximize the simplicity of creating and reading (parsing) XML formatted data. This simplicity translates into simpler software making it easier to build and support software that uses XML data formats. Jabber exploits XML's simplicity to make it easier to write Jabber software. XML also allows the Jabber protocols to target a wider variety of platforms such as embedded systems.

- *Flexible*—XML is a generic data formatting language. It provides mechanisms like schemas, DTDs, and namespaces to allow users to create customized definitions of XML documents for their own uses. Jabber heavily exploits DTDs and namespaces to harness this flexibility as well as preserve flexibility so users can further extend Jabber while staying compliant.

- *Portable*—XML documents are simple, marked-up text files that can be sent over the network and read on pretty much any platform. XML support transcends programming languages and operating systems. Most common programming environments such as Java, C/C++, Delphi/Pascal, Perl, and so forth support XML with standard libraries.

This book focuses on Java Jabber programming. It is logical to ask if Java and XML are a good combination. The answer is a resounding "Yes!" In fact, a common joke among Java enthusiasts is that "XML gives Java something to do," referring to the fact that before XML many considered Java a solution in search of a problem.

Sun Microsystems (www.sun.com)is aware of the use of Java and XML and created a standard Java XML library package with all Java XML technologies packaged together for easy use. XML parsing support is being added to the standard Java libraries in the 1.4 release of the Java Development Kit (JDK).

In fact, the buzz surrounding XML and Java is a stronger advantage for Jabber and its XML protocols than many of its other advantages. As with many software-related technologies, building a critical mass in the development community is more important than the technical merits of the technology itself. XML and Java is a perfect example of this.

The strong interest in XML and Java has created a huge market of tools, books, programming libraries, and third-party experts (consultants, contract programming firms, etc.). This market legitimizes both XML and Java, and helps to ensure that anything based on Java and XML will be compatible with future technologies. It appears that we'll be using XML for all sorts of programming problems for a some time to come. However, even if it doesn't work out that way, enough people are committed to XML that new technologies will almost certainly continue to offer XML support or conversion tools.

The use of XML in the Jabber protocols is an excellent start in creating an accessible, flexible IM system. However XML alone is not enough to make Jabber truly interesting. The complementary breakthrough with Jabber is its simple, scalable architecture.

1.2.2 *Jabber's simple architecture*

The Jabber messaging model follows the well-understood client/server architecture. Jabber clients only communicate with Jabber servers in their Jabber domain.[12] Jabber domains break the entire IM universe into separate zones of control, each supported and managed by a separate Jabber server. This is in contrast with most IM systems that use one centralized server for the whole IM system.[13] In Jabber, messages pass from the sender's client, to the sender's server, to the recipient's server,[14] to the recipient's client.

Jabber is client/server

The basic Jabber communication model follows the simple and well-understood client/server architecture model. In client/server systems, the client displays information to the end user and handles user requests. Information is passed from the client to a server that offers well-defined services (figure 1.5).

---

[12] This statement is an over-simplification. Normal Jabber messaging occurs through the server. However, clients are always free to send data directly to each other through any means at their disposal. How to do so, though, is not covered by the Jabber standards. Jabber does provide an out-of-band packet to help clients arrange for these direct, client-to-client communications. However the client-to-client exchange does not occur within the Jabber system.

[13] A central server is the IM system architecture for services like AIM, Microsoft Messenger, and Yahoo! Messenger.

[14] If the sender and receiver both use the same Jabber server, this step is not necessary.

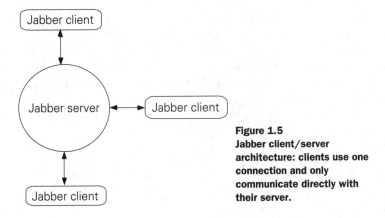

Figure 1.5
Jabber client/server
architecture: clients use one
connection and only
communicate directly with
their server.

In Jabber, the client/server model is heavily weighted to favor the creation of simple clients. Most of the processing and IM logic is carried out on the server. Minimal Jabber client responsibilities give Jabber client developers the most flexibility in creating Jabber IM clients that fit the needs of users. Embedded and other limited resource environments can support simple Jabber clients. Heavyweight Jabber clients can concentrate on the user interface and ease of use issues. Finally, the simplicity of creating Jabber clients encourages people to write more clients on different platforms using different programming languages, helping to spread Jabber access far and wide.

Unlike distributed systems, such as those based on peer-to-peer technology,[15] the simple Jabber client/server architecture provides an excellent opportunity to implement centralized control of Jabber domains and provides opportunities for enforcing quality of service guarantees. This is especially important for enterprises that may need to enforce corporate communication policies. In addition, as IM systems are used for mission-critical messaging beyond direct user communication, it will become increasingly important to ensure certain levels of quality of service can be met.

Jabber distributed servers build the Jabber network

Just as the current email system allows separate, distributed email servers to manage email domains, Jabber servers manage a Jabber domain. Like email, Jabber domains are defined by an Internet domain name. So a Jabber server that manages

---

[15] Peer-to-peer describes a family of technologies that allows network systems to be created without the use of a central server.

the `shigeoka.com` Jabber domain will handle all outgoing and incoming messages for Jabber users in that domain. Jabber addresses, known as Jabber IDs, specify the user's Jabber domain following an '@' character just as email addresses do.

This hub-and-spoke distributed server architecture (figure 1.6) is quite common in messaging systems. Email systems use this architecture. In addition, this is a standard architecture for enterprise messaging servers including the most popular ones that implement the JMS standard.

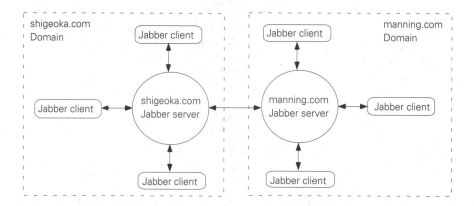

Figure 1.6   Distributed Jabber servers define and control Jabber domains in a hub and spoke architecture. Jabber servers that exchange messages with other Jabber servers create federated domains and expand their Jabber network. Here we see two Jabber servers (shigeoka.com and manning.com) federated to form a Jabber network encompassing both domains.

Creating a distributed Jabber server architecture limits a Jabber server's responsibilities to only handling messaging with its own users and other Jabber servers. A small Jabber server can support a single user and consume minimal resources while large Jabber servers may support hundreds of thousands of users and require large data centers.

Breaking up the server responsibilities so that each server is only in charge of its own Jabber domain helps the Jabber network to grow without requiring massive resources from any particular Jabber server or Jabber domain. As each Jabber domain adds more users, it is in charge of adding its own capacity for handling the increased traffic from those users. You can limit a Jabber server's resource requirements simply by limiting the number of users in its Jabber domain.

This divide-and-conquer strategy helps to level the playing field for Jabber participants. You don't need to be AOL or Microsoft to host your own Jabber system. In addition, it gives each Jabber domain control and autonomy over its own little corner of the Jabber IM network while encouraging interoperability so that your users can communicate with other Jabber servers. These same advantages have been the primary reasons why the current Internet email system is so pervasive and maintains such a high degree of cohesiveness.

In many ways, Jabber's simple, client/server architecture with distributed servers is old technology. There is nothing really innovative about Jabber's messaging model. In my opinion, this is a major strength rather than a weakness. IM's major innovation is the addition of presence to communication systems. Jabber's innovation is the use of an open XML data format for the data being sent in the communication system. Adding any more innovations at the same time would have probably resulted in a much less elegant and easy to build system.

1.2.3 Jabber's four core concepts

Four central Jabber concepts form the basis for Jabber systems. Before we can look at the Jabber protocols, we must understand these concepts as they exist in Jabber. They're straightforward but it is important for us all to be working with the same set of messaging concepts before setting off into Jabber's details. These four central concepts are:

- Jabber domains
- Users and resources
- Jabber IDs
- Presence

Jabber systems organized into networks and domains

The Jabber universe is broken down into several logical sets and subsets of entities. From the largest to the smallest, we have a Jabber:

- *Network*—All Jabber domains that exchange messages. A network must contain at least one domain.
- *Domain*—A subset of the network containing all entities that handle or belong to a domain. Jabber domains provide local control over parts of the Jabber network while still communicating with users outside of the Jabber domain. A domain is defined by:
  - A valid Internet domain name address.
  - The server that handles connections to that address.
- *Server*—A logical entity that manages a Jabber domain.
- *User*—An entity representing a *logical* message delivery endpoint. Jabber data packets are usually addressed to users, but are always delivered to a resource. Users are managed on the server with user accounts.

- *Resource*—An entity representing a *particular* message delivery endpoint for a user. All Jabber data packets are delivered to resources. Jabber clients play the role of Jabber resources.

A minimal Jabber network is composed of a single Jabber server handling one Jabber domain, and the Jabber clients that use that server, as shown in figure 1.7. Jabber servers can exchange messages using the `jabber:server` protocols. When servers do this, they are federating their Jabber domains to expand the Jabber network.[16]

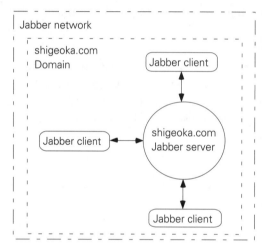

Figure 1.7
A minimal Jabber network with a single domain managed by a Jabber server and zero or more clients.

Server federations are the primary method for Jabber networks to grow. Many Jabber servers are configured to federate with any other Jabber server on Internet. This essentially creates a single Internet Jabber network containing thousands of users.

It is also possible to bridge Jabber systems by using the client protocols to exchange messages between domains as shown in figure 1.8. I'll refer to this process as *bridging* to differentiate it from the privileged server-side access that server federation requires.

---

[16] Jabber servers find each other by opening connections to the domain name address of other servers (see chapter 9 for more details). Jabber server administrators can play some "DNS tricks" such as allowing multiple physical machines to act as the same logical Jabber server. This trick, commonly referred to as *round-robin DNS*, creates *server farms* in advanced Jabber installations. Jabber servers are also free to develop their own proprietary server-to-server connections in addition to (or as a replacement for) support for standard Jabber server-to-server connections if needs demand.

In jabberd, the Jabber server reference implementation written in C, a hybrid bridging solution is provided by server components known as transports. They have privileged Jabber server access but typically use client protocols to access foreign systems.

For example, one of the most popular and most controversial is an AIM transport. The AIM transport lets Jabber users transparently send messages to AIM users and track AIM users presence, an important capability when most IM users are currently using AIM. However you should be careful about creating transports or bridges as it may violate the usage policies for foreign services. AOL in particular has been resistant to AIM transports.

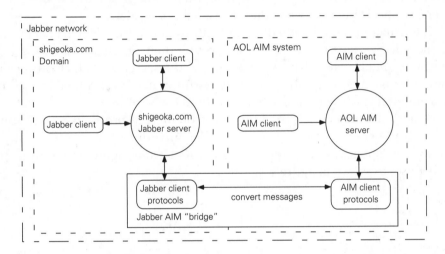

Figure 1.8   **Jabber clients or server components known as transports can bridge IM systems by serving as bridges. Here a Jabber AIM bridge acts on behalf of Jabber users to deliver AOL AIM messages.**

For example, imagine you have a small business with an intranet local-area network (LAN) that is isolated from the Internet. If you set up a Jabber server on that network and use Jabber clients on your workstations, you have created a companywide Jabber network. You can also create isolated Jabber networks on the Internet or other large networks by preventing your Jabber server from connecting to other Jabber servers. Your clients will only connect with your server, and your server can't connect with any other Jabber servers, creating a separate Jabber network.

Jabber entities: users and resources

Each Jabber domain hosts zero or more Jabber users. A Jabber user is a logical messaging endpoint usually representing a person or user account. However, Jabber users can be anything to which you would want to send a Jabber message. Users can include automated services and gateways to other messaging systems. A Jabber user is addressed by their username. Jabber usernames follow the email guidelines for email usernames.[17]

In the common case where a Jabber user represents a person, it is possible for a single user to be simultaneously using separate clients to access their Jabber server. For example, a user may log in to the server using their PC at work to check messages. When they're away from their desk, they may use their mobile phone to check messages while their PC remains logged in.

This situation is not handled by explicitly by email. Instead, email clients must decide how to trick the server into supporting their simultaneous access. This is usually accomplished by leaving messages on the server so each client receives a copy. It is not an entirely satisfying or successful strategy as anyone that uses multiple computers to access a single email account can verify.

Jabber's designers recognized this shortcoming and provided explicit support for multiple client access. To do this, they introduced the concept of *Jabber resources.* A Jabber resource represents particular messaging endpoint for each Jabber user as shown in figure 1.9.

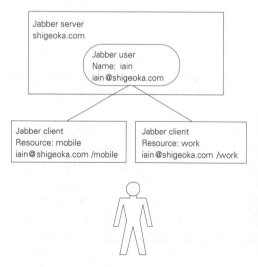

Figure 1.9
A user has two clients logged into the "iain" user account on the Jabber server shigeoka.com. They are represented in the Jabber network by two resources, creating three distinct messaging endpoints for the same user: the generic iain@shigeoka.com and the client endpoints iain@shigeoka.com/mobile, and iain@shigeoka.com/work.

---

[17] In general, usernames are alphanumeric names that can contain a few special characters like dots, underscores, and dashes, but must avoid other characters like quotes and the @ symbol.

In most cases, you send packets to users. Packets are always received at resources. The Jabber server takes care of properly routing packets sent to a user, to the best resource available for that user.

For example, I want to send a packet to the user "iain" in the Jabber domain shigeoka.com. I don't care how the packet gets to "iain." The server receives the packet, sees that it is addressed to user "iain" and checks to see what clients, if any, are connected. If none are, the packet is stored for later delivery. For this example, imagine that I have two clients connected to the server and logged into my Jabber user account. The clients use different resource names: mobile and work. The server detects this, determines that "mobile" is my preferred resource if available, and sends the packet to that client.

I can override the server's routing by addressing the packet to user "iain" at resource "work" using the address iain@shigeoka.com/work. This allows me to chat with user "iain" at the "work" resource even though the packet should go to the "mobile" resource by default. If the "work" resource becomes unavailable the server will automatically route the packet as if it were addressed to the user. In most cases, clients should accept the default packet routing provided by the server rather than specifying resource addresses.[18]

> **JABBER IMPLICIT ADDRESSING**
>
> The Jabber protocols make certain assumptions about addresses depending on the protocol and the context of a Jabber packet exchange. The server will often override any address you use in packets and replace it with these implicit addresses.
>
> For example, when your client connects with a server, it establishes a Jabber session. This session sets up certain implicit addresses. First, the user's account becomes the default address for all packets sent from the client. If you don't specify a packet recipient, the server will assume that the implicit recipient is the user's account. Second, when a client authenticates with the server as a user and sets its resource, that user and resource are used as the implicit sender address of all packets originating from that connection.
>
> Most Jabber servers will automatically set the sender address of packets to the session's sender address overriding anything the client may have set. This helps the server to prevent clients from sending messages with bad or purposefully wrong sender addresses. If you aren't aware of these implicit addresses you can run into unexpected behavior or errors.

---

[18] Obviously, there will be many cases where default packet routing is *not* the behavior you want. For example, if you are chatting with someone, you will want to send all messages in the conversation to the same resource regardless of their normal server packet delivery settings.

Jabber addressing using Jabber identifiers

As the earlier sections have shown, Jabber addressing involves properly specifying the Jabber domain, and optionally a username and resource. The Jabber protocols use a standard Jabber identifier, often referred to as a Jabber ID or JID, to format this information into a single, easy-to-use address: user@domain/resource.

For example, if I have a user "iain" on Jabber domain shigeoka.com with the resource "work" then a full URL would be: iain@shigeoka.com/work.

Both the user and resource components of the Jabber ID are optional. The most common form is to simply omit the resource: iain@shigeoka.com. This form is easy to remember and resembles the ubiquitous email address. In fact, I have a feeling that many Jabber systems will simply reuse email accounts so that users can have the same Jabber ID and email address.

There is an assumed anonymous Jabber user associated with the server address. You can address messages to a Jabber server by simply specifying the server name (the empty user part of the Jabber ID implies delivery to this anonymous server user): shigeoka.com.

The most common usage of server addresses is to send packets to Jabber servers outside of your own Jabber domain. To deliver packets from a client to its own server, it's more efficient to not specify the recipient address. The server knows that any unaddressed packets have the user's account as their implicit address. The server will handle these packets on behalf of the user, routing or processing them according to the Jabber protocols.

It is possible to send packets to a resource at the server: shigeoka.com/admin. This form is fairly rare, though, as most server messages are sent from clients to servers without regard for resources.

The compact and familiar format of the Jabber ID makes it easy to remember and use Jabber addresses. The only real danger in its format is the possibility of confusion between Jabber IDs and email addresses. Jabber domain administrators can reduce this confusion by simply using the same address for both so that Jabber messages or emails sent to a particular address will both go to the same user. It is also possible to bridge the two messaging systems so that users can use a single Jabber client to handle both Jabber messages and email, thus further reducing the chance for problems.

The final core Jabber concept is the IM concept of presence.

Jabber awareness using presence

IM systems frequently rely on the "instant" delivery of messages and real-time interaction between clients. These real-time interactions can be simple text chats, or they can be complex collaborative applications such as groupware and massively multiplayer, online games. Both features require the server and clients to be able to determine who is currently available to receive messages.

Jabber provides standard IM support of presence to indicate each user's online status. In most cases, the simple "available/unavailable" status is enough. However, Jabber allows users to customize their presence status to indicate any presence status such as "away to lunch" or "gone fishing." These custom presence states aren't as useful for automated tools, but they help users to interact in rich and flexible ways.

Jabber also allows you to create rosters, often referred to as buddy lists. This feature lets you maintain a list of other users and their current presence status. Jabber rosters are stored and maintained on the server so your rosters will always be available when you log into the Jabber system.

Finally, the Jabber presence protocols allow you to approve or disapprove presence subscription requests from other users. This feature allows you to protect your privacy and determine who has permission to see your presence status. You can also revoke previously approved presence permissions if you change your mind.

Jabber's presence system is flexible enough to apply to a variety of applications outside of simple user presence management. For example, imagine using a motion detector from a home automation kit to send Jabber updates indicating the "presence" of a car in a particular parking space. You can then write a simple Jabber client to watch for the "car in space" presence update and send you a message if your Jabber presence is set to "chat." That way, if you're Jabbering with your friends on the job and your boss arrives you'll be warned to get back to work, but it won't bother you if you're really working.

Now that we have a basic understanding of the core Jabber concepts, let's discuss the benefits and drawbacks of using Jabber for our Java IM system.

1.3 Benefits of the Jabber protocols

The Jabber protocols offer a wide variety of benefits to developers. One of the most important is its open nature where sharing, experimentation, and cooperation are always encouraged. This has led to the rapid growth of Jabber's user and developer communities. Developers have an amazing level of access to both the major creators of Jabber software, as well the option to influence the creation and evolution of Jabber standards.

From a technical standpoint, Jabber's simple XML packet format provides a nice compromise between a conversational, human readable format, and something that machines can easily interpret. It is easy to hack and explore the Jabber protocols by reading and typing in raw XML using simple tools like telnet. If Jabber had used binary data formats, special tools would be necessary to both read and send valid messages.

Jabber's XML design also permits the routing of any information that can be expressed as XML.[19] With the growing number of XML technologies being brought to fore, especially in advanced business systems, this places Jabber in an interesting position to become a core part of future XML messaging systems that goes beyond simple IM.

Jabber's XML protocols have also been designed to transparently accommodate extensions. Developers can use these extensions to support new applications on top of Jabber such as games and collaborative groupware. Work is already under way in the Jabber community to bridge Jabber systems to other communication systems like pagers and Short Message Service (SMS).

Finally, as we'll see in this book, the Jabber protocols are simple. A small team of developers using a modern language like Java can create a Jabber system in a very short time. This simplicity lets you concentrate on features beyond IM. Whether your goals are to create applications on top of Jabber, integrate Jabber into your current software, or create massively scalable Jabber software, the Jabber protocols won't get in your way.

1.4   *Drawbacks of the Jabber protocols*

Unfortunately, Jabber is not trouble-free. There are problems with the Jabber standards that you must be willing to accommodate in order to use the technology. The most glaring problem is the relative immaturity of the Jabber standards. In many cases, official documentation for Jabber standards and protocols are incomplete or outdated and the only definitive answer to protocol questions is to check the behavior of the Jabber open source reference server.

The Jabber community is working on addressing this shortcoming. The Jabber Software Foundation (foundation.jabber.org) has recently been formed to help manage the Jabber standards process. It is hoped that before the end of 2002, new Jabber standards under the guidance of the Jabber Software Foundation will provide definitive documentation for Jabber standards.

The Jabber protocols suffer from inefficiencies directly related to its conversational, XML-based nature. Binary data formats can greatly reduce the bandwidth

---

[19] In particular, the Jabber-As-Middleware and jabber-rpc working groups in the Jabber community (www.jabber.org) are looking into these very issues. The former is concentrating on what is needed to make Jabber enterprise ready, while the latter is specifically looking at transport bindings for XML-RPC over Jabber.

required by a system, as well as provide other features such as error detection and correction. However, the Jabber designers decided that gaining the XML-related benefits mentioned earlier outweigh the resulting inefficiencies. I agree that this was a good decision. However, if this overhead is unacceptable to your application, you may need to search for an alternative.

Another drawback with the Jabber system is its underdog status in a fragmented IM market. The current market leader by a long shot is AOL that controls both AIM and ICQ. Other large IM providers like Microsoft and Yahoo! also have much large user populations than Jabber. These IM leaders have also been resistant to interoperability and open IM standards that could jeopardize their control over their captive IM user communities.

Jabber has been fighting this problem by both pushing standards efforts and reverse-engineering the proprietary IM protocols to create transports[20] to bridge Jabber networks to these networks. Unfortunately, these standards efforts have not been very productive to date.

Jabber's strategy of creating unauthorized transports to bridge Jabber networks to other IM networks may also meet with problems in the future. Until recently Jabber has been a relatively small effort. However as the technology moves forward and larger organizations begin to use it, there may be legal and business problems with bridging to these networks without permission from their operators. Companies interested in using transports should thoroughly investigate the legal aspects of transports before adding them to their Jabber servers.

Finally, the Jabber protocols lack standard enterprise features like transactions and quality of service support. It will be impossible to build mission-critical applications on top of Jabber without adding these features. Fortunately, there is a working group in the Jabber community called Jabber-As-Middleware (JAM) looking into these issues. If you're interested in using Jabber for mission-critical applications, I highly encourage you to join the JAM working group, hosted by the Jabber Software Foundation, and help define these standards.

1.5   Conclusion

Despite some drawbacks, Jabber is one of the best ways for Java developers to build IM systems. Creating IM systems in Java is important as IM is poised to be the next great Internet communication revolution for both consumers and enterprise users. In the next chapter, we'll take a look at Jabber from a technical standpoint and examine how the Jabber protocols work.

---

[20] We'll discuss transports in more detail in chapter 9.

2

Jabber technical fundamentals

Our tour of the Jabber protocols begins with a technical discussion of the Jabber messaging model followed by a discussion of the three core Jabber protocols: message, presence, and info/query. The chapter ends with a walkthrough of an annotated Jabber session showing a full Jabber protocol exchange between a client and server. Getting to know what Jabber looks like under the covers removes the mystery associated with the Jabber protocols and illustrates how simple and powerful they truly are.

2.1   The Jabber messaging model

It is important that we understand the Jabber messaging model before we begin writing Jabber software. There are four important participants in any Jabber message exchange, as shown in figure 2.1:

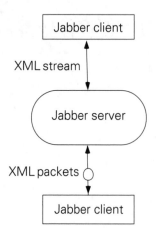

Figure 2.1
The Jabber messaging model is composed of four main elements: XML packets containing marked-up data, XML streams used to transport XML packets, and Jabber clients and servers that exchange XML packets over an XML stream.

- *Server*—The Jabber server participates in and manages all Jabber communication. Its primary responsibility is to provide Jabber services to clients. The most important services it offers to clients are packet routing and user account management.
- *Client*—Jabber clients typically act as user agents displaying information (such as messages) to the end user, and responding to user inputs. Jabber clients may also offer services autonomously to the Jabber network. When acting as a service provider, clients are referred to as chatbots.
- *Streams*—The network connection between the client and server is conceptualized as a pair of one-way streams. From an XML standpoint, the Jabber stream is a streaming XML document enclosed in `<stream:stream>` tags.

From a logical standpoint, the stream forms a session with associated context metainformation about the stream such as the client's full Jabber ID, the server's Jabber ID, a unique stream ID, and a stream state.

- *Packets*—XML fragments sent through the streams between client and server are called packets. Each packet is a self-contained, valid XML subdocument. The Jabber protocols specify the format of these packets, and the proper procedures for exchanging them.

A Jabber server, like other server applications, is started on a machine and listens for connection requests from clients. The Jabber standard establishes port 5222 as the standard port for Jabber servers. Secure client/server connections can be made over SSL (Secure Sockets Layer) by connecting to the Jabber server on port 5223. Jabber servers may accept connections on either port (or both) depending on the wishes of the server administrator.

Alternative ports may be used. However, most Jabber clients will assume Jabber servers are on ports 5222 and 5223 and the clients will need to be configured in an implementation-specific manner in order to connect to alternative ports.

A Jabber client creates a stream by connecting with the server and sending an opening `<stream:stream>` XML tag. The opening stream tag identifies the name of the server domain to which the client is attempting to connect. This is important even though a client used the server's domain as its address when it was making the connection. The reason this is important is that a single server may be acting as the Jabber server for multiple Jabber domains.

For example, I have two Jabber domains: shigeoka.com and manning.com (figure2.2). I can configure the domain name server (DNS) so that both Internet domain names map to the same IP address 10.0.0.1. A client wishing to join the shigeoka.com Jabber domain uses DNS to look up the appropriate Jabber server. It gets the IP address 10.0.0.1 and makes a connection to the machine there. Another client wishing to join the manning.com Jabber domain uses DNS to look up the server and also receives the 10.0.0.1 IP address and connects to it.

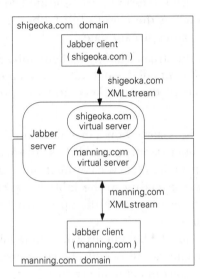

Figure 2.2
This figure shows a single Jabber server acting as two virtual Jabber servers. Each client's XML stream must identify the domain to which it belongs.

The Jabber server at IP address `10.0.0.1` knows it is a virtual server handling both `shigeoka.com` and `manning.com`. Unfortunately, as the server accepts connections to port 5222 it does not know to which domain the client is trying to connect. However, when the first client sends its opening `<stream:stream>` tag, it indicates that the intended server is shigeoka.com while the second client indicates it is connecting to manning.com. The server can associate this information with the connection so that it knows the domain to which each client belongs.

When a Jabber server accepts a client connection, it will respond to the client's `<stream:stream>` tag with its own `<stream:stream>` tag confirming the server's domain, and also assigning a random session ID to the stream. Both the client and server must keep track of the session ID associated with the stream as that information is used in other Jabber protocols. An error in the process will result in the server sending a `<stream:error>` packet explaining the problem followed immediately by the server closing the connection.

Once the streams have been opened between client and server, they can exchange Jabber packets according to the various Jabber protocols. In most cases, the server will only allow clients to participate in a restricted subset of the Jabber protocols until the client has authenticated itself with the server. Client authentication allows the server to verify that the client has permission to act on behalf of a user as a particular resource.

The Jabber standards do not specify what protocols should be available prior to authentication. At a minimum, most servers will allow clients to use the Jabber registration and authentication protocols.

Either the client or the server can close the stream at any time by sending a closing `</stream:stream>` tag. At that time, either can close the connection and end the Jabber session. It is polite but not necessary to allow the other entity to finish the transmission of any incomplete packet before shutting down the connection.

For clients, this boils down to a pretty straightforward messaging algorithm:

1   Connect with the Jabber server on port 5222.

2   Send an opening `<stream:stream>` tag containing the server address.

3   Wait for the server's `<stream:stream>` reply and record the stream's session ID.

4   Use the Jabber authentication protocol to log in to a user account as a resource.

5   Send Jabber packets to the server according to the Jabber protocols. The Jabber server routes the packets to appropriate recipients.

6   Send a closing `</stream:stream>` tag to close the stream.

7   Close the network connection.

In this messaging model, clients need only one network connection with their server. The connection is kept open as long as the client wishes to send or receive packets. To send a packet, the client addresses the packet to a recipient, and sends it to the server over their mutual XML stream. The server is in charge of properly routing the packet to its ultimate destination.

This simple client/server messaging model has several benefits and drawbacks.

2.1.1 *Benefits*

Jabber's distributed client/server messaging model has many benefits. Most importantly, it is a simple-to-use and well-understood model for network communication. Email uses an identical messaging model so the costs and benefits have been thoroughly explored and refined for best overall performance. This model has only two communication scenarios, client/server and server-server. For all the Jabber servers that do not interact with other servers and all Jabber clients, the distributed client/server messaging model reduces to a single set of simple, client/server protocols.

Client privacy and security are much improved because clients only talk to their server. Attackers on the network don't have any information about the client's location. In addition, the client never accepts connections like a server.

Eliminating the need for clients to act as a server avoids problems with clients behind firewalls and prevents a whole family of attacks that can occur against servers. Limiting the client's security exposure is a significant advantage of Jabber's client/server architecture when compared with peer-to-peer networks like Gnutella (figure 2.3).

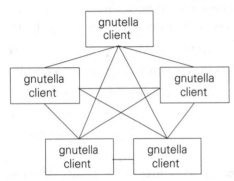

Figure 2.3
A Gnutella peer-to-peer network requires clients to connect directly with other clients.

Jabber's messaging model also benefits developers because it greatly simplifies the task of writing Jabber client software. Simpler clients mean that client applications can be brought to market more quickly and at a lower cost. In addition, minimizing the amount of IM code on the client allows client developers to concentrate on other aspects of the client such as the user interface, integration with other applications, ease of maintenance, and ease of deployment.

Finally, Jabber servers allow you to readily exert centralized control over a Jabber domain. You can create policies and enforce them on the server without having to modify clients or try to exert control over independent peers in a peer-to-peer network. For example, if you want to restrict the amount of data each user can send or receive in a 24-hour period, it is easy to track and limit usage on the server. Or alternatively, you might allow messaging to certain domains during business hours for most users, but allow certain users to still communicate with off-domain users, and lift those restrictions for all users during lunch and after business hours.

2.1.2 *Drawbacks*

Ironically, many of the benefits of Jabber's simple client/server messaging model also create drawbacks. For example, in most cases, server-managed privacy and security is convenient and efficient. However, if you cannot trust your server, a centralized, all-powerful server can be a major problem. There is nothing preventing someone with access to the server from recording and reading your messages without your permission (figure 2.4).

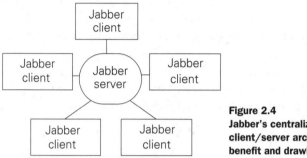

Figure 2.4
Jabber's centralized hub-and-spoke client/server architecture is both a benefit and drawback.

Jabber users are not entirely at the mercy of the Jabber server. You can send encrypted versions of your messages inside a normal Jabber message. Several commonly available encryption algorithms[1] can protect data from prying eyes and prevent integrity attacks such as unauthorized editing of messages. In addition, several Jabber protocols are designed to help protect you from server security problems. The zero-knowledge authentication Jabber protocol is a good example of this.

The possibility of server security exploits points to the greater problem of reduced user control in client/server architectures. The server is the ultimate authority on all things and the loss of control on the client can cause a lot of user dissatisfaction. In the earlier example of centralized server control, we saw that it is trivial for servers to restrict message delivery and place arbitrary restrictions on the number of types of messages sent through the server. These types of arbitrary restrictions are what make alternative architectures such as peer-to-peer so attractive to users.

Restrictive server control is a potential problem in the Jabber messaging model. The problem is more social than technical in nature. However, Jabber's model lends itself to certain types of problems that simply don't exist on other systems.

The server doesn't only represent a single point of control for a Jabber domain. It is also a single point of failure and a likely bottleneck for Jabber networks. A server failure disables an entire server domain so you must treat it like a

---

[1] Many of these algorithms are already implemented in the standard Java libraries in the `java.security.*` packages.

mission-critical server. Building reliable, highly scalable software is a difficult but achievable goal so this problem is not as serious as several others presented here.

All of the other major IM systems use a simple client/server messaging model so they suffer the same drawbacks as Jabber. However, Jabber doesn't settle for these simple trade-offs, but seeks to alleviate the drawbacks. It goes a step further than simple client/server messaging by introducing distributed servers to the messaging model in order to create a distributed client/server architecture. This architecture provides more flexibility in selecting a better middle ground between simple client/server and completely decentralized architectures.

2.1.3 *Relying on distributed servers*

Distributed servers address many of the drawbacks of the basic client/server messaging model. Rather than use a single Jabber server, Jabber explicitly provides for multiple Jabber servers in the same Jabber network using Jabber domains and server-to-server(S2S) communication. Packets bound for users in different domains are sent from the sender's server to the recipient's server using the jabber:server protocols, which are commonly known as the S2S protocols.

The S2S protocols are essentially a mirror of the jabber:client protocols (figure 2.5). A server wishing to open an S2S connection connects to a server using a single network connection and establishes a Jabber stream. The "sender server" that makes the connection acts as a client on behalf of all its users sending messages to the "recipient server" for delivery to users in that domain. If the recipient server wishes to send messages to users on the sender server, it must open its own S2S connection in the opposite direction.[2]

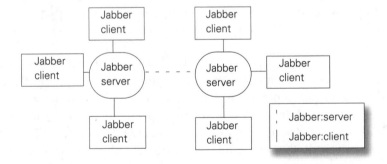

Figure 2.5 **Jabber client/server streams follow the** jabber:client **protocols while server-server streams follow the** jabber:server **protocols.**

---

[2] The S2S protocol is discussed in more detail in chapter 9 and covered in the Jabber reference section in appendix A.

Breaking the Jabber network into domains controlled by a separate server allows you to select how centralized the server will be, with all of the benefits and drawbacks associated with that centralization. On one extreme, you can have millions of users on a single Jabber server essentially creating a pure client/server system, thus maximizing the benefits and drawbacks of the client/server model.

On the other hand, you are free to completely decentralize the Jabber system, going to the far extreme of running a Jabber server for every client. This would convert Jabber into a peer-to-peer system with none of the benefits or drawbacks of the client/server model. Of course, as with most things, the best solution is usually a compromise between the extremes: federations of modest Jabber servers handling midsized domains. This compromise offers enough autonomy and control for users while still reaping the benefits of centralized management and control.

Distributed servers also allow the Jabber network to grow extremely large without requiring a high-capacity server installation like the one powering AIM. Instead, many inexpensive Jabber server nodes host the network. In addition, the cost of supporting the network is spread much more evenly with Internet Service Providers (ISPs) supporting their users, companies supporting their employees, and so forth.

With all these clients and servers, it is can be easy to lose sight of the actual simplicity and efficiency of the complete Jabber messaging model. This is best demonstrated by examining how packets travel through the Jabber network. Servers and their packet routing algorithms handle the entire process.

2.1.4 How Jabber packet routing works

The key to understanding Jabber's routing scheme is realizing that IM delivery is primarily between users, not client-to-client or computer-to-computer. In other words, an IM message is sent to a logical user, not to a particular machine or network location. It is the responsibility of the IM routing system to ensure that the packet reaches the user whenever and wherever the user happens to be on the network.

It is important to realize that instant messaging occurs across space and time. Messaging across space means packets travel across the network with the IM routing system determining where to deliver the packets and how to get it there.

Messaging across time means packets are sent at one moment in time, and arrive at its destination as soon as possible following that. Ideally the time is minimal, resulting in "instant" messaging. However, IM systems realize that users can't always be online to receive packets. The IM routing system transparently holds packets for delivery when recipients do become available online.

The routing process begins with the Jabber ID. Packets are addressed to recipients by setting the to attribute of the packet to the recipient's Jabber ID. The Jabber ID contains all the information the server needs to make its routing decisions.

Recall from chapter 1 that the Jabber ID contains the recipient's Jabber domain and can optionally include the recipient's user name and resource. A full Jabber ID takes the form user@domain/resource. From a software standpoint, the most difficult thing about dealing with Jabber IDs is parsing them. Rather than describe in words the Jabber ID parsing process, let's take a look at Java source code that does it.[3] Listing 2.1 shows a Java class that represents a Jabber ID.

Listing 2.1   The JabberID class members and access methods

```java
public class JabberID{

  String user;
  public String getUser() { return user; }
  public void setUser(String name){ user = name; }

  String domain;
  public String getServer() { return domain; }
  public void setServer(String name){ domain = name; }
  public String getDomain() { return domain; }
  public void setDomain(String name){ domain = name; }

  String resource;
  public String getResource() { return resource; }
  public void setResource(String value){ resource = value; }
```

The class begins with a simple set of member variables that store the user, domain, and resource for the Jabber ID. Appropriate set/get methods have been added to provide access. The member variables can then be used to provide a wide variety of equality tests, as shown in listing 2.2.

Listing 2.2   The JabberID class equality methods

```java
public boolean equalsDomain(String domain){
    if ( this.domain == null ^ domain == null ) {
      return false;
    }
```

---

[3] The full source code to everything presented in this book is freely available online. See the book preface for information on obtaining the source. To save space I've omitted many Java "extras" that are required by Java, but are not relevant to the discussion (e.g., import statements, package names, etc.). The full source contains all of these details.

```
    return this.domain.equalsIgnoreCase(domain);
}

public boolean equalsDomain(JabberID testJid){
  return equalsDomain(testJid.domain);
}

public boolean equalsUser(String user){
  if ( this.user == null ^ user == null ) {
    return false;
  }
  return this.user.equalsIgnoreCase(user);
}

public boolean equalsUser(JabberID testJid){
  return equalsUser(testJid.user);
}

public boolean equalsResource(JabberID test){
  return equalsResource(test.resource);
}

public boolean equalsResource(String test){
  if ( resource == null ^ test == null ) {
    return false;
  }
  return resource.equalsIgnoreCase(test);
}

public boolean equalsUser(String user, String resource){
  return equalsUser(user) && resource.equals(resource);
}

public boolean equals(JabberID jid){
  return equalsUser(jid) && equalsDomain(jid) && equalsResource(jid);
}

public boolean equals(String jid){
  return equals(new JabberID(jid));
}
```

The equality tests are fairly straightforward. There is some extra testing involved because any of the values except domain can be null, indicating no value has been set. The server software will use the equality tests extensively when matching recipients to resources.

As mentioned earlier, the real work occurs in parsing Jabber ID strings to locate its user, domain, and resource components. This functionality is encapsulated in the setJID() method, as shown in listing 2.3.

Listing 2.3   The JabberID class Jabber ID parsing method setJID()

```
public void setJID(String jid){
  if (jid == null){
    user = null;
    domain = null;
    resource = null;
    return;
  }
  int atLoc = jid.indexOf("@");
  if (atLoc == -1){
    user = null;
  } else {
    user = jid.substring(0, atLoc).toLowerCase();
    jid = jid.substring(atLoc + 1);
  }

  atLoc = jid.indexOf("/");
  if (atLoc == -1) {
    resource = null;
    domain = jid.toLowerCase();
  } else {
    domain = jid.substring(0, atLoc).toLowerCase();
    resource = jid.substring(atLoc + 1).toLowerCase();
  }
}
```

The setJID() method is used in the JabberID constructor. In addition, we see the opposite process used in the toString() method to recreate a JabberID as a simple string. (Listing 2.4)

Listing 2.4   The JabberID class constructor and toString() method.

```
public JabberID(String user, String domain, String resource){
  setUser(user);
  setDomain(domain);
  setResource(resource);
}

public JabberID(String jid){
  setJID(jid);
}

public String toString(){
  StringBuffer jid = new StringBuffer();
  if (user != null){
```

```
        jid.append(user);
        jid.append("@");
    }
    jid.append(domain);
    if (resource != null){
        jid.append("/");
        jid.append(resource);
    }
    return jid.toString();
  }
}
```

So how is the Jabber ID used by the Jabber routing system? The process begins with the client (playing the role of a Jabber resource) generating a packet and setting its to attribute to the recipient's Jabber ID.[4] The client sends the packet to the server, where the packet is then forwarded from the sender's server to the recipient's server. The packet is then delivered to a recipient resource when one is available.

Unfortunately, the process is not always as straightforward. Complications arise when a user has more than one resource available to receive messages. In these cases, the server must select which resource to direct messages. The situation is simple when the recipient Jabber ID matches a specific resource Jabber ID. However if the resource is not available, or the recipient Jabber ID specifies the user but no resource, the server must choose the best resource to receive the message.

Since there is no way for the server to automatically detect which resource the user prefers, the user must tell the server its delivery preferences. This is done using the presence protocols and the <priority> element.[5] (figure 2.6). Essentially, the presence protocol lets each resource (user client) indicate its messaging status (available or unavailable) and priority (numbers starting at 0 and going up) to the server. The server uses this information to deliver messages addressed to the user to the resource with the highest priority that is available for receiving messages.

---

[4] If the client omits the to attribute, the server's Jabber ID is used as an implicit recipient address for the packet.

[5] We'll cover in detail how presence interacts with message routing in chapter 8.

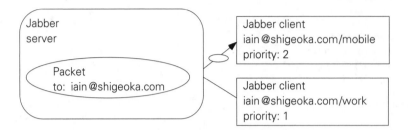

Figure 2.6 The Jabber server routes user addressed packets to the highest priority resources. In this case, the mobile resource has the highest priority and will receive all packets addressed to iain@shigeoka.com and all other iain@shigeoka.com resource addresses including iain@shigeoka .com/mobile. Only packets sent to iain@shigeoka.com/work will be sent to the work resource. Priorities are set using the Jabber presence protocols.

2.1.5 *Step-by-step: a message's path through Jabber*

Imagine we are a Jabber client playing the role of a resource with Jabber ID bigwig@manning.com/work. We want to send a `<message>` packet to user "iain" in the shigeoka.com Jabber domain. The packet might look like:

```
<message to='iain@shigeoka.com'/>
```

Next, we send the packet to our manning.com server. The server examines the recipient Jabber ID, adds the implicit sender address in a `from` attribute, and forwards the packet to the shigeoka.com Jabber server:

```
<message to='iain@shigeoka.com' from='bigwig@manning.com/work'/>
```

The shigeoka.com server reads the iain@shigeoka.com address and sees that the packet is addressed to user "iain." If there are no resources logged into the "iain" account, the message is stored for later delivery. When a resource is available, the shigeoka.com server can deliver the final `<message>` packet to the resource. The following packet is what would be received:

```
<message from='bigwig@manning.com/work'/>
```

Notice that the recipient address has been stripped off. In this case, the client will assume that the message was addressed to itself. Jabber servers don't have to strip off the recipient address so clients should be able to handle packets with or without recipient addresses.

2.2   *The core Jabber protocols*

The Jabber protocols define a set of data structures and conventions for exchanging them to carry out IM-related tasks. The Jabber protocols are simple and flexible, giving systems that use them a great deal of power and flexibility. They build upon other standard Internet technologies such as TCP/IP, Universal Resource Identifiers (URI), and the XML so the learning curve for developers is greatly reduced.

There are only three core Jabber protocols:

- Message
- Presence
- Info/Query

Each of these protocols fills a crucial niche in the Jabber system. Let's take a brief look at each of them to get a feel for what they offer us.

2.2.1 *Message: Delivering data*

The message protocol is the simplest of the Jabber protocols. In most cases, the majority of packet traffic on the Jabber network falls under the message protocol, so its simplicity and ease of use pays off in better messaging. This simplicity follows the common design philosophy of making common things easy and rare things possible.

As you can probably guess, the message protocols are used to send human-readable messages between users. These messages can resemble full-scale email messages or form the line-by-line messages in chat sessions.

The message protocol uses the `<message>` packet and is covered in depth in chapter 4.

2.2.2 *Presence: updating user online status*

The other frequently used core Jabber protocol is the presence protocol. This protocol governs the subscription, approval, and update of presence information in the Jabber system. As with the focused message protocol the presence protocol is designed for simple, efficient Jabber presence management.

The presence protocol uses the `<presence>` packet and is covered in depth in chapters 5 and 8.

2.2.3 *Info/Query: handling everything else*

The Info/Query (IQ) protocol is the last core Jabber protocol and serves as the catch-all Jabber protocol. If a protocol is not sending a message, or managing presence, it is an IQ protocol. IQ is a generic request-response protocol with low overhead. It is designed to be easily extensible with IQ extension protocols.

The general format of an IQ packet contains an `<iq>` "envelope" that generically describes what type of IQ protocol will take place and the query recipient, often called the IQ handler. Within the `<iq>` envelope are zero or more `<query>` packets. The `<query>` packets establish a default namespace, and each `<query>`packet can contain its own namespace-specific subpackets. The namespace keeps the `<query>` packet contents from clashing with any Jabber element names and provides an easy way to identify what IQ extension protocol is being used.

For example, if a client wishes to conduct an IQ `get` query using the `jabber:iq:auth` IQ extension protocol, the packet may look like the following:

```
<iq type='get' to='handlerJID'>
 <query xmlns='jabber:iq:auth'>
   <username>iain</username>
 </query>
</iq>
```

There are over twenty standard or proposed standard IQ extension protocols. These protocols cover everything from Jabber account registration and authentication to querying the local time or software version of a client or server. In addition, developers are free to create their own IQ extension protocols as long as they don't use the same namespaces as the standard IQ extension protocols.[6]

This simple extension mechanism allows developers the freedom to extend the Jabber system quickly and easily. In addition, because the query's contents are protected in an XML namespace and Jabber routing information such as the packet recipient is contained in the outer `<iq>` envelope, custom IQ extension packets can be sent over the Jabber system without any need for modifications of the rest of the Jabber software. Only the sender and recipient/handler need to understand the IQ extension protocol. Clients or servers that don't support a given IQ extension protocol simply send an error to the sender indicating the lack of support.

For example, imagine we create a new IQ extension protocol `http://shigeoka.com/game/character` for a Jabber online game that describes the user's game character to other users in the game. A client may send the following IQ packet to the server:

```
<iq type='set' to='evilwizard@shigeoka.com'>
  <query xmlns='http://shigeoka.com/game/character'>
    <name>Mario</name>
    <sex>male</sex>
    <occupation>plumber</occupation>
    <lives>3</lives>
```

---

[6] The `jabber:iq:*` namespace is reserved for Jabber standard IQ extensions. It is recommend that you use a URL format for private or proprietary IQ extensions. For example, if your company has a registered domain name `shigeoka.com` and you are creating a new `time` IQ extension, a good namespace would be `http://shigeoka.com/time`.

```
    <level>5</level>
    <score>4200</score>
  </query>
</iq>
```

The completely unmodified Jabber server receives this packet and forwards it to the `shigeoka.com` server. The unmodified shigeoka.com server delivers it to its "evilwizard" user. The "evilwizard" user's client receives the packet and updates its game display. Neither of the servers used to transport the custom IQ packet knows anything about the `http://shigeoka.com/game/character` IQ extension but both can properly deliver the packet.

The potential for new Jabber applications built upon protocol extensions is an exciting area of exploration for Jabber developers.

Now that we have reviewed how Jabber works from a technical standpoint, let's take a look at a real Jabber communication session to get a solid feel for the system.

2.3 Jabber session example

Although we only know the basics of how the Jabber protocols work, it is enough to understand any Jabber communication session from a high level. The best way to truly understand what is happening is to take a look at the raw Jabber protocols being passed across the network.

Jabber's XML-based packet format makes the examination of "raw" Jabber data simple. Unlike protocols that rely on binary data formats, XML uses simple, marked-up text that looks familiar to anyone who's seen HTML. You don't need special tools to decode incoming data into some human readable format, nor do you need to have special tools to generate outgoing data. We can manually act as a Jabber client and connect to any Jabber server using the ubiquitous telnet application, reading raw XML as it arrives, and typing raw XML using a standard keyboard. In this section, we'll step through a heavily annotated, sample Jabber session.

To begin, start your telnet program. On some platforms, your telnet program may be a nice graphical application started on the desktop. However, every operating system that I'm aware of has a simple text telnet program that you can access by simply typing "telnet server port" at a command prompt (Windows) or terminal window (Unix and MacOS X). You have to replace "server" and "port" with the Jabber server's address and port. For example, you may use the open `shigeoka.com` server by typing: telnet shigeoka.com 5222

The telnet program will respond with some opening information then wait for you to type something.

In the telnet example session included in this section, what I type is in bold with the responses in normal font. I've reformatted the XML data to be a little easier to read. I suggest if you're trying to do this on your own, that you type your packets into a text editor and then paste them into the telnet session.[7] Doing this will allow you to reuse your packets and avoid mistakes.

In this example, we'll go through a simple Jabber authentication and message sending exercise. To send and receive messages, we'll use two client sessions, logged into two different user accounts. By doing so, we can see messages being sent between users. The procedure is as follows:

Basic telnet actions for exploring the Jabber protocols

Iain	Smirk

1. Connect with the Jabber server shigeoka.com.
2. Open a Jabber stream.
3. Create user account "iain," password "secret" on domain shigeoka.com.
4. Authenticate with the server as user "iain," password "secret" on domain shigeoka.com with resource "test."
     5. Connect with the Jabber server shigeoka.com.
     6. Open a Jabber stream.
     7. Create user account "smirk," password "secret" on domain shigeoka.com.
     8. Authenticate with the server as user "smirk," password "secret" on domain jabber.org with resource "test."
9. Send a message to user "smirk."
10. Update presence status to "available."
     11. Update presence status update to "available."
     12. Receive message from "iain."
     13. Send message to "iain."
14. Receive message from "smirk."
15. Close stream.
     16. Close stream.

The two sequences, steps 1–4 and steps 5–8, are almost identical. We'll take a look at how steps 1–4 are carried out for logging into the "iain" account. We want both

---

[7] Telnet doesn't send what you type until you press Enter. Each packet should be followed by pressing Enter in order to send it to the server.

client connections to be active simultaneously so once you complete steps 1–4, you then repeat them with 5–8 so that you end up with two connections.

The first step is to connect with the Jabber server using telnet.

Step 1: Connecting to the Jabber server using telnet

"Raw" telnet screen	What is happening
`% telnet shigeoka.com 5222`	Start a telnet connection to the server.
`Trying shigeoka.com...`	Telnet application information.
`Connected to shigeoka.com.`	Extra text may vary.
`Escape character is '^]'.`	

To begin speaking with the server, we need to open a Jabber XML stream. The `<stream>` element is defined in the `http://etherx.jabber.org/streams` namespace and must be declared for every valid Jabber stream. We are also using the client/server protocols, so we must define the `jabber:client` default namespace for elements within `<stream>`. In addition, to support virtual Jabber servers, the opening `<stream>` tag contains a `to` attribute specifying the name of the server with which we are expecting to connect.

Step 2: Opening the Jabber XML stream

"Raw" telnet screen	What is happening
`<?xml version='1.0'?>`	XML version (optional).
`<stream:stream`	Opening stream element.
`xmlns:stream=` `'http://etherx.jabber.org/streams'`	`<stream>` namespace.
`xmlns='jabber:client'`	Default namespace for `<stream>`.
`to='shigeoka.com'>`	Tell server connection domain requested.
`<?xml version='1.0'?>`	XML version (optional).
`<stream:stream`	Opening stream element.
`xmlns:stream=` `'http://etherx.jabber.org/streams'`	`<stream>` namespace.
`id='3C0FB738'`	The random "session ID" for this connection.
`xmlns='jabber:client'`	Default namespace for `<stream>`.
`from='shigeoka.com'>`	Tell client connection granted.

Once we have established the session, it is time to create a user account on the server. In most cases, your account will already exist on the server. In fact, only open Jabber servers like the one at jabber.org will allow you to create new accounts using the `jabber:iq:register` IQ extension protocol we'll see here. Other Jabber servers will have other procedures for creating user accounts just like there are many ways to create email accounts. If you already have a Jabber account set up on the server, you can skip this step.

Step 3: Creating a user account on the server

"Raw" iain client session	What is happening
`<iq type='set'`	Account registration is an IQ set protocol.
`    id='reg_id'>`	We use a unique ID to track this query.
`  <query xmlns='jabber:iq:register'>`	jabber:iq:register IQ extension protocol.
`    <username>iain</username>`	The user name for the account.
`    <password>secret</password>`	The password for the account.
`  </query>`	
`</iq>`	
`  <iq type='result'`	Empty result indicates success.
`      id='reg_id'/>`	Match queries and results using ID.

Now that you have a user account on the server, we can authenticate with it using the `jabber:iq:auth` IQ extension protocol. There are several authentication protocols available. In this example, we'll use the simplest: the "plain authentication" protocol.

Step 4: Authenticating with the server

"Raw" iain client session	What is happening
`<iq type='set'`	Authentication is an IQ set protocol.
`    id='auth_id'>`	We use a unique ID to track this query.
`  <query xmlns='jabber:iq:auth'>`	This is a jabber:iq:auth IQ extension protocol.
`    <username>iain</username>`	The user name for the account.

Step 4: Authenticating with the server (continued)

"Raw" iain client session	What is happening
`<password>secret</password>`	The password for the account.
`<resource>test</resource>`	The resource for this client.
`</query>`	
`</iq>`	
`<iq type='result'`	Empty result indicates success.
`    id='auth_id'/>`	The packet ID tells us what IQ query was successful.

That was pretty easy wasn't it? Now we repeat the same steps in a second telnet window so we have two Jabber sessions logged into the "iain" and "smirk" accounts. Other than the large amount of typing you have to do, opening a Jabber session and authenticating with the server is a fast, straightforward procedure. I'll show the raw telnet session for steps 5–8 without comments:

Step 5-8: The "smirk" client authenticating with the server

"Raw" smirk client session

```
% telnet shigeoka.com 5222

Trying shigeoka.com...

Connected to shigeoka.com.

Escape character is '^]'.

<?xml version='1.0'?>

<stream:stream xmlns:stream='http://etherx.jabber.org/streams'

xmlns='jabber:client'

to='shigeoka.com'>

<?xml version='1.0'?>

<stream:stream xmlns:stream='http://etherx.jabber.org/streams'

id='3C0FB73C'

xmlns='jabber:client'
```

Step 5-8: The "smirk" client authenticating with the server (continued)

"Raw" smirk client session

```
from='shigeoka.com'>
```

```
<iq type='set'>
  <query xmlns='jabber:iq:register'>
    <username>smirk</username>
    <password>secret</password>
  </query>
</iq>
```

```
<iq type='result'/>
```

```
<iq type='set'>
 <query xmlns='jabber:iq:auth'>
  <username>smirk</username>
  <password>secret</password>
  <resource>work</resource>
 </query>
</iq>
```

```
<iq type='result'
    id='pthsock_client_auth_ID'/>
```

Now that we're authenticated with the Jabber server, we can send messages. We'll begin by using the "iain" client to send a message to the "smirk" client using the Jabber message protocol, as shown in step 9.

Step 9: The "iain" client sends a message to the "smirk" client

"Raw" iain client session	What is happening
`<message to='smirk@shigeoka.com'>`	A message packet addressed to "smirk."
`<subject>Hello</subject>`	The "subject" for this message.
`<body>This is the message text</body>`	the "body" of the message.
`</message>`	

What we are doing is instant messaging so we should expect that the message is delivered immediately to the "smirk" client. Look at the smirk client session. Was the message packet delivered? There should be no message. The message was not delivered. Why not?

The answer lies in Jabber presence. Recall that presence tells the server if a client is available to receive messages. When a client first logs in, the session's presence status is set to `unavailable`. We have to set our presence status to `available` in order to receive messages.

Let's update our presence status to `available` for both clients beginning with the "iain" client, as shown in step 10.

Step 10: The "iain" client updates its presence status to available

"Raw" iain client session	What is happening
`<presence type='available'/>`	Presence update.
`<message from='shigeoka.com'`	Server message.
`    to='iain@shigeoka.com'>`	Addressed to "iain" client.
`<subject>Welcome!</subject>`	The message's "subject."
`<body>Welcome to Jabber! </body>`	The message's "body."
`<x xmlns='jabber:x:delay'`	Optional server delay "X extension."
`  from='iain@shigeoka.com'`	Indicates account where message delayed.
`  stamp='20011206T18:22:09'>`	The time the message was sent/received.
`Offline Storage`	Message explaining the delay.
`</x>`	
`</message>`	

As soon as the "iain" client becomes available, the server delivers a message to the client. The message is from the server and displays "welcome information." Jabber servers will often send a message to users as they log in to update them on news, or server status. This is optional so your server may not send any message.

This particular message example also shows a `jabber:X:delay` X extension. This is a packet added by the server to messages to let clients know that a message has been delayed. In this case, the server has delivered a message to the client as soon as authentication occurred. However, the message could not be delivered because the client was unavailable. The `delay` X extension is not a mandatory feature of the Jabber protocols so your Jabber server may not include these packets in delayed messages.

Check your "smirk" client. telnet session. Notice that nothing has changed there. Its presence is still `unavailable` so the server won't send messages to it. Let's update its presence to `unavailable` and see what happens. The process follows what we just did on the "iain" client session. However, let's use a shortcut. The `<presence>` packet default type is `unavailable` so we can omit it to save bandwidth (and typing). These actions are shown in steps 11 and 12.

Steps 11 and 12: The "smirk" session updates its presence to available and receives two messages. One is from the server, the other is the message we sent from the "iain" session

"Raw" smirk client session	What is happening
`<presence/>`	Presence update (available is default).
`<message from=' shigeoka.com'`	Server message.
`   to='smirk@shigeoka.com'>`	Addressed to "smirk" client.
`  <subject>Welcome!</subject>`	The message's "subject."
`  <body>Welcome to Jabber! </body>`	The message's "body."
`  <x xmlns='jabber:x:delay'`	Optional server delay "X extension."
`   from='smirk@shigeoka.com'`	Indicates the account message delayed at…
`   stamp='20011206T18:22:38'>`	The time the message was sent/received.
`   Offline Storage`	Message explaining the delay.
`  </x>`	
`</message>`	
`<message to='smirk@shigeoka.com'`	Message to "smirk."
`   from='iain@shigeoka.com/test'>`	from iain's "test" resource.
`  <subject>Hello</subject>`	The message's "subject."
`  <body>message text.</body>`	The message's "body."
`  <x xmlns='jabber:x:delay'`	Optional server delay "X extension."
`   from='smirk@shigeoka.com'`	Indicates the account message delayed at…
`   stamp='20011206T18:23:54'>`	The time the message was sent/received.
`   Offline Storage`	Message explaining the delay.
`  </x>`	
`</message>`	

As we expected, once the "smirk" client became available, we received the messages waiting for it. In this case, the server's "welcome" message, and the message we sent to "smirk" from "iain" in step 9. Once again, the server has added a `delay` X extension to the message. You server may not have done so.

Look back at the "iain" session. No new packets should have appeared. As you can see, neither the message or presence protocols have a server reply. The IQ protocols on the other hand will send replies to each request. The assumption is that once a `<message>` or `<presence>` packet has been sent from the client to the server, the server guarantees its delivery. No reply means success.[8] Failures will result in the server sending an error packet back to the sender.

It has been nice to see that messages will eventually be delivered to clients when they become available. However, this is instant messaging so let's see what happens when we send a message to someone that is available. We'll use the "smirk" session to send a message to "iain," as shown in step 13.

Step 13: The "smirk" session sends a message to "iain."

"Raw" smirk client session	What is happening
`<message to='iain@localhost'>`	A new message to "iain."
`<body>I love messages</body>`	The message's "body."
`</message>`	

We don't expect a reply for the `<message>` packet so nothing should appear when you send the message. However, if you look at the "iain" session, you should "instantly" see the packet as shown in step 14.

Step 14: The "iain" session receives a message from "smirk."

"Raw" iain client session	What is happening
`<message to='iain@shigeoka.com'`	A new message to "iain."
`from='smirk@localhost/test'`	The sender is "smirk" on resource "test."
`<body>I love messages</body>`	The message's "body."
`</message>`	

---

[8] The proposed "event" Jabber protocol allows senders to request delivery confirmation for packets.

Notice that the packet is missing the delay X extension because there was no server delay for the message. You can play around with sending messages between the two sessions. When you're finished, close the stream on both the "iain" and "smirk" sessions. Once you close the stream, the server will automatically close down the telnet connection, as shown in steps 15 and 16.

Steps 15 and 16: Closing the Jabber XML stream.

"Raw" client session	What is happening
`</stream:stream>`	Close the stream.
`Connection closed by foreign host.`	Telnet application information: server has closed connection.
`%`	Command prompt.

Despite the fact that we know nothing of the Jabber protocol details, the basics of the core Jabber protocols and the various Jabber packets are pretty intuitive. The structured, but still human-friendly nature of XML makes the Jabber sessions easy to follow along even with our limited knowledge of Jabber details.

2.4   Conclusions

The Jabber system is technically simple, flexible, and surprisingly intuitive. Looking at the XML data that is passed between client and server, we can easily understand, analyze, and debug the Jabber protocols. These developer-friendly properties come from the clever use of XML by Jabber.

In the next part of this book, we'll look at the Jabber protocols in greater depth; building the detailed knowledge we need to implement these protocols in software. Along the way, we'll develop Java software that can understand, analyze and exploit the Jabber protocols. The end result will be a thorough coverage of the core Jabber protocols, and a few important IQ extension protocols. In addition, we'll create a Java client and Java server. You can use that software to explore Jabber and expand it for your own Jabber software needs.

Part II

Protocols, code, and advanced IM

In this part of the book, we cover the core Jabber protocols in enough detail that you can implement Jabber-compliant software. We'll build a Jabber server and client in Java to clearly illustrate the Jabber protocols and we'll examine the tradeoffs facing Jabber developers. The part ends by examining advanced Jabber features not included in the current Jabber standards. We'll also explore how you can build applications that exploit these enterprise instant messaging frameworks to create next-generation, IM-based systems.

IM concepts and Jabber protocols

The foundation for the Jabber software that we'll continue to develop through the remaining chapters begin here. We will start with the development of a basic Jabber server. Using the code developed here as a framework, each subsequent chapter will add more Jabber capabilities.

3.1 A basic Java Jabber server

If you have ever written code for a server, the basic design of a Jabber server will be very familiar to you. If not, don't worry. Server software, in its basic form, is surprisingly simple. Most of the cost, complexity, and work that goes into large-scale server software lies in adding extra features that allow the server to handle large numbers of users simultaneously and to do so in a secure, reliable manner.

The Jabber server in this book is designed to be as simple as possible while implementing the Jabber protocols. This simplicity makes it easy to understand and modify—two features that for our purposes (learning) are more important than the typical server features that interest programmers. Once you understand the Jabber software, you can easily modify it to add features as you need them.

Our simple Jabber server does three things:

- Handles network connections with Jabber clients
- Reads and writes Jabber XML streams
- Reacts to input from Jabber clients

Surprisingly, we can create a server to do these things in just a few Java classes. In this section, we'll create a basic Jabber server that carries out all three tasks.

3.1.1 Goals for our server

Before writing a piece of software, it helps to have a clear set of project goals. Goals provide general guidelines that drive design and implementation decisions. For the Jabber server we'll use the following design goals:

- *Simple*—Simple things appeal from a purely aesthetic point of view. In addition, simple software tends to be more robust, easier to understand, and easier to modify. The latter two are also project goals we'll cover later. By keeping things simple, we have a head start on meeting our other goals as well.
- *Standards compliant*—We're developing the Jabber server software to explain and illustrate the Jabber protocols. Obviously we want to make sure that it implements the Jabber protocols correctly or it loses its educational value. In addition, compliant servers will be interoperable with the significant amount of Jabber software available today.

- *Easy to understand*—The software must be easy to understand. It is difficult to learn from confusing software and it is even harder to explain it well. The clearer the software the less work both of us have to do.

- *Easy to modify*—Although this software is an educational tool, hopefully some of you will want to use it in the real world. In most cases, you will need to modify it to meet your needs (its present form is severely limited in capability). We should make it as easy as possible to modify while still meeting our other goals.

It is also vital that we establish what the server is *not* trying to do. The Jabber server software in this book is not intended to be secure, scalable, manageable, robust (transactional), efficient, or fast. On a reasonably fast machine the server should be able to provide non-mission-critical IM to about 20 users: perfect for a small workgroup but not enough for most small- to medium-sized businesses.

3.1.2 *Our server software*

The server software in this chapter will accept and handle incoming client connections, parse an XML stream over that connection, and react to Jabber commands sent over the XML stream. The software will be extremely limited to start, but as we cover new Jabber protocols code supporting them will be added to the server, expanding the server's features and capabilities.

All of the software in this book is available for download from the book's web site at Manning Publications (www.manning.com/shigeoka). I'm releasing the software under a modified Apache (BSD) license. The license permits you to do almost anything you want with the software including copying it, selling it, or incorporating it into commercial products. Send a note through the book's website, letting me know what you're doing with the software.

There are several interesting directions that you can take the software including implementing the advanced Jabber features. Covered in chapter 10, they include implementing server security, embedding Jabber functionality into existing applications, or integrating it into other enterprise resources.[1] In addition, the server is useful as a normal Jabber server for small workgroups. You may want to work on optimizations in I/O (input/output), threading, parsing, distributed processing, management/administration, transactions/journaling, size, space, or

---

[1] These bridges to enterprise resources are often referred to as *middleware*, and Jabber's use in this area would fall under the topic of MOM.

memory consumption. The last three optimizations are very important when Jabber is used in small, resource-constrained, embedded systems.[2]

3.1.3 *The basic server design*

My Jabber server is broken up into three basic functional modules:

- *Session pool*—A collection of Jabber client/server sessions. Each session manages a `java.net.Socket` connection and metainformation such as the associated session ID and Jabber ID. A session index allows other server modules to locate a session by Jabber ID.

- *XML parser*—The XML parsing classes handle the incoming Jabber XML data and transform it into Java packet objects that can be used by the Jabber server. The XML parsing classes rely on the Simple API for XML (SAX) parser in the Xerces XML Java library.

- *Packet handlers*—The server reacts to incoming packets. In most cases, the server simply routes packets to a particular delivery endpoint. However many packets must be processed by the server, generating one or more reply packets.

The modules are joined together by a `PacketQueue` that holds Jabber `Packet` objects:

- *PacketQueue*—This class is a basic queue data structure for `Packet` java objects.[3] The `PacketQueue` joins the packet handlers to the XML parser module by allowing the XML parser to deposit `Packet` objects into the `PacketQueue`. The packet handlers remove `Packet` objects from the `PacketQueue` and handles them. The `PacketQueue` is designed to be thread-safe allowing separate server threads to work with the `Packet-Queue` simultaneously.

- *Jabber packets*—The `Packet` class stores information about the Jabber XML data packets that are sent between a Jabber client and server.

The general architecture is shown in figure 3.1.

---

[2] Who would run a Java Jabber server in an embedded system? There is a whole category of embedded systems called "home gateways" or "digital hubs" that manage home networks, primarily for automation and entertainment. Many run Java and could benefit from embedded Jabber servers for communication and presence.

[3] A *queue* is a basic first-in, first-out (FIFO) list. Items placed into the queue are taken from it in the order they entered.

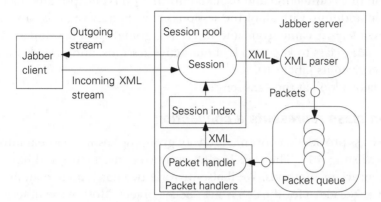

Figure 3.1   The basic server modules joined by the PacketQueue

The basic server operation begins when a client connects to the Jabber server. The server will create a session object for the connection and start an XML parser reading incoming XML. The XML parser generates Java `Packet` objects that are pushed onto the packet queue. A set of packet handlers takes packets from the queue, processes them as necessary, generates XML for outgoing packets, uses the session index to find the correct `Session` object's outgoing XML stream, and writes the outgoing XML to that stream.

    The session pool, XML parser, and packet queue work together to support processing Jabber packets. We will implement the various Jabber protocols in the packet handler classes. For now we will provide rudimentary routing for all incoming packets. As we cover new Jabber protocols we'll add more packet handlers.

3.2   *The session pool maintains client connections*

A typical Jabber server will maintain many simultaneous, long-lived connections with clients. Each of these sessions defines a context for the packets being passed between the client and server. The session's context must remain associated with each connection. It includes information such as:

- The Jabber ID associated with the session
- The Stream ID associated with the session
- The `java.net.Socket` and corresponding `java.io.Reader/Writer` objects used by this session
- The status of the session (disconnected, connected, streaming, authenticated)

This collection of a connection and its metainformation is encapsulated in a `Session` object. In addition, with all of the sessions active in a server, it is easy to lose track of where a `Packet` came from, and where it is going. We'll develop a centralized `SessionIndex` class to keep track of our active sessions, and provide a way to find a `Session` given its Jabber ID.

Let's first take a look at the `Session` class.

3.2.1 *The Session class represents a connection*

The `Session` class provides a convenient way of grouping session context information together (listing 3.1). The class begins with two constructors and basic data fields and their access methods. We'll also provide two convenience methods to produce `Writer/Readers` for the `Session`'s `Socket` object. Most of the time, a `Session` object is used to get a `java.io.Writer` in order to write information to the `Session` `Socket`'s `OutputStream`, or a `java.io.Reader` to read information. By creating and saving a `Reader` and `Writer`, users of the class won't have to get the `Socket`, get the `Input/OutputStreams`, and create a `Reader/Writer` themselves.

> **Listing 3.1   The Session class**

```
public class Session{

  public Session(Socket socket) { setSocket(socket);        }
  public Session()              { setStatus(DISCONNECTED); }

  JabberID jid;
  public JabberID getJID()             { return jid;  }
  public void     setJID(JabberID newID) { jid = newID; }

  String sid;
  public String getStreamID()             { return sid;     }
  public void    setStreamID(String streamID) { sid = streamID; }

  Socket sock;
  public Socket getSocket()             { return sock;  }
  public void    setSocket(Socket socket) {
    sock = socket;
    setStatus(CONNECTED);
  }

  Writer out;
  public Writer getWriter() throws IOException {
    if (out == null){
      out = new BufferedWriter(new OutputStreamWriter(sock.getOutputStream()));
    }
    return out;
  }
```

```
   Reader in;
public Reader getReader() throws IOException {
   if (in == null){
     in = new BufferedReader(new InputStreamReader(sock.getInputStream()));
   }
   return in;
}
```

The most interesting part of the Session class is its status management code. There will be several classes that will want to know the status of a Session as well as to take action when the status changes. This is especially true of client software that we will develop in the next chapter. To support this, we'll use a session status event model similar to that found in the Swing classes.

In the event model (listing 3.2), listeners register themselves for event notification. When an event is triggered (in our case by changing the status using the setStatus() method), the Session will notify its registered listeners of the event. The process can be a bit confusing the first time you see it, but it is a great way to solve the problem of having many objects watch a variable on another object.

Listing 3.2   The Session class status event code

```
LinkedList statusListeners = new LinkedList();

public boolean addStatusListener(StatusListener listener){
   return statusListeners.add(listener);
}

public boolean removeStatusListener(StatusListener listener){
   return statusListeners.remove(listener);
}

public static final int DISCONNECTED   = 1;
public static final int CONNECTED      = 2;
public static final int STREAMING      = 3;
public static final int AUTHENTICATED = 4;

int status;
public int getStatus() { return status;  }

public synchronized void setStatus(int newStatus){
   status = newStatus;
   ListIterator iter = statusListeners.listIterator();
   while (iter.hasNext()){
     StatusListener listener = (StatusListener)iter.next();
     listener.notify(status);
```

```
    }
  }
}
```

A `java.util.LinkedList` class is used to maintain a list of listeners for the `Session`. This makes adding and removing status listeners simple. All status event listeners must implement the `StatusListener` interface:

The StatusListener interface

```
public interface StatusListener {
  public void notify(int status);
}
```

This simple interface has a single `notify()` method that is used in the `setStatus()` method to send the event information to the listeners. For consistency, I also defined some standard values for the four status states that I anticipate for the `Session` class.

The `Session` class represents a single network connection and Jabber session between a client and server. The server will need to handle many simultaneous `Sessions` and provide a mechanism for organizing them and locating `Sessions` by their Jabber ID. The `SessionIndex` class handles these responsibilities.

3.2.3 *The SessionIndex class provides session lookup*

The primary responsibility of the `SessionIndex` class is to look up `Session` objects by Jabber ID. Locating the correct `Session` object by Jabber ID is important for the server because the majority of incoming Jabber packets will be addressed to Jabber users. The server must locate the `Session` corresponding to the recipient's Jabber ID and deliver the packet to that client.

To accomplish this, the `SessionIndex` class maintains two `java.util.Hashtable` objects: `userIndex` and `jidIndex`.. The `userIndex Hashtable` maintains a mapping between the `Session`'s user name and the `Session` object. The `jidIndex` maintains a mapping between the `Session`'s full Jabber ID string, and the `Session` object.

This allows the `SessionIndex` to conduct `Session` lookups using the following algorithm:

- Check if the recipient Jabber ID is in the `jidIndex`. The comparison uses an exact match allowing clients to send messages to other specific clients.
- If there is no matching Jabber ID in the `jidIndex`, then see if the Jabber ID's user name is in the `userIndex`.[4]
- If no match is found, return a `null` object.

Using this algorithm the server will display a reasonable message routing behavior. For example, imagine that a client with the Jabber ID iain@shigeoka.com/home is connected to the server. A message is sent to iain@shigeoka.com/home. The `SessionIndex` will look up the Jabber ID, find it in the `jidIndex`, and return the correct `Session`. Now imagine the message is addressed to iain@shigeoka.com. The `SessionIndex` class will search the `jidIndex` and not find a match. However when the `SessionIndex` looks in the `userIndex`, it will find a match for "iain" and return the `Session` connected to iain@shigeoka.com/home.

Finally, consider a message addressed to iain@shigeoka.com/work. The `SessionIndex` class will fail to find it in the `jidIndex`, but will find the matching "iain" entry in the `userIndex` and return the `Session` attached to iain@shigeoka.com/home. Thus, the message is delivered to the correct user but at an alternate resource. This behavior is consistent with the Jabber message routing standard.

The implementation of the class (listing 3.3) is a fairly straightforward management of these mappings.

Listing 3.3   The SessionIndex class

```
public class SessionIndex {

  Hashtable userIndex = new Hashtable();   ← Username to Session mapping
  Hashtable jidIndex = new Hashtable();    ← Full Jabber ID string to Session mapping

  public Session getSession(String jabberID){
    return getSession(new JabberID(jabberID));
  }

  public Session getSession(JabberID jabberID){
    String jidString = jabberID.toString();
    Session session = (Session)jidIndex.get(jidString);
    if (session == null){
      LinkedList resources = (LinkedList)userIndex.get(jabberID.getUser());
      if (resources == null){   ← User offline (not connected to server)
        return null;
      }
      session = (Session)resources.getFirst();
    }
```

---

[4] I also assume messages are always sent to clients at this server so I can ignore the server part of the Jabber ID.

```
    return session;
  }

  public void removeSession(Session session){

    String jidString = session.getJID().toString();
    String user = session.getJID().getUser();

    if (jidIndex.containsKey(jidString)){
      jidIndex.remove(jidString);
    }
    LinkedList resources = (LinkedList)userIndex.get(user);
    if (resources == null){
      return;
    }
    if (resources.size() <= 1){
      userIndex.remove(user);
      return;
    }
    resources.remove(session);
  }

  public void addSession(Session session){
    jidIndex.put(session.getJID().toString(),session);
    String user = session.getJID().getUser();
    LinkedList resources = (LinkedList)userIndex.get(user);
    if (resources == null){
      resources = new LinkedList();
      userIndex.put(user,resources);
    }
    resources.addLast(session);
  }
}
```

As you can see by my use of a LinkedList of Sessions for each username in the
userIndex, messages are routed to users on a first-come first-served basis. In other
words, if I connect the following clients in this order:

```
iain@shigeoka.com/home
iain@shigeoka.com/work
iain@shigeoka.com/laptop
```

a message sent to iain@shigeoka.com will be delivered to iain@shigeoka.com/
home. If iain@shigeoka.com/home disconnects (the server calls removeSession()
on the SessionIndex), then messages sent to iain@shigeoka.com will be delivered to
iain@shigeoka.com/work.[5] This is not standard Jabber routing behavior but it is the
best we can do until chapter 8 when we add user accounts, user presence, and supporting protocols. When we have the user presence protocol support in place, we'll
implement the more sophisticated, priority-based Jabber routing scheme that is speci-

fied by the Jabber standards. The primary user of the `SessionIndex` is the packet-handling classes associated with the `QueueThread` class.

3.3   XML parsing subsystem

XML parsing is the most complicated task that the Jabber server does at this point. However, for Java coders, the task is child's play because we will rely on the standard Java SAX parsing library to do the actual work of XML parsing. We only need to react in the form of event handler methods to the XML data that the parser finds.

The job of the server's XML parsing classes is to take streaming XML information, convert it to `Packet` objects, and store those packets in the `PacketQueue` as shown in figure 3.2. We'll start our coverage of the XML parsing process with the `Packet` and `PacketQueue` classes.

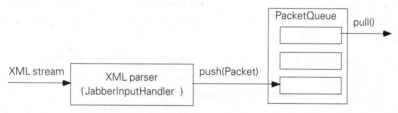

Figure 3.2   The server's XML parsing classes act like a transformation filter, taking in an XML text stream and producing a stream of `Packet` objects to be pushed into the `PacketQueue`.

3.3.1   Representing Jabber packets

The Jabber protocols involve the exchange of XML fragments between the client and server. We'll refer to these XML fragments as Jabber packets. We will represent them as Java objects which are easier to work with than XML strings. Using Java objects enables us to exploit Java's many object-oriented features such as strong type checking, inheritance, and object polymorphism.[6]

A quick glance at the Jabber protocol specification shows that there are only three "core" Jabber packets to worry about:

---

[5] In chapter 6, we'll see how authenticated users can override this behavior to prioritize the delivery of messages to alternative resources.

[6] Polymorphism means many forms and refers to the ability of Java objects to act as different classes through the use of class inheritance and the implementation of Java interfaces.

- *<message></message>*—A standard Jabber message packet. I'll cover the message packet and protocols in detail in chapter 4.

- *<presence></presence>*—A standard Jabber presence packet. I'll cover presence packet and protocols in detail in chapter 5.

- *<iq></iq>*—A standard Jabber IQ packet. The IQ protocols cover all Jabber tasks that are neither messaging nor presence. The IQ protocols include authentication, account management, and configuration. I'll cover the these packet and protocols in detail in chapter 6.

In addition, we must recognize and react to the opening and closing stream tags and the stream error packet:[7]

- *<stream:stream>*—The opening XML stream tag. This signals the start of a Jabber XML session. I have to react to the tag immediately so it gets full packet status in the server.

- *<stream:error></stream:error>*—A Jabber stream error packet. This packet is used to indicate a problem with a stream (usually indicating an improperly formatted stream).

- *</stream:stream>*—The closing XML stream tag. This signals the conclusion of a Jabber XML session. As with the opening stream tag, I have to react to the closing tag so it gets full packet status as well.

Supporting these packets and tags at the most basic level is quite simple. By the end of this chapter, our Jabber server will be able to recognize and handle them all. The first step in supporting Jabber packets is to recognize the common traits of all packets and encapsulate them in a Java class.

Jabber packets are XML fragments that can be thought of as "mini" XML documents. There are many ways to represent XML documents in Java. One of the most popular is to follow the W3C Document Object Model(DOM) standard. Most Java XML parsing libraries include standardized Java classes to support W3C DOM. In DOM, the XML document is represented in a tree-like data structure.

Our needs for XML representation aren't as generic as that provided by the DOM standards. We know what kinds of XML documents we'll be receiving and we can specialize our Java objects accordingly. In addition, avoiding DOM will free our code from dependencies on DOM libraries and lower the amount of code

---

[7] The stream protocol is defined in the `jabber:stream` namespace while `message`, `presence`, and `iq` are defined in the `jabber:client` and `jabber:server` namespaces.

needed to build our server. Finally, our `Packet` class must do more than represent the XML fragment's information. The `Packet` class must fill two primary roles:

- *Packet store*—The `Packet` class is primarily a data storage class. The information can be set up using standard Java method calls. We'll store `Packets` in a tree-like data structure just like that used in the W3C DOM.[8]

- *XML writer*—The `Packet` class knows how to create its own XML string representation. This feature allows other classes to generically convert `Packet` objects from Java objects to their XML `String` representation.

A separate XML parsing class covered later in this chapter will build `Packet` objects from incoming XML strings. The data structure for a `Packet` class mirrors the structure of XML fragments. For example, consider an XML packet:

```
<message to='recipient'>
  <subject>hello</subject>
  <body>How are you doing?</body>
</message>
```

We can organize it into three packets, arranged in a tree:

```
Packet: message (attribute to='recipient)
  Packet: subject
    String (value "hello")
  Packet: body
    String (value "How are you doing?");
```

In such a data structure, we can see that a `Packet` has an "element name," zero or more attribute name/value pairs, and zero or more children. A `Packet` object's children are either `Strings`, or other `Packet` objects. In addition, each `Packet` has an associated namespace.

As a Java class, we can store the list of a `Packet`'s children in a simple `java.util.List`, its attributes in a `java.util.Hashtable`, and its other values as `Strings`. To aid in navigation, the `Packet` class also keeps track of its parent `Packet`. If the `Packet` has no parent, the `Packet`'s parent variable is set to `null`.

The class begins with three constructors:

The Packet class constructors

```
public class Packet {

  public Packet(String element){
    setElement(element);
  }
```

---

[8] Our `Packet` class closely resembles the DOM `Node` class (rather than the `Document` class).

```
public Packet(String element, String value){
  setElement(element);
  children.add(value);
}

public Packet(Packet parent,
              String element,
              String namespace,
              Attributes atts){
  setElement(element);
  setNamespace(namespace);
  setParent(parent);

  //Copy attributes into hashtable
  for (int i = 0; i < atts.getLength(); i++){
    attributes.put(atts.getQName(i), atts.getValue(i));
  }
}
```

The parent and `children` member variables maintain the tree structure of Packets and their children. We'll use the `java.util.LinkedList` class to store child Packets and Strings. In addition, the namespace and element name for the packet must be stored as Strings.

```
String namespace;
  public void    setNamespace(String name) { namespace = name; }
  public String getNamespace()            { return namespace; }

  String element;
  public void    setElement(String element) { this.element = element; }
  public String getElement()               { return element;           }

  Packet parent;
  public Packet getParent()                 { return parent;          }
  public void    setParent(Packet parent){
    this.parent = parent;
    if (parent != null){
      parent.children.add(this);
    }
  }

  LinkedList children = new LinkedList();

  public LinkedList getChildren() {return children;}
```

The Packet class provides several convenience methods for working with the Packet data. Imagine we have an XML packet that looks like the following:

```
<item>
  ItemValue
  <sub-item>sub-item value</sub-item>
  <sub-item>another value</sub-item>
</item>
```

The `Packet` class provides several convenience methods for working with the `Packet` data. Imagine we have an XML packet that looks like the following:

```
<item>
  ItemValue
  <sub-item>sub-item value</sub-item>
  <sub-item>another value</sub-item>
</item>
```

There are three typical tasks that other classes will need to carry out on the `Packet`:

- Obtaining the first child `Packet` with a given element name (the `Packet` representing the sub-packet `<sub-item>sub-item value</sub-item>`).
- Obtaining the first string value for the `Packet` (the `String` "ItemValue").
- Obtaining the `String` value associated with the first child `Packet` with a given element name (the `String` "sub-item value").

The first convenience method locates the first child `Packet` of a given element name. This is implemented in the `getFirstChild()` method. For example, consider our earlier `<item>` XML packet. You can call `getFirstChild("sub-item")` on the `<item>` packet object in order to find the first subpacket with an element name of `sub-item`.

```
public Packet getFirstChild(String subelement){
    Iterator childIterator = children.iterator();
    while (childIterator.hasNext()){
      Object child = childIterator.next();
      if (child instanceof Packet){
        Packet childPacket = (Packet)child;
        if (childPacket.getElement().equals(subelement)) {
          return childPacket;
        }
      }
    }
    return null;
}
```

Another common task is to obtain the String value associated with an element. For example, when we receive the `<sub-item>` sub-Packet, we will want to know its value ("sub-item value"). You can get this by calling the getValue() method on the `<sub-item>` Packet object.

```
public String getValue(){
  StringBuffer value = new StringBuffer();
  Iterator childIterator = children.iterator();
  while (childIterator.hasNext()){
    Object valueChild = childIterator.next();
    if (valueChild instanceof String){
      value.append((String)valueChild);
    }
  }
  return value.toString().trim();
}
```

Even more likely is the scenario where we want to know the value of the `String` child of a sub-`Packet`. In the previous examples, we obtained the value of the first `<sub-item>` sub-`Packet` by calling `getFirstChild("sub-item")` to obtain the sub-`Packet` and then calling `getValue()` to get its string value. Since these are convenience methods, let's make it more convenient by combining the steps into a single `getChildValue()` method.

```
public String getChildValue(String subelement){
  Packet child = getFirstChild(subelement);
  if (child == null){
    return null;
  }
  return child.getValue();
}
```

Incoming `Packets` often rely on their session context for routing and other behavior. Each client/server connection in our Jabber server will have an associated `Session` object to track this session context. The `Packet` stores a reference to this `Session` object.

```
Session session;
public void      setSession(Session session) { this.session = session; }

public Session  getSession() {
  if (session != null){
    return session;
  }
  if (parent != null){
    return parent.getSession();
  }
  return null;
}
```

Many of the Jabber protocols rely on `Packet` attributes (key/value pairs) for vital information regarding the `Packet` and its behavior. The `Packet` class stores the attributes in a `java.util.Hashtable`. In addition, it supplies several convenience methods for accessing the most common `Packet` attributes:

- *to*—The packet's recipient.
- *from*—The packet's sender.
- *id*—The packet ID uniquely identifying the packet.
- *type*—The packet's type. The meaning depends on the protocol.

```java
Hashtable attributes = new Hashtable();

public String getAttribute(String attribute) {
  return (String)attributes.get(attribute);
}

public void  setAttribute(String attribute, String value) {
  if (value == null){
    removeAttribute(attribute);
  } else {
    attributes.put(attribute,value);
  }
}


public void removeAttribute(String attribute){
  attributes.remove(attribute);
}

public void clearAttributes(){
  attributes.clear();
}

public String getTo()                { return (String)attributes.get("to");    }
public void    setTo(String recipient) { setAttribute("to",recipient);          }

public String getFrom()              { return (String)attributes.get("from");  }
public void    setFrom(String sender){ setAttribute("from",sender);             }

public String getType()              { return (String)attributes.get("type");  }
public void    setType(String type){ setAttribute("type",type);                 }

public String getID()                { return (String)attributes.get("id");    }
public void    setID(String ID)     { setAttribute("id",ID);                    }
}
```

Finally, the `Packet` class will write itself to a `java.io.Writer` as an XML string. The process of creating an XML representation involves the methodical traversal of the `Packet` tree, outputting the appropriate elements, attributes, and children.

```java
public void writeXML() throws IOException {
  writeXML(session.getWriter());
}

public void writeXML(Writer out) throws IOException{
```

```java
    out.write("<");
    out.write(element);

    //Output the attributes for the element
    Enumeration keys = attributes.keys();
    while (keys.hasMoreElements()){
      String key = (String)keys.nextElement();
      out.write(" ");
      out.write(key);
      out.write("='");
      out.write((String)attributes.get(key));
      out.write("'");
    }

    //Empty element
    if (children.size() == 0){
      out.write("/>");
      out.flush();
      return;
    }

    out.write(">");
    //Iterate over each child
    Iterator childIterator = children.iterator();
    while (childIterator.hasNext()){
      Object child = childIterator.next();
      //Send value to Writer
      if (child instanceof String){
        out.write((String)child);
      //Or recursively write its children's XML
      } else {
        ((Packet)child).writeXML(out);
      }
    }
    out.write("</");
    out.write(element);
    out.write(">");
    out.flush();
  }

  public String toString(){
    try {
      StringWriter reply = new StringWriter();
      writeXML(reply);
      return reply.toString();
    } catch (Exception ex){
    }
    return "<" + element + ">";
  }
}
```

Packets are placed into, and retrieved from, a single, serverwide packet queue.

3.3.2 *The PacketQueue class as server focal point*

The PacketQueue class is a basic data structure class with a limited set of responsibilities. However, it serves as a focal point for the flow of information in the server. Packets from the server's many clients fan in to the PacketQueue. The Packets are then fanned out to the packet handlers according to the packet's element name. Many threads of operation will be active at once in the server and all of them synchronize on the PacketQueue and the packets within it.

COMMAND PROCESSOR DESIGN PATTERN

For those familiar with design patterns, our packet handling system is a minor variation on the Command Processor design pattern.[9]

"The Command Processor design pattern separates the request for a service from its execution. A command processor component manages requests as separate objects, schedules their execution, and provides additional services such as the storing of request objects for later undo."

In our Jabber server, the XML parser acts as the command controller accepting requests (our XML stream) and converting them into commands (our Packet objects). The QueueThread acts as the command processor taking the packets and scheduling their execution. Unlike the command processor design pattern however, the Packets don't handle their own execution. Instead our packet handler classes act as dual-function command processor suppliers and command processors to provide the entire Packet processing functionality.

The benefits of the command processor pattern apply to our design as well, and they are:

- *Flexibility in the way requests are activated*—Supporting alternative activation methods makes it easier to bridge our Jabber server to other messaging systems.

- *Flexibility in the number and functionality of requests*—Especially important with the rapidly changing Jabber protocols.

- *Programming execution-related services*—In particular, we can easily log packets and replay Jabber sessions by making minor modifications to the QueueThread.

---

[9] Buschmann et al, *Pattern-oriented Software Architecture: a System of Patterns* (John Wiley & Sons, 1996), p. 277. The Command Processor pattern is also covered in *Design Patterns: Elements of Reusable Object-Oriented Software* (Addison-Wesley, 1994), by Gamma et al, and is referred to in that text as the Command pattern.

- *Testability at application level*—The `QueueThread` is an excellent point of entry into the system for testing the XML parsing as well as packet handling parts of the server. Once again, the ability to log and replay sessions can be a big help.

- *Concurrency*—`Packets` and their handling is a relatively isolated computation. The `QueueThread` can easily distribute processing by handling packets in parallel threads of execution.

The commander processor pattern has some liabilities, however:

- *Efficiency loss*—Converting data formats and providing intermediate processing steps requires additional computation time and storage.

- *Potential for excessive number of command classes*—We avoid this issue for the most part by representing all packets with a single, generic `Packet` class. We pay for the simplicity in reduced efficiency of the general representation. In addition, a generic `Packet` class can represent an infinite number of packet classes. Our server has to create extra logic to resolve which packet we're dealing with (a <message> packet, <presence> packet, etc.)

The `PacketQueue` (figure 3.3) must:

- *Store Packets*—Accept `Packet` objects pushed onto the back of the `Packet-Queue`, maintaining the order of items pushed.

- *Retrieve Packets*—Allow `Packet` objects to be pulled off the front of the `Pack-etQueue`, removing the item.

- *Be thread-safe*—Allow multiple threads of execution to push and pull `Packets` from the `PacketQueue` without problems.

- *Provide thread synchronization*—If the `PacketQueue` is empty, attempting to pull `Packets` from the front will cause the caller to wait (block) until a new `Packet` is pushed onto the back of the queue or the thread is interrupted. Threads can use this feature to synchronize their actions and conserve server resources.

Threads that operate on `Packet` objects can do so efficiently by pulling `Packet` objects from the `PacketQueue` in an infinite loop. The `PacketQueue` itself will make sure that these worker threads only execute when there are available `Pack-ets` in the `PacketQueue`

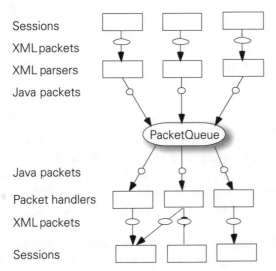

Sessions

XML packets

XML parsers

Java packets

PacketQueue

Java packets

Packet handlers

XML packets

Sessions

Figure 3.3
The PacketQueue accepts
packets from parallel XML
parsing streams, and feeds
parallel packet handlers.

The implementation of the PacketQueue is extremely simple. A java.util
.LinkedList object is used to store the Packets[10] and a sprinkling of Java thread
primitives is added to support the server's multithreaded environment.

In listing 3.4 I have highlighted the thread support code in bold. Notice that
the methods push() and pull() are synchronized to protect them from being
executed by overlapping threads. Every push() method call causes notify-
All() to wake up any threads waiting on a pull() method call. The pull()
method blocks on its internal wait() method call while the queue is empty.

Listing 3.4   The PacketQueue class

```
public class PacketQueue {
  //Actual storage is handled by a java.util.LinkedList
  LinkedList queue = new LinkedList();

  public synchronized void push(Packet packet){
    queue.add(packet);
    notifyAll();
  }

  public synchronized Packet pull(){
    try {
      while (queue.isEmpty()) {
```

---

[10] The Java library contains many excellent classes that will save you from reinventing the wheel. It is well
worth your time to familiarize yourself with it.

```
      wait();
    }
  } catch (InterruptedException e){
    return null;
  }
  return (Packet)queue.remove(0);
  }
}
```

The loop is necessary because push() calls notifyAll(), waking up all threads waiting on pull(). If only one Packet is pushed onto the queue, the first thread to execute will remove the Packet from the queue. All the other waiting threads will then run (they won't run simultaneously because pull() is synchronized), the queue will be empty, and they will have to block on the wait() call again until the next Packet arrives.

If you don't understand Java threading code you can trust that this works, write some test code to verify it, or learn more about Java threads. I have tried to keep the amount of threading code to a minimum in the book's source code but server code tends to be heavily threaded. If you wish to learn more about threads, there are several excellent books about Java threads. In addition, the JavaSoft online documentation (java.sun.com) provides a free tutorial on using Java threads.

Now that we're ready to take care of XML parsing using the JabberIn-putHandler class.

3.3.5 *SAX parsing in Java*

The JabberInputHandler XML parsing class coordinates the three main XML parsing entities: the Packet class under construction, the Java SAX parser, and the PacketQueue. Of the three, only the parser remains to be tackled.

SAX parsing is a standard programming interface to XML parsers. SAX hides the details of XML parsing. Instead, interesting XML data is reported to the programmer using XML content events. SAX programmers simply write a SAX content handler class that responds to these content events. For Jabber parsing, we only need to handle the content events that correspond to the beginning and end of an element, and to character data within the element.

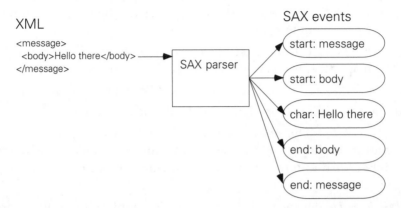

Figure 3.4   A SAX parser reads XML text, and issues corresponding SAX content events for handlers to process.

The `JabberInputHandler` is a SAX content handler class. Its primary task is coordinating the building of packet objects from the SAX events generated by the Xerces SAX parser. The `JabberInputHandler` accomplishes this in a fairly generic way by watching the depth of embedded elements within an XML document.

In order to build our `Packet` classes into a tree structure we will track the depth of a particular element within the XML document tree. The depth increases by one with every start element and decreases by one for each end element. This depth-first ordering of element tags makes tracking your current position in the tree relatively simple.

The actions for each SAX event are summarized here:[11]

- *startElement()*—For the start of each new element, add one to the depth counter and if:
  - *[depth == 0]*—The element should be a `<stream:stream>` tag. Instantiate a special open stream `Packet` with name `stream:stream`. It doesn't need an end element to be completed. Instead, it is immediately pushed onto the `PacketQueue`. This is the root of the Jabber stream.

---

[11] Note: SAX gurus will notice that my parser ignores processor instructions and does not validate the Jabber XML against the Jabber DTDs. Processing instructions are not used in Jabber XML streams and validation is too resource-intensive to use in most Jabber servers.

- *[depth == 1]*—Create a parentless `Packet` object. When we complete this packet, we'll push it onto the `PacketQueue`. The packet becomes the active packet under construction.

- *[depth > 1]*—Create a `Packet` object and set its parent to the active packet. The new packet becomes the active packet under construction.

- *characters()*—Add the given `String` as a child to the active packet.

- *endElement()*—Subtract one from the depth counter and if:

  - *[depth == 0]*—The active packet should be a `</stream:stream>` tag ending the Jabber XML stream. Instantiate a special close stream `Packet` with element name `/stream:stream` and push it onto the `PacketQueue`.

  - *[depth == 1]*—The active Jabber `Packet` is complete. Push the completed `Packet` onto the `PacketQueue`.

  - *[depth > 1]*—The active packet's parent `Packet` is still being built. Set the active packet to the current active packet's parent.

To process the XML stream, the `JabberInputHandler` needs to carry out the following configuration steps:

- *Create SAX parser*—We need to instantiate a parser object. You can do this in a generic way using a SAX parser factory class or directly by specifying a particular parser implementation class. The advantage of using the factory class is that you can easily plug in different **SAX** parser implementations (e.g., replace Xerces) without changing code by simply setting system properties. I directly create the Xerces SAX parser because I must set it up for XML streaming.

- *Set up the parser*—In this case, the parser is the `JabberInputHandler` class. We also have to install a new reader factory into the Xerces parser so that it will incrementally parse the incoming XML.

- *Parse*—Parsing is a simple matter of calling the parser's `parse()` method, handing it an `InputSource`. The SAX parser will parse the entire XML stream, calling content handler methods as necessary, before returning from `parse()` method. The `parse()` call only returns when the stream has been closed or an uncaught exception is thrown.

PARSING XML STREAMS WITH SAX

◆ Not all SAX XML parsers are created equal. Most assume you have a complete XML document resulting in parsers that buffer incoming XML for greater efficiency. Unfortunately for us, these parsers refuse to parse XML stream data as it arrives: resulting in a "stuck" Jabber server.

The Xerces SAX parser allows us to override its buffering data reader with a streaming reader by creating and installing a custom reader factory. This factory produces reader objects that Xerces uses to read the XML.

> **NOTE**   If you are using another SAX parsing library you need to find out if it supports streaming (often called incremental XML parsing) and turn the feature on.

There is no standard way of telling a SAX parser you want to handle streaming data so you must consult your SAX library documentation for details. For Xerces, the following class is all you need:

```
public class StreamingCharFactory
        extends DefaultReaderFactory {

    public XMLEntityHandler.EntityReader createCharReader(
                    XMLEntityHandler  entityHandler,
                    XMLErrorReporter errorReporter,
                    boolean sendCharDataAsCharArray,
                    Reader reader,
                    StringPool stringPool)
    throws Exception {
        return new StreamingCharReader(entityHandler,
                                    errorReporter,
                                    sendCharDataAsCharArray,
                                    reader,
                                    stringPool);
    }

    public XMLEntityHandler.EntityReader createUTF8Reader(
                    XMLEntityHandler entityHandler,
                    XMLErrorReporter errorReporter,
                    boolean sendCharDataAsCharArray,
                    InputStream data,
                    StringPool stringPool)
    throws Exception {
        XMLEntityHandler.EntityReader reader;
        reader = new StreamingCharReader(entityHandler,
                                    errorReporter,
                                    sendCharDataAsCharArray,
                                    new InputStreamReader(
                                                    data,
                                                    "UTF8"),
```

```
                                                    stringPool);
        return reader;
    }
  }
```

Although the process of configuring the SAX parser may sound a bit complicated for a simple XML parser, it isn't. In fact, I think the code speaks for itself. Let's start by examining the constructor for the `JabberInputHandler` class.

The JabberInputHandler Constructor

```
public class JabberInputHandler extends DefaultHandler {

  PacketQueue packetQ;
  Session session;

  public JabberInputHandler(PacketQueue packetQueue) {
    packetQ = packetQueue;
  }
```

The constructor allows us to set the PacketQueue once for the handler. I did this in anticipation of reusing JabberInputHandlers objects to process different XML streams. The current server doesn't take advantage of this.

Now for creating the parser, configuring it, and parsing our XML stream.

The JabberInputHandler process method starts the parsing work

```
public void process(Session session)
  throws IOException, SAXException {

    //Directly create a Xerces SAXParser
    SAXParser parser = new SAXParser();

    //Content handler for the SAX parser
    parser.setContentHandler(this);

    //Handle streaming XML
    parser.setReaderFactory(new StreamingCharFactory());

    //Save the session
    this.session = session;


    //Start the SAX parser parsing
    parser.parse(new InputSource(session.getReader()));
  }
```

The `process()` method is the launch pad for starting the parsing process. There are two nonstandard things going on here. First, we create a Xerces `SAXParser` class directly[12] rather than using the SAX parser factory, and we customize the

SAXParser with our custom reader factory to support XML streaming. Second, we use the Session object to obtain a java.io.Reader object for the XML stream. By hiding the details of how the reader is created in the Session object, we provide a lot of flexibility for future changes without having to modify the JabberInputHandler class.

> **SERVER OPTIMIZATION**
>
> The JabberInputHandler is not designed for efficiency. Resources such as object instances are relatively expensive to create, store in memory, and garbage-collect. If you have a large-scale server, you may need to handle thousands of XML streams at once. Rather than create a JabberInputHandler for each connection, you can share them between streams, only processing XML as it becomes available. The JabberInputHandler unfortunately creates a new SAXParser every time it calls the process method. If you do plan on reusing the JabberInputHandler in high capacity servers, you should consider methods for reusing expensive resources like SAXParser instances.

Now the only remaining part of the JabberInputHandler class is the event handlers. They are pretty straightforward now that you know how the PacketQueue and Packet classes work.

Listing 3.5   JabberInputHandler event handler methods

```
                              Active packet
                              being built          XML element
                                                   tree depth
Packet packet;  <———————————
int depth = 0;  <———————————————————————————

public void startElement(String namespaceURI,
                         String localName,
                         String qName,
                         Attributes atts)
                throws SAXException{               Only a
                                                <stream:stream>
                                                packet is allowed,
   switch (depth++){                             throw exception
                                                   otherwise

   case 0:
     if (qName.equals("stream:stream")){
       Packet openPacket = new Packet(null,qName,namespaceURI,atts);
       openPacket.setSession(session);
       packetQ.push(openPacket);
       return;
     }
     throw new SAXException("Root element must be <stream:stream>");
```

---

[12] SAXParser is imported with import org.apache.xerces.parsers.SAXParser to force the use of the Xerces parser.

```
   case 1:                                              Only a new message,
     packet = new Packet(null,qName,namespaceURI,atts);  presence, or <iq>
     packet.setSession(session);                         packet is allowed
     break;

   default:
     Packet child = new Packet(packet,qName,namespaceURI,atts);   Add a child
     packet = child;                                              Packet
   }
 }

public void characters(char[] ch,
                       int start,
                       int length)
           throws SAXException{

  if (depth > 1){
    packet.getChildren().add(new String(ch,start,length));
  }
 }

public void endElement(java.lang.String uri,
                       java.lang.String localName,
                       java.lang.String qName)
                throws SAXException {

  switch(--depth){

  case 0:                                               We're done;
    Packet closePacket = new Packet("/stream:stream");   this should be a
    closePacket.setSession(session);                     closing stream
    packetQ.push(closePacket);                           packet
    break;

   case 1:                          Active packet done;
     packetQ.push(packet);          push it onto the
     break;                         PacketQueue

   default:                         Move back
     packet = packet.getParent();   up the tree
   }
 }
}
```

As you can see, event handling is so very simple with the help of other classes. I must emphasize, however, that this is not the quickest, or most efficient, way of handling XML parsing.

For example, the majority of message packets enter the Jabber server and are immediately sent out to a Jabber client or server. There is no reason for the Jabber server to process the message contents, and no advantage for creating a Java object to represent that message. In fact, these short-lived Java objects can become a huge performance problem as we create and destroy thousands of these objects and the garbage collector struggles to keep up.

I took this approach because it is simple, and easier to understand. Once you start optimizing for performance, robustness, or scalability, you will be forced to add complexity and shortcuts that are hard to follow. I will leave these improvements to you as you experiment with and expand the Jabber server for your own uses.

3.4 *Packet handling and server threads*

The final Jabber server subsystem I need to cover is the server's packet handling classes and the threads that run the server. The packet handlers are simply classes that implement the `PacketListener` Java interface and process `Packet` objects. We'll use the packet handler classes to implement each of the Jabber protocols as we cover them.

In this chapter, we'll create three packet handler classes:

- An `OpenStreamHandler` class to create a `Session` object for each connection when the opening `<stream:stream>` tag is sent.
- A simple `MessageHandler` class that implements a crude version of Jabber packet routing.
- A `CloseStreamHandler` class to shut down the connection when the client sends its closing `<stream:stream>` tag.

The server's threading system is composed of three classes, each of which represents a separate thread of execution:

- *Server*—The main application class and main execution thread. This class creates the Jabber server socket and accepts new Jabber client connections.
- *ProcessThread*—This thread class handles connections accepted by the server. It creates a `JabberInputHandler` and processes the incoming XML stream. A separate `ProcessThread` thread handles each connection.
- *QueueThread*—This thread class takes `Packets` from the `PacketQueue` and hands them to the appropriate packet handler class. There is only one `QueueThread` object active in the Jabber server.

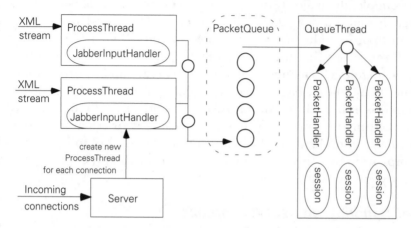

Figure 3.5 The server consists of one server, one `PacketQueue`**, one** `QueueThread`**, and many** `ProcessThreads` **(one for each connected Jabber client).**

The Jabber server may have many threads running at the same time. However, there are only three types of threads to worry about, and only the `ProcessThread` will have more than one instance running in the server. To better understand how the server works, look at the sequence diagram in figure 3.6, which shows what is happening in the server over time.[13]

We see that the `Server` main application class starts first. Its first task is to create a `QueueThread` class. The new `QueueThread` immediately calls `pull()` to receive a `Packet` from `PacketQueue`. `QueueThread` blocks because there are no packets in the queue. The `Server` then waits for incoming connections by calling `java.net.ServerSocket.accept()`.

---

[13] Sequence diagrams show the interaction between objects or threads over time. Time increases as you go down the diagram with vertical bars representing a particular entity (object or thread). You can learn more about sequence diagrams by reading a UML book (they're also called Booch interaction diagrams). However, I think you'll find them pretty intuitive.

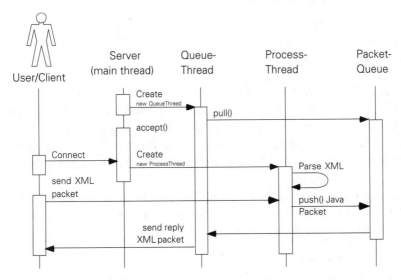

Figure 3.6   Sequence diagram of the server thread operations

A client connects to the server. This causes the Server to create a ProcessThread. The ProcessThread begins parsing incoming XML from the stream using the SAX parser and our JabberInputHandler class. As the client sends XML packets to the server, the ProcessThread's parser classes create Packet objects and calls push() to append them to the PacketQueue.

New Packets in the PacketQueue wake up the QueueThread (the pull() call returns). The QueueThread determines the Packet it has pulled from the queue, and processes it with the correct Packet handling class. The Packet handlers send any outgoing XML packets back to the connected clients.

Note that there is only one Server thread accepting connections, and one QueueThread processing Packet objects from the PacketQueue. However, there is one ProcessThread active for every connected client. There are ways to share threads of execution for handling the incoming client connections. In addition, servers with a lot of packets to process should probably run more than one QueueThread. However, in our server, we'll avoid these complications in order to keep the operation of the server as simple as possible.

Since the Server main class creates the QueueThread and ProcessThread, let's look at these two helper thread classes first, before examining the main Server class. The QueueThread is the more complicated so we'll begin there.

3.4.1 Packet handling in QueueThread

The QueueThread operates like a separate program. The Server starts one QueueThread at the very beginning of the program, and then lets it work independently. The QueueThread's sole job is to pull Packets from the PacketQueue and handle them.

There are a large number of things you may want to do with a packet to handle it. In fact, there are probably situations where you may want multiple handlers to have a chance to process a particular packet. For example, you may want to log each packet that passes through the server in addition to handling it in a normal manner. Or you may want to filter the messages to provide higher priority to certain users or types of traffic.

The situation is similar to the status update design problem facing the Session class. Like the status event model, a Packet event model will also work well here. To make this work, I need a PacketListener interface:

The PacketListener interface

```
public interface PacketListener {
  public void notify(Packet packet);
}
```

The single event notify() method passes the Packet as the event parameter. This makes it very simple for PacketListener implementation classes to handle the Packet without worrying about how to use the PacketQueue or what the QueueThread is doing. The QueueThread manages the event model in a very familiar manner.

There is one trick with the design of the QueueThread packet event listener code. When you register a PacketListener, you indicate the element name of Packet classes you are interested in handling. When a Packet arrives in the PacketQueue, the QueueThread calls the pull() method to obtain the Packet object from the PacketQueue and then goes through its list of PacketListeners. The QueueThread checks to see if the Packet's element name matches the interests of any registered PacketListener (see code in bold in listing 3.6). Only interested listeners will be passed the Packet in their notify() methods.

Listing 3.6   The QueueThread class

```
public class QueueThread extends Thread {

  PacketQueue packetQueue;
```

```
public QueueThread(PacketQueue queue) {
  packetQueue = queue;
}

HashMap packetListeners = new HashMap();
public boolean addPacketListener(PacketListener listener, String element){
  if (listener == null || element == null){
    return false;
  }
  packetListeners.put(listener,element);
  return true;
}

public boolean removePacketListener(PacketListener listener){
  packetListeners.remove(listener);
  return true;
}

public void run(){

  for( Packet packet = packetQueue.pull();
       packet != null;
       packet = packetQueue.pull()) {

    try {
      synchronized(packetListeners){
        Iterator iter = packetListeners.keySet().iterator();
        while (iter.hasNext()){
          PacketListener listener = (PacketListener)iter.next();
          String element = (String)packetListeners.get(listener);
          //An empty string "" indicates match anything
          if (element.equals(packet.getElement())
              || element.length() == 0){
            listener.notify(packet);
          }
        }
      }
    //Continue to process packets no matter what happens
    } catch (Exception ex){ }
    }
  }
 }
}
```

The QueueThread class is simple, but manages the very complex problem of routing packets to their proper processing handlers. Next, let's take a look at the three Packet handling classes (listings 3.7, 3.8, and 3.9) in the basic server.

For the server, we are interested in doing three things for the three major types of packets it knows about:

- <stream:stream> our special open stream packet, should result in the server returning an opening stream tag and assigning a stream ID to the `Session`. Once the stream is established, the Session should be added to the server's `SessionIndex`.

- </stream:stream> the special close stream packet, should result in the server returning a closing stream tag, closing down the `Session`, and removing it from the server's `SessionIndex`.

- All other Jabber packets (`message`, `presence`, and `iq`) will be delivered to its recipient. If the server doesn't know how to deliver the packet, it is simply dropped.

The `OpenStreamHandler` class implements `PacketListener` and handles open stream packets. It has three primary responsibilities:

- Verify the open stream tag has the correct contents. The only requirement for now is a valid `from` address. We'll use the `from` address to specify the Jabber ID for the `Session`. Assigning a Jabber ID to the `Session` based on the opening stream tag is a workaround until we add user accounts and client authentication in chapter 6. Standard Jabber servers should reject client streams containing a `from` address so this workaround must be very temporary.

- Update the `SessionIndex`.

- Create a return open stream tag to return to the client. This involves switching the `from` and `to` addresses of the packet and assigning a unique stream ID to the packet.

Listing 3.7   The OpenStreamHandler class

```
public class OpenStreamHandler implements PacketListener{

  static int streamID = 0;
  SessionIndex sessionIndex;

  public OpenStreamHandler(SessionIndex index) {
    sessionIndex = index;
  }

  public void notify(Packet packet){

    try {
      Session session = packet.getSession();
```

```
    String from = packet.getFrom();       │ Verify the packet
    if (from == null){                     │ contains valid
      session.getSocket().close();         │ Jabber ID
      return;
    }

    session.setJID(new JabberID(from));                         │ Update
    session.setStatus(Session.STREAMING);                       │ SessionIndex
    session.setStreamID(Integer.toHexString(streamID++));       │
    sessionIndex.addSession(session);                           │

    packet.setTo(packet.getFrom());          │ Send response
    packet.setFrom(Server.SERVER_NAME);      │ OpenStreamPacket
    packet.setID(session.getStreamID());     │ to client
    packet.writeXML();                       │

  } catch (Exception ex){
    ex.printStackTrace();
  }
 }
}
```

Notice that the generation of a unique stream ID is a simple matter of assigning an increasing integer value to the stream for each connection. The stream ID is used in some of the authentication protocols for added security. Servers that support those authentication protocols will need to generate stream ID values in a random manner to prevent hackers from breaking authentication security.[14]

Closing the stream is simpler than opening it. All the `CloseStreamHandler` packet handler must do is:

- Send a reply close stream tag `</stream:stream>`. This is optional and the reference Jabber server does not do this.
- Close the `Session`'s `Socket`.
- Remove the `Session` from the `Server`'s `SessionIndex`.

---

[14] We'll discuss the issue in more depth in chapter 6.

The code is shown in listing 3.8.

Listing 3.8   The CloseStreamHandler class

```
public class CloseStreamHandler implements PacketListener {

  SessionIndex sessionIndex;

  public CloseStreamHandler(SessionIndex index) {
    sessionIndex = index;
  }

  public void notify(Packet packet){
    try {
      packet.writeXML();

      Session session = packet.getSession();
      session.getSocket().close();

      sessionIndex.removeSession(session);

    } catch (Exception ex){
      sessionIndex.removeSession(packet.getSession());
    }
  }
}
```

The final packet handling class is `DeliveryHandler`. This class simply sends packets to their recipients. It uses the `SessionIndex` to match the recipient Jabber ID with a `Session` for sending the packet. The resulting routing behavior was already explained in the `SessionIndex` class discussion. The majority of the routing work is done in the `SessionIndex` class so the `DeliveryHandler` is short and simple. (Listing 3.9)

Listing 3.9   The DeliveryHandler class

```
public class DeliveryHandler implements PacketListener {

  SessionIndex sessionIndex;

  public DeliveryHandler(SessionIndex index) {
    sessionIndex = index;
  }

  public void notify(Packet packet){
    String recipient = packet.getTo();
```

```
        //Messages sent to the server are ignored
        if (recipient.equalsIgnoreCase(Server.SERVER_NAME))
          return;
        }

        try {
          Session session = sessionIndex.getSession(recipient);

          if (session != null){
            //Deliver the packet
            packet.writeXML(session.getWriter());
          //Recipients that are not online are dropped
          } else {
            return;
          }
        } catch (Exception ex){
          ex.printStackTrace();
        }
      }
    }
}
```

The event-driven design of the QueueThread will let us make small changes to the various packet handling classes to add new Jabber features without affecting other parts of the server. This is going to be especially important for the DeliveryHandler class. We will be adding new delivery options to the Jabber server throughout the rest of the book.

For now, this simple QueueThread and its packet handling classes will let us explore the Jabber message protocols in the next chapter. Next, we will discuss the ProcessThread class that works in coordination with the QueueThread through the PacketQueue.

3.4.2 *Parsing XML in the ProcessThread*

If the PacketQueue is emptied by the QueueThread, it must be filled by another thread. We already know that the JabberInputHandler XML parser puts Packets into the PacketQueue given a Session object. Unfortunately, it can only handle one incoming XML stream at a time. In addition, it doesn't complete its processing until the stream it is working on is closed. To support multiple simultaneous connections, we need to create a separate thread of execution for each client/server connection. This is the task of the ProcessThread class (listing 3.10).

The server will create a `ProcessThread` for each client connection. The `ProcessThread` is then started and processes the incoming XML stream using a `JabberInputHandler`.

Listing 3.10   The ProcessThread class

```
public class ProcessThread extends Thread {

  Session session;
  PacketQueue packetQueue;

  public ProcessThread(PacketQueue queue, Session session){
    packetQueue = queue;
    this.session = session;
  }

  public void run(){
    try {
      JabberInputHandler handler = new JabberInputHandler(packetQueue);
      handler.process(session);
    } catch (Exception ex){
      ex.printStackTrace();
    }
  }
}
```

Notice that the thread calls `process()` and then exits, and that there is no looping. Recall from section 3.3.3 that the `JabberInputHandler` reads data from the `Session`'s `Reader` until the connection is closed. Once the connection is closed, the `process()` method call returns and we don't need this thread any more (the client has left).

THREAD POOLS
Large-scale server programmers are always looking to recycle and share valuable resources, a technique often called *resource pooling*. Valuable resources for servers are network connections, threads of execution, and live objects (memory). The `ProcessThread` contains all three. Yet we use a separate `ProcessThread` instance with all its valuable resources for each client connection. Our goal of supporting a small workgroup of clients makes this design acceptable. However, if you need to support thousands of users you will need to rethink the `ProcessThread` and come up with ways to reduce its resource consumption.

3.4.3 *The main application Server class*

The Server class launches the Jabber server and creates all of its threads and objects. The other threads and classes we have discussed are pretty intelligent so the Server is relatively simple. It has a limited number of tasks:

- Creating a PacketQueue that all threads share.
- Creating a QueueThread, configuring it with packet handlers, and starting it.
- Going into an infinite loop accepting new network connections and creating ProcessThreads to handle them.

The code that accomplishes these tasks contains no surprises so I'll let it speak for itself (listing 3.11).

Listing 3.11   The Server class

```
//Hardcoded info should be in configuration files
final static public int    JABBER_PORT = 5222;
final static public String SERVER_NAME = "127.0.0.1";

static public void main(String [] args){

  System.out.println("Jabber Server -- " + JABBER_PORT);

  //The shared PacketQueue
  PacketQueue packetQueue = new PacketQueue();

  //Creating and starting QueueThread
  QueueThread qThread = new QueueThread(packetQueue);
  //Daemon threads don't keep an application running;
  //We rely on the main thread to do that
  qThread.setDaemon(true);

  //Register the packet handler classes with the QueueThread
  qThread.addPacketListener(new OpenStreamHandler(index),
                            "stream:stream");
  qThread.addPacketListener(new CloseStreamHandler(index),
                            "/stream:stream");
  qThread.addPacketListener(new DeliveryHandler(index),
                            "");

  qThread.start();

  ServerSocket serverSocket;

  try {
    //Begin listening on Jabber port
    serverSocket = new ServerSocket(JABBER_PORT);

  } catch (IOException ex){
    //If port not available, server shuts down
    ex.printStackTrace();
```

```
      return;
    }

  while (true){
    try {
      //Accept new connections forever
      Socket newSock = serverSocket.accept();
      Session session = new Session(newSock);

      //Create and start a thread to handle new connection
      ProcessThread processor = new ProcessThread(packetQueue,
                                                  session);
      processor.start();
    } catch (IOException ie){
      ie.printStackTrace();
    }
  }
 }
}
```

The Server class performs basic application setup then accepts incoming client connections. Notice that the class contains hard-coded application settings for the server's domain name and port. One of the first things you may want to play with is storing these settings in a configuration file so that it is easier to change the server's settings. In addition, there is no way to stop or restart the server once it is started.[15] Another glaring omission is the lack of test and logging code in the server.

You will need to obtain the full server source online (www.manning.com/shigeoka) and follow the instructions to unpack, compile, and run the server. Once you have the server installed and running, you can begin manually testing the server using telnet.

3.5 *Testing the server*

One of the simplest ways (if not the most tedious) to test the server is to use telnet.[16] First start the server. I have included a simple Windows batch file named server.bat with the online source code to start the server on Windows. I've also included a simple Unix shell script that will do the same on Unix[17] and MacOS X.

---

[15] You can stop the server by terminating the Java Virtual Machine (JVM): usually this can be done by pressing CTRL+C.

[16] Telnet is a simple networking tool that should be included as part of any complete TCP/IP stack. It is available as part of all of the Windows OSs, as well as MacOS X, and all Unix versions.

The server should start and print its banner "Jabber Server – ####" where #### is the port number it is using. By convention, the port number for Jabber is 5222.

To test the server, open a console/terminal window and type: "telnet hostname port" where "hostname" is the Internet domain name or network address of the computer the server is running on and "port" is the port number that the Jabber server reported in its startup banner. If you're running the server and telnet on a computer without a network you can use `127.0.0.1` as the host name (e.g., "telnet 127.0.0.1 5222" without the quotes).

Telnet will connect with the Jabber server and wait for you to type something. Type in the opening stream tag:[18]

```
<stream:stream from='user@server/resource' to='server'>
```

The server will respond with its stream tag, including a stream ID. Now close the stream by typing:

```
</stream:stream>
```

The server will respond with its closing stream then close the connection. Telnet will exit and you'll be back at the prompt. A typical session should look something like the following:

Telnet testing the server
```
% telnet 127.0.0.1 5222
Trying 127.0.0.1...
Connected to 127.0.0.1.
Escape character is '^]'.
Send: <stream:stream
Send:    from='iain@shigeoka.com/work'
Send:    to='shigeoka.com'
Send:    xmlns='jabber:client'
Send:    xmlns:stream='http://etherx.jabber.org/streams'>
Recv: <stream:stream
Recv:    from='shigeoka.com'
Recv:    to='iain@shigeoka.com/work'
Recv:    xmlns='jabber:client'
Recv:    xmlns:stream='http://etherx.jabber.org/streams'
Recv:    id='0'>
Send: </stream:stream>
Recv: </stream:stream>
Connection closed by foreign host.
```

---

[17] I include Linux and the BSDs like FreeBSD in the Unix category.

[18] Our server does not check for the stream namespace attribute: `xmlns='http://etherx.jabber.org/streams'` although it should. It is required by the Jabber protocols. The open source reference Jabber server rejects streams without this namespace.

Now try the same thing with two telnet sessions in two console/terminal windows at the same time with different "from" Jabber ID's to make sure the server can handle more than one connection at a time. Experiment by sending message packets addressed to the other telnet session to see how the server routes messages. A message packet is typically of the form shown here:[19]

Sample Message Packet

```
<message from='iain@shigeoka.com/work' to='iain@shigeoka.com/home'>
  <body>
    This is the message
  </body>
</message>
```

The server provides a good starting point for future explorations into the Jabber protocols. Now that we have a basic Jabber server, we need a basic Jabber client. Having both a client and server will allow us to test them against each other rather than debugging them using telnet.[20] We'll develop a Jabber client in the next chapter.

3.6   Conclusion

The code for a basic Jabber server introduced in this chapter can handle Jabber packets and valid Jabber XML streams. Throughout the rest of the book, we will add to this server to support other parts of the Jabber protocols.

The code demonstrates how simple—and powerful—the Jabber platform is. It allows us to quickly build Jabber software and embed it into all sorts of devices and applications. Using Jabber IM we can concentrate on building software systems to do what we want without wasting time and resources on basic messaging infrastructure.

To show just how simple and fun Jabber can be, the next chapter introduces the most important and useful Jabber core protocol: message.

---

[19] We'll look at the message packet in detail in the next chapter.

[20] Testing with telnet is a bit crude but shows the advantage of using XML rather than binary data formats. We sacrifice network bandwidth efficiency but gain the ability to directly play with the protocols without any tools beyond telnet. Rather than type XML packets directly into telnet, though, I find it much easier to type into a text editor and then cut and paste into the telnet window. That way I can edit the packets and reuse them.

The Jabber
message protocols

4

101

Messaging is the heart and soul of every IM system. The Jabber <message> protocols provide a simple yet powerful framework for sending and receiving messages. In this chapter, we will discuss the Jabber message protocol and how it works. To demonstrate, we will create a basic Jabber client that can send and receive messages through the Jabber server we developed in the last chapter.

4.1 *Messaging is the heart of IM*

Sending messages is the primary responsibility of the Jabber system. Jabber supports six primary types of <message> packets: normal, chat, groupchat (conferences), headline, error, and out-of-band messages. Each uses a different model of communication and is best suited for different situations. The following table summarizes the various message options.

Table 4.1   Jabber message types and messaging model.

Message Style	Type	Model	Typical interface
Normal	normal	Email-like messages (default)	Message editor
Chat	chat	One-on-one online chat	Line by line chat
Groupchat	groupchat	Online chatroom	Line by line chat
Headline	headline	Scrolling marquee message	"Stock Ticker"
Error	error	Message error occurred	Alert dialog box
Out-of-Band	X Extension jabber:x:oob	Direct client to client file exchange. Defined in an X extension in <message> element.	Napster/FTP

The first five message types fall within the Jabber <message> protocol. Each sends its contents within the <message> element. These are the most common types of messages sent in Jabber systems. In this chapter, we'll build a client that supports them.

Out-of-band messages provide a mechanism for clients to directly exchange data (typically files). The out-of-band protocol uses the Jabber server to exchange information about how the clients will talk to each other (usually by sending a web URL for downloading the file).

You can send out-of-band tags as either an X extension within a <message> element, or as an Info/Query packet[1]. We'll briefly cover the X extension version of the out-of-band message in this chapter. The IQ protocol is explained in detail in chapter 6, and the exact usage of the out-of-band IQ extension is detailed in appendix A.

---

[1] X Extensions are simple Jabber packets in an <x> element. They provide an extension mechanism for adding custom content to standard Jabber packets. I'll discuss this in more detail later in the chapter.

4.2   *The message protocol*

The message protocol is extremely simple: message packets are sent from a sender to a recipient. By default, there is no acknowledgement when the recipient receives the message. If a message is sent and the recipient is not reachable, the server is obliged to store the message and deliver it when the recipient becomes available,[2] a process referred to in messaging systems as *store and forward*.

A basic message packet consists of a `<message>` element with the typical Jabber `from`, `to`, and `id` packet attributes. The message packet supports four standard subelements[3] shown in table 4.2.

Table 4.2   The sub-packets allowed within a `<message>` packet.

Sub-Packet	Description
`<subject>`	Indicates the subject of the message similar to the subject field in an email message.
`<thread>`	A client generated identifier to help track messages belonging to a single "thread" of conversation.
`<body>`	The message body is enclosed in this element.
`<error>`	If an error occurred, the standard Jabber error packet is enclosed in the message.

Let's take a look at the XML for a complete message packet. This message is being sent from "iain" to "smirk." Most message packets do not contain an `id` attribute (it is optional).

Sample message packet

```
<message from='iain@shigeoka.com/work'
         to='smirk@jabber.org/home'
         id='messageid1'>
  <thread>threadid_01</thread>
  <subject>The message's subject</subject>
  <body>The text in the message body</body>
</message>
```

---

[2] In the Jabber server developed in the previous chapter, I cheated a little and we simply dropped messages addressed to someone that is offline. This flaw will be fixed in chapter 7 when we create user accounts on the server.

[3] There are several X extensions that are also supported within a `<message>` packet. I'll cover what an X extension is and show an example when I discuss the out-of-band X extension later in this chapter.

The <thread> packet is used to keep different threads of messages together.[4] In this example, our thread ID is threadid_01. All messages sent between clients with the same thread ID will be displayed together[5]. In most graphical user interfaces (GUIs) this would be shown in a line-by-line chat interface. This allows you to chat with several people at once and keep each conversation separate.

When clients send messages to servers, the sender is implied to be the client's Jabber ID, and the recipient is assumed to be the server if no recipient is specified. Some Jabber servers may not allow you to send messages with a sender address that does not match the sender's session address. A perfectly valid (and typical) message sent to the server is:

```
<message to='smirk@jabber.org'>
  <body>howdy</body>
</message>
```

The server fills in implied fields for final delivery as shown in this example:

```
<message from='iain@shigeoka.com/work'
         to='smirk@jabber.org'>
  <body>Howdy</body>
</message>
```

4.2.1 *Normal messages*

The default message type is a *normal message.* These messages are typically created and displayed using interfaces similar to that used in email applications (figure 4.1). Like email, normal messages are sent to Jabber users who aren't necessarily online. These messages tend to be longer than other message types and resemble letters or memos.[6]

Message packets that do not contain a type attribute are considered normal messages (figure 4.1). In addition, you can explicitly indicate a message is a normal message by setting the type attribute to normal as shown in the following example.[7]

---

[4] The <thread> packet is an aid to the Jabber client for correctly displaying related messages. It is not required, however, and clients should be able to display messages missing the <thread> packet.

[5] The id attribute indicating the packet ID is also used to link related packets. However, the packet ID links request packets to response packets, or any packet and its associated error messages. The Info/Query protocols covered in chapter 6 rely heavily on the packet ID for its request-response process.

[6] Typically, normal messages contain static content intended for offline delivery or more formal communications. Chat messages (covered in the next section) are intended for short messages where the user may or may not be online (all message types will be stored offline and delivered later). Think of normal messages as letters, while chat messages are Post-It notes.

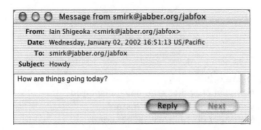

Figure 4.1
A typical normal message being
displayed in the JabberFOX client
(jabberfox.sourceforge.net).

Sample normal message packet

```
<message from='iain@shigeoka.com/work'
         to='smirk@jabber.org/home'
         id='messageid2'
         type='normal'>
  <thread>threadid_02</thread>
  <subject>The message's subject</subject>
  <body>The text in the message body</body>
</message>
```

It is typical for Jabber client applications to offer users the ability to start chatting with the sender of a normal message.

4.2.2 Chat messages

Jabber users send chat messages back and forth to other users who are online at the same time they are. These messages tend to be short and conversational, like the type of communication you do over a telephone. Chat messages are typically displayed in a line-by-line interface.[8] When you write a chat line-by-line interface, you must place a copy of the messages you send into the chat window so the user can see both sides of the conversation.

Chat messages (figure 4.2) must have their `type` attribute set to `chat`. In addition, the message should contain a `<thread>` subelement. Jabber clients link messages into a threaded conversation using the `<thread>` ID. All chat messages that belong to a single conversation should use the same `<thread>` ID. It is common for the `<subject>` to be omitted in chat messages.

---

[7] There are few good reasons to force the normal message type. If you're sending a normal message, leave the `type` attribute out. It's more efficient. The only reason I can see to force it is if your software is not flexible enough to send packets without a `type` attribute.

[8] There are many innovative ways of displaying chat messages. Some clients display them as "thought bubbles" above animated cartoon characters, while others may use virtual reality or text-to-speech software to enhance the chat experience.

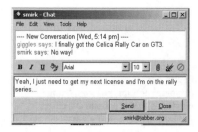

Figure 4.2
A typical chat message being displayed and edited in the Jabber Instant Messager client (www.jabber.com).

Sample chat message packet

```
<message from='iain@shigeoka.com/work'
         to='smirk@jabber.org/home'
         id='messageid3'
         type='chat'>
  <thread>threadid_03</thread>
  <body>The text in the message body</body>
</message>
```

Chat is useful for conducting one-on-one online conversations. When you need to converse with many people at once, you need to use groupchat messages.

4.2.3 Groupchat messages

Groupchat messages are similar to chat messages but they are designed to support online conversations within groups. Instead of a one-on-one conversation like chat, groupchat allows many users to send and receive messages from an entire group of people.[9] Everyone participating in the group, including the sender, receives a copy of the message.

When creating your groupchat user interface (figure 4.3), your interface should send groupchat messages to the group and update the groupchat interface with incoming messages. Groupchat servers automatically send groupchat messages to participants (including the sender). This feature relieves you from manually copying your outgoing messages to the groupchat window.[10]

A groupchat server manages groupchat conversations. In most Jabber servers, the groupchat server will be built into the Jabber server although it is possible to design a separate Jabber server that functions solely as a groupchat server. Groupchat conferences may be enhanced, supplemented, or replaced in the future

---

[9] Jabber groupchats are often called conferences, chatrooms, or forums.

[10] In chat message interfaces you must manually copy your outgoing messages into the chat window so the user sees both sides of the conversation. The server will not send you a copy of your own messages like it does in groupchat messaging.

by conferences using the `jabber:iq:conference` IQ extension protocol. I expect that the two will coexist in future Jabber servers. See the `jabber:iq:conference` IQ extension specification in this book located in appendix A.

Figure 4.3
A typical chat message being displayed and edited in the Jabber Instant Messenger client (www.jabber.com). Notice that the presence of participants is shown on the right.

Groupchat message packets are like chat packets except the type attribute is set to `groupchat`. Notice that you are sending messages to the groupchat server and not directly to another Jabber user. Groupchat groups use special Jabber IDs. The standard format for a groupchat group address is: [group name]@[groupchat server]/[user nickname]

Users can choose an arbitrary groupchat nickname for each group they join. It doesn't necessarily have anything to do with their regular Jabber user name. For example, we have a user name of "iain," with a Jabber ID of "iain@shigeoka.com/work." We want to send a message to the groupchat group named "java-users" on the groupchat server `conference.shigeoka.com`. We've already joined the group using the nickname "hacker." Our client sends a `<message>` packet to the group (java-users@conferences.shigeoka.com) that looks like the following:

Sample groupchat message outgoing packet

```
<message from='iain@ shigeoka.com/work'
         to='java-users@conference.shigeoka.com'
         id='messageid4'
         type='groupchat'>
  <thread>threadid_04</thread>
  <body>The text in the message body</body>
</message>
```

The groupchat server receives the message and sends it to all members of the java-users group including our Jabber client.

Sample groupchat message incoming packet

```
<message from='java-users@conference.shigeoka.com/hacker'
         to='iain@shigeoka.com/work'
         id='messageid4'
         type='groupchat'>
  <thread>threadid_04</thread>
  <body>The text in the message body</body>
</message>
```

One of the great things about this design is that the other members of the group never see my real Jabber ID. The only information they know is that the messages are coming from java-users@conference.shigeoka.com/hacker. This prevents people from hanging out on the groupchat server and scraping Jabber IDs from the groups for spam lists or stalking users outside of the conference.

There is something missing from the groupchat message protocol, though. If you were paying close attention to the outgoing groupchat packet example, you'll notice that there is no information in it telling the server that I'm using the nickname "hacker." Nor can the conference server determine who is in the conference just from the message itself.

Mapping Jabber IDs to nicknames, managing conference membership, and other administrative issues concerning Jabber groupchat groups are handled using the Jabber presence protocols.[11] An advanced form of groupchat called conferencing is being proposed and uses the IQ protocols.[12]

4.2.4 *Headline messages*

Headline messages are Jabber messages designed for display in scrolling marquees, status bars, or other client interfaces designed for streaming information. It is common for automated chatbot services to generate headline messages concerning current events and news such as weather reports, severe weather alerts, and stock quotes.

Headline messages use a type attribute of `headline` and typically don't require a `<thread>` or `<subject>` subelement.[13]

---

[11] Presence protocols are discussed in chapter 5 where we'll implement support for basic groupchat.

[12] Info/Query protocols are discussed in chapter 6. The conferencing protocol is included in appendix A.

[13] There is an exception to the lack of `<subject>` tags in headline messages. When creating streaming news services, it is common to use the `<subject>` for a news subject line, `<body>` for the news article itself, and the oob X extension to provide a URL for more information. This is similar to RDF Site Summary (RSS) functionality (purl.org/rss/1.0/spec).

Sample headline message packet

```
<message from='quote-bot@stockbroker.com'
         to='iain@ shigeoka.com/work'
         id='messageid5'
         type='headline'>
  <body>SUNW 10</body>
</message>
```

The last message type that is supported by the <message> packet is the standard Jabber error message.

4.2.5 *Error messages*

When you send a message, there is always a chance that something will go wrong or the recipient will refuse the message. The error message type is used to notify the sender that the message they sent has encountered problems. The error packet shown in listing 4.1 is the standard Jabber error packet that we covered in the last chapter.

Listing 4.1   Sample error message packet

```
Send: <message from='iain@shigeoka.com/home'
Send:           to='hotbabe@ shigeoka.com'
Send:           id='messageid6'
Send:           type='normal'>
Send:   <subject>Doing anything tonight?</subject>
Send:   <body>Hi, how about a date!</body>
Send: </message>
Recv: <message from='hotbabe@shigeoka.com/jacuzzi'
Recv:           to='iain@shigeoka.com/home'
Recv:           id='messageid6'
Recv:           type='error'>
Recv:   <error code='400'>
Recv:     Go away!
Recv:   </error>
Recv: </message>
```

Notice that the message id attribute (messageid6 in this example) is preserved from the original message to the error message. This allows the client to match up the message it sent with the error message it received. Remember that messages are normally sent one-way so you may have sent many other messages before receiving an error message response.

> NOTE   Error messages don't necessarily refer to the last message you sent
> You must match error messages to their cause by examining the
> packet ID.

4.2.2 Out-of-band messages

The last type of standard Jabber message, an out-of-band message, isn't really a Jabber message at all. Instead, it is a message X extension that is sent inside of a standard Jabber `<message>` packet (usually a message of type `normal`).

An out-of-band message contains information, typically a URL, that clients can use to conduct a direct client-to-client data transfer that bypasses the normal client-server-client Jabber message routing. Jabber clients will typically implement this by running a web server or FTP server either separately or as part of the Jabber client. The out-of-band message then tells the downloading client what URL to use to hit the web/FTP server and download the file.

Out-of-band messages are typically used to arrange sending large files that would cause severe server bandwidth shortages were routed through the server. For example, you may want to add music trading to your Jabber client application. The chat and song searching functions can occur over the Jabber server, but transferring multimegabyte MP3 files through the server would quickly bring your server to its knees. Ideally these high bandwidth transfers can be done directly between the clients resulting in:

- Reduced server load
- Possibly faster transfers
- Support for streaming network broadcasts

OUT-OF-BAND SECURITY RISKS

Note that the advantages of out-of-band messaging don't come without a cost. Since clients must directly communicate with each other, the client's security and privacy can be violated in ways that are impossible when all communication occurs through the Jabber server. In addition, network issues such as getting through firewalls and proxy servers are multiplied when clients must act as file servers.

These issues lie beyond the Jabber standards so Jabber client developers are often left on their own when trying to create robust and secure out-of-band systems. In addition, your solution may not work with other Jabber clients unless everyone agrees on how the out-of-band transfers will take place. Out-of-band messaging is an area of great interest and debate in the Jabber community. Hopefully in the future, the protocols for carrying out an out-of-band transfer will be standardized and added to the Jabber standards.

Two protocols are involved in carrying out an out-of-band transfer. The first uses the oob X extension for exchanging URLs used for the transfer, the second uses the oob IQ protocol for initiating the transfer.

Two protocols are involved in carrying out an out-of-band transfer. The first uses the oob X extension for exchanging URLs used for the transfer, the second uses the oob IQ protocol for initiating the transfer. We'll cover the Info/Query protocol in chapter 6. Let's take a look at the X extension technique here. In order to understand how the out-of-band X extension works, we first need to understand X extensions in general.

X extensions

The Jabber designers know that although the Jabber packets can handle the majority of IM tasks, there will always be additional features that people would like to support. To keep the protocol extension process under control, the Jabber core protocols support X extensions.

An X extension is simply an `<x>` packet within the core Jabber packet types: `<message>`, `<presence>`, and `<iq>`. By making `<x>` packets a valid subelement of the core packets, you can comply with the Jabber DTD and create a valid Jabber packet that contains this mysterious `<x>` packet.

The `<x>` packet has no default sub-elements.[14] To create an X extension, you must define a new namespace within the `<x>` packet, and then insert any XML information you want in the packet. The XML namespace ensures that you won't violate the validity of the resulting XML fragment. Sometimes it is easier to show an example than to try to explain. So let's take a look at the out-of-band X extension.

The out-of-band X extension

The out-of-band (oob) X extension is a standard Jabber X extension that allows you to specify an out-of-band transfer mechanism. Think of it as a URL passer.[15] It resides in the `jabber:x:oob` namespace and contains two subelements:

- *<url>*—The URL describing the out-of-band transfer.
- *<desc>*—A text description of the data to be transferred.

---

[14] For XML gurus, the `<x>` packet is defined in the parent packet DTDs so that it is a valid subpacket that conforms to the Jabber DTDs. However the `<x>` packet itself has no default subpackets allowing you to define its contents independently using an XML namespace.

[15] The actual file exchange is initiated using the out-of-band IQ protocol `jabber:iq:oob`. You can learn more about the Info/Query protocol in chapter 6 and the specifics of the `jabber:iq:oob` protocol in appendix A.

The out-of-band X extension tells the receiving client where to get the file (figure 4.4). It does not actually contain the file (otherwise it would have passed through the server). In general, out-of-band transfers are an advanced feature typically found in only the more sophisticated Jabber clients

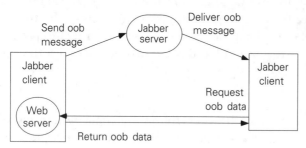

Figure 4.4
Out-of-band data is sent as an oob message through the Jabber server. The recipient must request the actual oob data directly from the sending client using some other protocol such as HTTP or FTP (here a web server and HTTP is used).

An out-of-band X extension in a message packet might be presented in a Jabber client with an email with attachments interface.

A message packet with out-of-band X extension

```
<message from='iain@shigeoka.com/work'
         to='iain@shigeoka.com/home'
         id='messageid8'
         type='normal'>
  <subject>Work files</subject>
  <body>Attached are some work files I may need</body>
  <x xmlns='jabber:x:oob'>
    <url>http://workserver/book.zip</url>
    <desc>Archive of my book</desc>
  </x>
</message>
```

In the interest of focusing on core Jabber protocols, we'll end our discussion of X extensions here. Although they are important parts of the Jabber protocols, X extensions are not essential for IM. By reading the reference section on the existing X extensions at the end of this book, it should easy to determine what X extensions are important for your project.

The client software we develop in this book will not support out-of-band transfers.

4.2.3 *Reality check: one message, many user interfaces*

The six messages types covered here represent the full range of messaging options available in a standard Jabber server. From this limited selection of message types, rich communication experiences have been created. In fact, from a packet and protocol standpoint, the messages are all similar and it is perfectly valid to consider them all the same packet from a software standpoint.

The real difference in the Jabber message types lies not in the packet structure or protocols but in the interface that Jabber clients provide for the user to interact with the different message types. In fact, I believe that Jabber clients and the Jabber IM experience are driven by the user interface, not the quality of the technical implementation of the protocols.

The Jabber protocols are simple. The real challenge facing Jabber developers is to create friendly, enjoyable, exciting, and productive Jabber user experiences using them. To help you explore these issues, we'll create a bare-bones Jabber client that you can use for your own user interface experiments.

4.3 Java Jabber client

Jabber servers have a fairly well-defined role handling Jabber connections and properly responding to requests. Jabber clients on the other hand can appear in a bewildering variety of forms. The most common is a stand alone IM client that operates similarly to well-known IM clients such as AIM or ICQ.

Jabber clients don't have to be written that way, though. You can add Jabber client capabilities to your existing application offering your users built-in IM or simple chat features. Alternatively, many people are writing chatbots, Jabber client programs that act as servers in their own right, offering services on top of the Jabber system.

For example, you could write a chatbot that looks like another Jabber user on the Jabber server. If you send an IM to the chatbot, it might respond by telling you the local weather forecast or your bank account balance. The Jabber services provided by chatbots are similar to the heavily hyped web services programming model that uses XML over the Internet for similar purposes. Chatbots and other advanced uses for Jabber clients are covered in more depth in chapter 10.

Table 4.3 Typical types of Jabber client applications. Most users are familiar with the graphical user agent clients they use on their desktop. However, developers will probably find the most opportunities in developing chatbots and test clients.

Client type	Relationship with human "user"	Example applications
User agent	Tool for using Jabber	IM messaging application, chat feature in games
Chatbot	Provides "services" via Jabber IM	A weather service, a stock quote service
Test client	None	Standards compliance, stress testing, benchmarking

This section will show you the code for a basic test client. Throughout the rest of the book we'll use the client to test the Jabber server and to demonstrate client features of the Jabber protocols. In addition, you can use the Jabber client software developed here in your own Jabber client software projects.

4.3.1 *Goals*

As with the Jabber server software, we want the client to be simple, standards-compliant, easy to understand, and easy to modify. In addition to these goals, the client code is designed to be easily usable both in applications where it has a user interface, and those where it does not. Although most people's initial fascination with IM software lies in creating IM clients, I believe a few players will come to dominate this market just as they do for web and email clients. I anticipate that the real market for most developers of IM software is implementing Jabber functionality inside of other applications, in embedded systems, and offering Jabber chatbot services over the IM network.

The Jabber client developed in this book will not be particularly useful as a user-friendly IM client. The reason is practical. There simply is not enough room in this book to cover the source code needed to build a full-featured user interface with features such as extensive error checking, user customization, and help files that should be part of any user application.

User applications contain a bewildering amount of minor user interface details that are straightforward to implement, but are composed of a large quantity of mundane, tedious code. It would be a waste of paper to print the source code for all of that. In addition, it is exactly these details that will differentiate your Jabber client from another one. If you need a fully functional Jabber client to use with the Jabber server created in this book, you can either expand the Jabber client code to create a GUI, or simply download one of the many free Jabber clients that are available (see www.jabber.org to get started).

Although a full-blown user agent program is beyond the scope of this book, you should be able to create one from the source in this book. To keep things manageable, the client in this book will only support the Jabber features that I cover in detail in this book:

- *Messaging*—Sending and receiving Jabber IM.
- *Presence*—Sending and receiving presence information.
- *Info/Query*—Basic information exchange between Jabber entities. This is a broad area and I'll restrict myself to three protocols from the full set IQ protocols:

- *Roster Management*—Subscribing and maintaining your online presence status.
- *Registration*—Creating user accounts on open Jabber servers.
- *Authentication*—Logging in to a Jabber server.

4.3.2 *The client design*

Our Jabber client is an extremely simple piece of software. Right now, it needs to complete the following basic tasks:

- Connect to a Jabber server.
- Send an opening `<stream:stream>` tag.
- Send `<message>` packets.
- Receive and display `<message>` packets.
- Send a closing `</stream:stream>` tag.
- Exit.

To aid us in debugging and to let the user know what is happening, we also want the client software to indicate to the user what the status is of the Jabber session, and to provide a listing of all the raw data being sent between the client and server.

We will use the Model-View-Controller (MVC) design pattern (figure 4.5) to facilitate the use of the client software with graphical user interfaces (GUI) as well as in applications with a limited or absent user interface. The MVC design pattern is described by Buschmann et al[16] as follows:

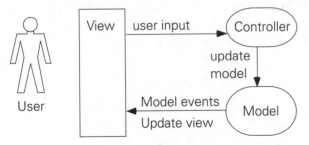

Figure 4.5 **The Model-View-Controller design pattern separates the user's display (View), from interpretation of user inputs (controller), and the data and functionality of interest (Model).**

---

[16] Buschmann et al, *Pattern-oriented Software Architecture: a System of Patterns* (John Wiley & Sons, 1996), p. 125.

The Model-View-Controller architectural pattern (MVC) divides an interactive application into three components. The model contains the core functionality and data. Views display information to the user. Controllers handle user input. Views and controllers together comprise the user interface. A change-propagation mechanism ensures consistency between the user interface and the model.

In this book, we will focus on discussing the client model classes from the MVC pattern. In this chapter, the client model must manage the Jabber connection, keep a status model, and log the Jabber XML stream. The client model will reuse most of the server code covered in the previous chapter so this is not as much work as it sounds.

We'll create a rudimentary test harness around the model to show how to use it, and to drive our client/server tests. I don't want to place too much emphasis on the user interface aspects of the client code so the client won't have one. User interfaces are something I leave to you to design for your own needs and tastes.

I hope that you will be able to use this book's source code to create your own user interfaces and attach them to our client model. You can therefore build and control the look and feel of your Jabber client, while using the book code to manipulate Jabber functionality and data. In addition, if you don't need a user interface, you can build an application that directly manipulates the client model we build here.

With that said, let's take a look at the client model source code.

4.3.3 *The client model*

The client model classes will handle all of the Jabber responsibilities of the client. Recall that for this chapter, we want to open a Jabber stream, send messages, receive messages, and close the stream. We have already developed software that does these things as part of the server in chapter 3. We can simply reuse that code here to create a client model, as shown in figure 4.6.

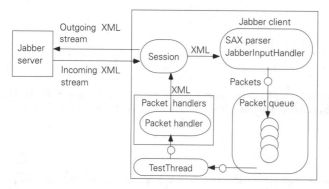

Figure 4.6 The client follows a similar architecture to the server, and reuses many of the server's classes.

We are not just reusing the server's design. Many of the main server classes, like the `JabberInputHandler` and `ProcessThread` are directly reused from the server. This makes the client-specific code compact enough that we can easily package it into a single model class, the `JabberModel`.

The `JabberModel`'s primary job is to make Jabber related tasks simple. Packet handling is carried out by a combination of `TestThread` actions and packet handling classes similar to that on the server. The `JabberModel`'s basic operations are outlined in the sequence diagram shown in figure 4.7.

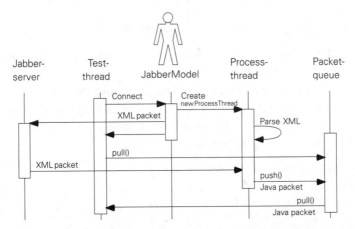

Figure 4.7 The `TestThread` (replacing the server's `QueueThread`) uses the `JabberModel` to create a `ProcessThread` and its associated packet handling classes. The `TestThread` operates by sending packets using the `JabberModel` and pulling responses from the `PacketQueue`. The `TestThread` also hands Packets to packet handling classes for special handling.

The JabberModel class constructor

```
public class JabberModel {

  JabberModel(TestThread qThread) {
    packetQueue = qThread.getQueue();
    qThread.addListener(new OpenStreamHandler(),"stream:stream");
    qThread.addListener(new CloseStreamHandler(),"/stream:stream");
    qThread.addListener(new MessageHandler(),"message");
  }

  Session session = new Session();
  PacketQueue packetQueue;
```

The `JabberModel` constructor should look familiar. We saw similar code in the Server class from chapter 3 to set up the `QueueThread` with `PacketListeners`. The `JabberModel` similarly configures the `TestThread` with `PacketListeners` to handle incoming packets. The packet-handling interface to the TestThread is closely modeled on the QueueThread. The client uses different versions of the PacketListener classes than the server because we want it to exhibit different behavior when packets arrive. We'll cover the new PacketListener classes later in this chapter.

Even without seeing them, you know from this constructor that I'm registering:

- An OpenStreamHandler class to handle the special <stream:stream> opening tag.
- A CloseStreamHandler class to handle the special </stream:stream> closing tag.
- A MessageHandler class to handle <message> Packets.

The TestThread will drop all other incoming packets because it does not have any PacketListeners to handle them.

The JabberModel contains a few member data fields and their access methods. These fields are a convenience for setting up default values throughout the client application. A real client application would have a separate user options object and store these options in configuration files.

The JabberModel class data fields and access methods

```
String jabberVersion = "v. 1.0 - ch. 4";
public String getVersion(){ return jabberVersion; }

String sName;
public String getServerName()              {return sName;}
public void    setServerName(String name)  {sName = name;}

String sAddress;
public String getServerAddress()              {return sAddress;}
public void    setServerAddress(String addr) {sAddress = addr;}
String sPort;
public String getPort()                    {return sPort;}
public void    setPort(String port)        {sPort = port;}

String user;
public String getUser()                    {return user;}
public void    setUser(String usr)         {user = usr; }

String resource;
public String getResource()                {return resource;}
public void    setResource(String res)     {resource = res;}

public void addStatusListener(StatusListener listener){
   session.addStatusListener(listener);
}

public void removeStatusListener(StatusListener listener){
```

```
    session.removeStatusListener(listener);
}

public int getSessionStatus() {
    return session.getStatus();
}
```

There are two interesting features of the code. The first is that there are some convenience methods for registering StatusListeners with the Jabber-Model's Session object and obtaining the Session's status. These convenience methods allow us to keep the Session object completely encapsulated within the JabberModel and prevents any outside classes from directly manipulating the Session.

The second thing to note is that we have a separate serverName and serverAddress field. In normal clients you will only need a server's name (e.g., "shigeoka.com"). The Socket class automatically figures out the server's address (e.g., "217.13.31.1") using DNS lookup. However, I tend to develop on isolated development machines and offline laptops. By providing both a server name and a server address, I can have the client act as if it is talking with a server shigeoka.com while connecting to a hardcoded address that may not have any real DNS name.

In this case, I can use the loopback address 127.0.0.1 so that I am able to run the client and server on the same machine without any network connection at all.[17] The client and server both think that the server is at shigeoka.com, allowing me to use Jabber IDs like iain@shigeoka.com/work rather than iain@127.0.0.1/work.

Next, the JabberModel implements the three remaining tasks that the client model must fulfill: connecting, sending messages, and disconnecting. The most code-intensive is the connect() method shown in listing 4.2.

Listing 4.2   The JabberModel class connect method

```
public void connect(String server,
                    int port,
                    String serverName,
                    String user,
                    String resource)

    throws IOException {
```

---

[17] The loopback address is a logical network address available to all TCP/IP clients. The address always points to the localhost: the machine you are currently working on. Thus the address provides a virtual loopback connection to yourself.

```
session.setSocket(new Socket(server,port));  ◁──┐   Create a
                                                 │   socket for
session.setStatus(Session.CONNECTED);  ◁────────┘   the session

(new ProcessThread(packetQueue,session)).start();  ◁──────

String senderJabID = user + "@" + sName + "/" + resource;

Writer out = session.getWriter();
session.setJID(new JabberID(user,sName,resource));
out.write("<?xml version='1.0' encoding='UTF-8' ?>");
out.write("<stream:stream to='");
out.write(sName);
out.write("' from=');
out.write(senderJabID);
out.write("' xmlns='jabber:client' ");
out.write("xmlns:stream='http://etherx.jabber.org/streams'>");
out.flush();
}
```

Annotations:
- **Session connected as soon as we open the Socket**
- **Start JabberIput Handler in the ProcessThread**
- **Send opening <stream:stream> tag**

Connecting to the Jabber server is relatively simple and resembles the creation of a Jabber session in the server. We can even reuse the ProcessThread class from the server to parse the incoming Jabber XML and place Packet classes into the PacketQueue.

Disconnecting and sending messages are supported by even simpler methods as shown in listing 4.3:

Listing 4.3   The JabberModel class disconnect and sendMessage methods

```
public void disconnect() throws IOException {
  session.getWriter().write("</stream:stream> ");
  session.getWriter().flush();
}

public void sendMessage(String recipient,
                        String subject,
                        String thread,
                        String type,
                        String id,
                        String body) throws IOException {

  Packet packet = new Packet("message");

  if (recipient != null){
    packet.setTo(recipient);
  }
  if (id != null){
    packet.setID(id);
```

```
  }
  if (type != null){
     packet.setType(type);
  }
  if (subject != null){
     packet.getChildren().add(new Packet("subject",subject));
  }
  if (thread != null){
     packet.getChildren().add(new Packet("thread",thread));
  }
  if (body != null){
     packet.getChildren().add(new Packet("body",body));
  }
  packet.writeXML(session.getWriter());
  }
}
```

The disconnect() method simply sends the closing </stream> tag. It does not have to close the socket because the server will automatically close it when it receives the client's closing stream tag.

The sendMessage() method creates a Packet object and fills it with the information it needs to generate the correct XML for a Jabber <message> packet. The sendMessage() method is a convenient way of sending Jabber messages from within Java code.

Now that we know which Packet classes we must handle, the final step in building the client model is constructing the client packet handler classes. The client packet handling classes straddle the line between the model and view because they must know how to deal with the Jabber Packet classes (part of the model) as well as how to update the user interface (part of the view). Our test client has almost no user interface so these classes remain extremely simple.

The client OpenStreamHandler class

The first packet we should react to is the open stream packet that the server sends us.

The client OpenStreamHandler class

```
public class OpenStreamHandler implements PacketListener{

  public void notify(Packet packet){
     Session session = packet.getSession();
     session.setStreamID(packet.getID());
     session.setJID(new JabberID(packet.getTo()));
     session.setStatus(Session.STREAMING);
  }
}
```

Recall that the client initializes the stream so we have already sent the `<stream:stream>` tag to the server. When we receive the server's return opening stream tag, we just need to extract the stream ID from it, and update the session with its new status and information.

Unlike the server, we don't need a `CloseStreamHandler` class in the client. Once we send a closing stream tag using `disconnect()`, the server will close the `Socket` at its earliest opportunity. We will likely never see a closing `</stream:stream>` tag. Notice that if the stream closes without sending a closing `</stream:stream>` tag, the XML document will not be valid and the SAXparser will generate a `SAXException`. We must be ready to receive this error and ignore it. (We expect it to happen).

The most important packet handler is the message handler class, which is discussed next.

The Client MessageHandler Class

The client handles all `<message>` packet types::

- Chat
- Normal
- Groupchat
- Headline
- Error

- Jabber:x:oob (out-of-band X extensiton)

In clients with a user interface, most of your time will be spent making the display of these messages intuitive and fun for the user. Our simple test client, on the other hand, uses incoming messages for different purposes.

For example, if we wanted to measure the server's message throughput, a test client only needs to count how many messages sent and received during the test. Similarly, a messaging latency test can be conducted by a client sending a message to itself and measuring the time it takes for the message to make its round trip through the server.

In our client, we only need to know that packets are being properly routed to their destination. We can see this by looking at the raw XML passed over the connection. The task can be made easier by simply printing the message when we get a `<message>` packet.

The client MessageHandler class

```
public class MessageHandler implements PacketListener {

  public void notify(Packet packet){
    String type = packet.getType() == null ? "normal" : packet.getType();
    System.out.println("Received " + type + " message: "
                       + packet.getChildValue("body"));
    System.out.println("    To: " + packet.getTo());
    System.out.println("  From: " + packet.getFrom());
  }
}
```

We could make the message simpler or more verbose, log the message to a file or database, or myriad other possibilities. For now though, this implementation will meet our needs.

The last step in creating our test client is driving the JabberModel. We'll accomplish this with the TestThread and SimpleMessageClient class.

4.3.4 *Using the client model*

The JabberModel class deals with all the details of Jabber communications. However, by itself, it won't do anything. Like all models in the MVC design pattern, the JabberModel is a passive class that reacts to inputs. We must write a class that plays the role of the user as well as the view and controller from the MVC design pattern. The TestThread class fulfills this role.

Our TestThread class will pull packets from the PacketQueue as shown in figure 4.8. However, unlike the QueueThread, we know what packets to expect on the PacketQueue so we can dispatch the packets with more intelligence. In addition, the TestThread is aware of both incoming and outgoing packets. This gives us the opportunity to send and receive packets in an expected order. Deviations from the expected order of outgoing or incoming packets signal a failure of the test. This turns our client programming model into a pseudo blocking method call system rather than the server's event based model.

In blocking systems, you send a packet by calling a method. The method returns with the appropriate response or when the protocol enters its next state. For example, a blocking call to JabberModel.connect() would only return when we receive a success result (a failure would throw an exception). The blocking method call system eliminates the entire event-handling model we've been using so far.

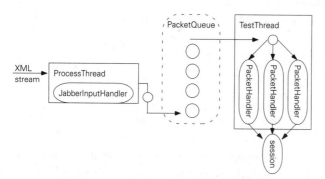

Figure 4.8 The `TestThread` class replaces the `QueueThread`. It intelligently routes packets and triggers tests by sending packets in response to incoming packets and its current state.

It is easier to program networked clients by blocking rather than using events. This is true with Jabber clients as well as those that support common network protocols like NNTP (Usenet news) and POP (email). The tradeoff is relatively straightforward. Event-based systems are easy to make multithreaded, easy to make responsive by running them in multiple threads, and easy to scale by using multiple processors or multiple machines to handle events.

All of these factors make event-based systems ideal for servers. Most of the Jabber server's interactions only require "local" information that is often present in the packet being processed or contained in the session context. You can design most of its actions as a simple, one-packet response.

Clients, on the other hand, usually use protocols in long, complex sessions where the context of events is just as important as the event itself.[18] For example, a client may wish to send a message. This simple goal ends up requiring a number of steps that must be carried out in the correct order. We know that we can't send a message without being authenticated. In addition, we can be authenticated without having established a Jabber XML stream with the server and having an account on the server. Finally, we can't establish a Jabber XML stream without being connected with the server.

---

[18] It can be complex enough that it may become worth the effort to use state-machines to carry out client tasks. In fact, I would recommend that designers of fully featured clients invest the effort to write or purchase a state-machine framework. Your client code will become easier to manage. In addition, it provides the groundwork for easy extensibility via scripting languages or plug-ins and allows you to automate Jabber clients. State-machines are a standard computer science model of computing systems. To learn more about state-machines, consult an introductory computer science textbook.

The client has little need for multitasking within its packet handling system. It will typically participate in one conversation at a time. Finally, clients usually don't need to be designed to be scalable. They are almost always limited by the abilities of the user to create input events and understand incoming information.

Our protocol tests will be carried out in a simple blocking style by sending a packet and waiting for the correct reply packet. This is similar to the approach we take when interacting with the server using telnet:

1   Send a packet.

2   Wait for a result.

3   See if it matches what we expect.

4   If so, go to the next step in the conversation.

For our first version, the client connects, sends a message, and disconnects. We need to carry out the two sides of the conversations in different threads so they can occur in parallel. Hence, the TestThread is a java.lang.Thread child class to allow more than one to run simultaneously.

The TestThread class is actually a base class of the test-specific classes we'll use in each chapter. It provides the basic packet-handling features we've seen in the QueueThread. In addition, we'll add a helper method that will allow the TestThread subclasses to wait for packets.

The TestThread class (listing 4.4) begins just like the QueueThread. The sole exception is the empty run() method and a simple way of assigning a Jabber-Model to the TestThread using the setModel() method. Subclasses will override the run() method to provide test specific code.

Listing 4.4   The TestThread class packet handling code

```java
public class TestThread extends Thread {

  public void run(){
  }

  JabberModel model;
  public void setModel(JabberModel newModel){
    model = newModel;
  }

  PacketQueue packetQueue = new PacketQueue();
  public PacketQueue getQueue() { return packetQueue; }

  HashMap packetListeners = new HashMap();
```

```
public boolean addListener(PacketListener listener, String element){
  if (listener == null || element == null){
    return false;
  }
  packetListeners.put(listener,element);
  return true;
}

public boolean removeListener(PacketListener listener){
  packetListeners.remove(listener);
  return true;
}
```

The packet listener management code is essentially the same as that in the QueueThread.[19] We can copy the code from the QueueThread's run() method into a notifyHandler() method to provide the same treatment of packet handlers in the TestThread.

The TestThread class notifyHandler method sends packets to registered handlers

```
void notifyHandlers(Packet packet){
  try {
    Packet child;
    String matchString = packet.getElement();;

    synchronized(packetListeners){
      Iterator iter = packetListeners.keySet().iterator();
      while (iter.hasNext()){
        PacketListener listener = (PacketListener)iter.next();
        String listenerString = (String)packetListeners.get(listener);
        if (listenerString.equals(matchString)){
          listener.notify(packet);
        }
      }
    }
  } catch (Exception ex){
    Log.error("TestThread: ", ex);
  }
}
```

As mentioned earlier, subclasses will conduct tests by sending packets out, and then wait for the correct packet to arrive. We can create a convenience method that makes waiting for specific packets simpler:

---

[19] The similarities suggest a good opportunity for creating a common base class for TestThread and QueueThread.

The TestThread class waitFor method waits for the "correct" packet

```
Packet waitFor(String element, String type){
    for( Packet packet = packetQueue.pull();
         packet != null;
         packet = packetQueue.pull()) {
      notifyHandlers(packet);
      if (packet.getElement().equals(element)){
        if (type != null){
          if (packet.getType().equals(type)){
            return packet;
          }
        } else {
          return packet;
        }
      }
    }
    return null;
  }
```

The waitFor() method uses the packet's element name, and optionally a particular type attribute to filter out the packet we're looking for. All other packets are sent to their packet handlers using the notifyHandlers() method. The waitFor() method returns the first matching packet it finds.

We'll create two TestThread subclasses as inner classes of the Simple MessageClient class shown in listing 4.5. The SimpleMessageClient class is a main application class that can be launched as a Java application. We provide the standard main() method for that purpose. The constructor takes care of most of the work, setting up the two test threads and models.

Listing 4.5   The SimpleMessageClient class

```
class SimpleMessageClient {

  public static void main(String[] args){        The client application
    Client client = new Client();               simply Creates Client
  }                                              object

  public SimpleMessageClient(){
    String server =  System.getProperty("jab.server.name",   "localhost");
    String address = System.getProperty("jab.server.address","127.0.0.1");
    String port =    System.getProperty("jab.server.port",   "5222");

                                                          Extract
                                                       settings from
    BuffyTestThread buffyTT = new BuffyTestThread();        system
    JabberModel buffyModel = new JabberModel(iainTT);     properties
    AngelTestThread angelTT = new AngelTestThread();
    JabberModel angelModel = new JabberModel(angelTT);
```

```
buffyModel.setServerName(server);
buffyModel.setServerAddress(address);
buffyModel.setPort(port);

buffyModel.setUser("buffy");
buffyModel.setResource("dev");

angelModel.setServerName(server);
angelModel.setServerAddress(address);
angelModel.setPort(port);

angelModel.setUser("angel");
angelModel.setResource("dev");

buffyTT.setModel(buffyModel);
buffyTT.start();        ◁————————┐
                                  │  Start two test
angelTT.setModel(angelModel);     │  threads
angelTT.start();        ◁————————┘
}
```

The actual tests are conducted in the two inner classes, `BuffyTestThread` and `AngelTestThread`, shown in listings 4.6 and 4.7. We'll simulate a short conversation between "buffy" and "angel." Buffy will start by sending a message and waiting for a reply. Angel will receive Buffy's message and reply. Angel doesn't need to wait for a reply so the `AngelTestThread` will disconnect as soon as it sends the reply message.

Listing 4.6   The BuffyTestThread inner class

```
public class BuffyTestThread extends TestThread {

  public void run(){
    try {
      model.connect();
      waitFor("stream:stream",null);
      model.sendMessage("angel@" + model.getServerName(),
                        "Want to patrol?",
                        "thread_id",
                        "normal",
                        "msg_id_buffy",
                        "Hey, do you wanted to patrol with me tonight?");
      waitFor("message",null);
      model.disconnect();
```

```
      } catch (Exception ex){
        ex.printStackTrace();
      }
    }
  }
```

Our blocking style of programming is well-suited to client interactions where we typically need to do one thing at a time. This is in contrast to the event-based model used by the server's `QueueThread` where we expect many things to be happening in parallel. The `AngelTestThread` provides the other side of the Jabber conversation.

Listing 4.7   The AngelTestThread inner class

```
public class AngelTestThread extends TestThread {

    public void run(){
      try {
        model.connect();
        for (Packet packet = waitFor("message",null);
             packet.getFrom().startsWith("buffy");
             packet = waitFor("message",null)){
        }
        model.sendMessage("buffy@" + model.getServerName(),
                          "Re: Want to patrol?",
                          "thread_id",
                          "normal",
                          "msg_id_angel",
                          "Sure, I'd love to go.");
        model.disconnect();

      } catch (Exception ex){
        ex.printStackTrace();
      }
    }
  }
}
```

Notice that the `AngelTestThread` uses an empty `for` loop to ensure that it waits for a message from "buffy" before sending a reply. Many Jabber servers send a welcome message to clients when they log on so we want to make sure we don't react to that. Of course, a normal Jabber server will require you to authenticate and indicate that you are available to receive messages before any are sent. However, our client is testing our server which lacks these features so we can skip these authentication steps until we add these features in future chapters.

EXPLOITING THE STATUS EVENT MODEL

Every GUI application is riddled with little bits of minutiae that can drive you crazy. One of them is the need to maintain a consistent application state at all times. In large applications, code scattered all over your application can change the state of your application at any time. The rest of the application classes, and most importantly the GUI, must be updated appropriately.

`Session` status is just one of many situations where we must continuously maintain a consistent application state. In this situation, a user-friendly application should be updating the appearance and the enabled status of menu items, buttons, and windows according to the `Session`'s status. We can use the status event notification feature we designed in the `Session` class to help automate the state update process.

As your application grows, you will be forced to decide whether to perform all status updates in one `StatusListener` class or to split the role among many smaller `StatusListener` implementation classes. Typically code will naturally evolve as a single large `StatusListener` class. Unfortunately, throwing "everything but the kitchen sink" into one class is usually not a good idea.

To eliminate the need for one `StatusListener` class, a Swing-based GUI client might use a specialized `javax.swing.JButton` that implements the `StatusListener` interface. The code might look like this:

```
class StreamEnabledButton extends JButton
  implements StatusListener{

public void notify(int status){

  switch(status){

  case Session.DISCONNECTED:
    setEnabled(false);
    break;

  case Session.STREAMING:
    setEnabled(true);
    break;
  }
 }
}
```

You can then add the `StreamEnabledButton` as a `StatusListener` to the `JabberModel` and it will automatically enable and disable itself when appropriate.

All buttons that you want to enable when the `Session` object is in the streaming state can use this class rather than `JButton`.

In addition, there are many Jabber features that Jabber servers will not allow unless you are authenticated.[20] These features can use a similar customized `Status-Listener` implementation and a new `Session` status for AUTHENTICATED to automatically enable and disable these features as well.

4.3.8 Results

Does it seem possible that in two short chapters we have created a Jabber client and server that can support basic IM? Well, try it out for yourself. Start the server from chapter 3, and then launch our Jabber client.

The `SimpleMessageClient` uses `java.lang.System` properties for many of its settings. You can set these properties on the command line using JVM options. For standard JVMs the –D option is used to pass these values. For example, I want to start the client so that it uses the server address `10.0.0.5`:

```
java –Djab.server.addess=10.0.0.5 SimpleMessageClient
```

A shell script or batch file can reduce the amount of typing you need to do, and help to launch the clients sequentially or simultaneously. Does the client send messages to itself as we would expect?

Try creating two `BuffyTestThreads` in the client with the different resource names. Where does Angel's reply message go? Messages should be delivered on a first-come, first-served basis. Are they? Is the server's message delivery behavior consistent with the server packet routing behavior we implemented in chapter 3? If you have two or even three computers on a network, it is even more impressive to create separate client applications that you can run on separate machines.

Congratulations! You're Jabbering!

NOTE   Client Is a Work in Progress   Be careful using the client "as-is". It lacks some critical "spit and polish" to make it safe for heavy use. For example, try sending a message with the '<' or '>' characters in the message body. It will crash the parser. Our client does not "normalize" the text before placing it into the Packet. Normalizing XML text changes the '<' character to the string ">" which is then safe to transport inside of XML character data.

---

[20] Authentication is covered in chapter 7.

4.4   *Conclusions*

The simplicity of the Jabber protocols and the power of Java have allowed us to create a miniature IM system in only two chapters. Playing with the current client and server will reveal how powerful even this simple Jabber system is. In fact, just a little user interface customization can make this system perfect for a lightweight communication system in a small home or office LAN.

The crucial IM feature missing from the software is support for presence. Presence lets us know who is online and if they are willing to communicate with us. This critical protocol enables features like chat to meet their full potential and is essential before we can conduct groupchat conferences. We'll dive into the Jabber presence protocols, and add groupchat conference support to the server and client in the next chapter.

The presence protocols

133

Instant messaging is differentiated from email by its instant delivery and the ability for users to project and detect each other's online presence. In the online world, the need for presence information is vital. You can't stick your head over the cubicle and see if someone is present when he is halfway across the world.

5.1 The need for presence

I once worked in a place that had a big white pegboard hanging on one wall. The board was split into rows labeled with each employee's name and columns with labels like "In the Office," "In the Warehouse," "In Meeting," "On Job Site," "Out of Town," and so forth. Each person would move the cardboard marker into the column that best matched his or her status. At a glance, people would know who was where, and what they were doing.

That big white pegboard was a manual method of managing employee presence. IM is a way to keep track in the online world.

Enabling users to keep track of each other's presence is especially troublesome for IM systems. We want to send instant messages, collaborate, and chat with people. In order to do that, we need to know who is online. In addition, because IM is always on, IM can become a problem if everyone you know is constantly sending you instant messages. It is important not only to know that someone is online, but also whether they are available to IM or are busy working.

Finally, if IM systems provide presence information, there is a danger that the information will fall into the wrong hands. For example, we don't want everyone in the world to know when we are at lunch or out of town. IM presence systems must provide a way for us to determine who is given permission to see our presence.

Jabber provides all of these features in its presence protocols. As you'll see in this chapter, the presence protocols, like all the Jabber protocols, are simple, flexible, and easy to use.

5.2 The presence protocol

The basic presence protocol is used in two primary contexts:

- *Presence update*—Informs people of your current presence state.
- *Presence subscription management*—Allows people to subscribe to another user's presence update packets and control who has access to their own presence.

In both cases, the Jabber server acts as an arbitrator between the presence information generator and the presence recipients. The server does not have the freedom to passively route presence packets. It must actively participate in the presence protocols to ensure their proper operation.

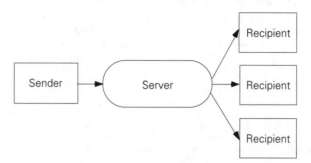

Figure 5.1 The Jabber server is an arbitrator in all presence exchanges.

The presence update protocol uses a simple, one-way message. A client sends the presence update packet to the server. The server forwards copies of the packet to every interested party on the user's presence subscription list. These subscription lists are called rosters in Jabber, but are more commonly referred to as buddy lists from their name in AIM.[1] The intent of the protocol's design is to keep the client's responsibilities to a minimum, offloading the difficult tasks like packet forwarding and maintaining rosters on to the server.

Maintaining user rosters on the server is handled using the second form of the presence protocol.[2] In this version of the presence protocol, the client sends and receives "subscribe" and "unsubscribe" requests and responses. From the client perspective, these requests and responses are handled like messages. The server appears to be passively passing the information between the sender and recipient. In reality, the server must snoop into these packets and use them to update the user's roster. We'll need to add similar server presence snooping in this chapter as we implement presence support for the groupchat protocols.[3]

The presence packet uses the `<presence>` element with the standard Jabber to, from, and type attributes for addressing the packet and determining its type. The presence types are summarized in table 5.1.

---

[1] Rosters and roster management is discussed in detail in chapter 8.

[2] Metainformation about rosters (chapter 8) is managed using the IQ protocol (chapter 6). However, presence management of rosters is handled by the presence protocol.

[3] We'll put off the serious use of presence and rosters until chapter 8.

Table 5.1 Presence packet types and the presence protocols in which they are used.

Presence type	Protocol type	Comment
available	Update	User is able to receive messages (default).
unavailable	Update	User is unable to receive messages.
subscribe	Management Request	Request a subscription to a user's presence.
unsubscribe	Management Request	Request removal of an existing presence subscription.
subscribed	Management Response	Subscription to the sender's presence has been accepted.
unsubscribed	Management Response	Subscription to the sender's presence has been removed.
error	Standard Jabber Error	The standard Jabber Error packet for presence problems.
probe[a]	Server-to-Server Request	Sends all presence information from one server to another (servers only).

[a]The `probe` presence type is not part of the Jabber client/server protocols. We'll discuss it in chapter 8.

In addition to the presence packet's attributes, the presence protocols allow four subelements in the `<presence>` packet:

- *<status>*—A free-form, text description of the user's status ("Away to lunch," "Gone fishing")
- *<priority>*—The numerical delivery priority of this resource. Higher numbers have higher priority. Only non-negative (zero or greater) integer numbers are allowed. Messages are routed to the resource that has the highest priority and is available.
- *<error>*—The standard Jabber error packet.
- *<show>*—One of four standard states that clients can use to modify the `available` presence state.[4] Clients will typically use the show state to display standard presence icons, sound alerts, and so forth. If a `<show>` state is not indicated, the user is in a `normal` or `online` state.[5] The standard states for `<show>` are:
  - *chat*—The user is actively seeking to chat.
  - *away*—The user is away from their Jabber client for a short period of time.

---

[4] The `show` state modifier applies only to users with an `available` presence state. If you are `unavailable`, you can't modify your presence state with `<show>`.

[5] Technically that makes five states: `normal` (no `<show>`), `chat`, `away`, `xa`, and `dnd`.

- *xa*—(extended away) The user is away from their Jabber client for a long period of time.

- *dnd*—(do not disturb) The user does not wish to receive any messages.

A sample presence update packet is shown in listing 5.1.

Listing 5.1   Sample update presence packet

```
<presence from='iain@shigeoka.com/home'
          to='shigeoka.com'
          type='available'>
  <status>I'm bored out of my mind, talk to me</status>
  <priority>10</priority>
  <show>chat</show>
</presence>
```

I normally put all of the optional fields in a packet to make the example clearer. Presence packets, though, thrive on context and minimal size. Presence packets from a client to the server often rely on the implied sender and recipient addresses associated with the session and the default presence type of `available`. A perfectly legal and useful presence update is simply: `<presence/>`. You are essentially saying, "I (the sender) am present!" A more typical presence packet that a client sends to the server may look like the following:

Compact update presence packet

```
<presence>
  <status>I'm bored out of my mind</status>
  <show>chat</show>
</presence>
```

The server would look up its internal roster of users that are subscribed to my presence and send the presence packet, slightly modified, to them. For example, if my friend Hieu were subscribed to my presence, he would receive:

Server update presence packet

```
<presence from='iain@shigeoka.com/work'
          to='hieu@vanillanet.com'>
  <status>I'm bored out of my mind</status>
  <show>chat</show>
</presence>
```

Presence subscription management packets use a request-response protocol. Here's what my client would see when successfully subscribing to the presence of my friend Hieu:

Subscription request and response packets

```
Send: <presence from='iain@shigeoka.com/work'
Send:            to='hieu@vanillanet.com'
Send:            type='subscribe'/>
Recv: <presence from='hieu@vanillanet.com/notebook'
Recv:            to='iain@shigeoka.com/work'
Recv:            type='subscribed'/>
```

A lot of time can pass between sending the subscribe request and receiving the subscribed reply. If Hieu were offline, he may not see the request until a day or more has passed. When he finally logs in, his client will show him the presence request and ask him whether it should grant permission to allow me to subscribe to his presence. If he agrees, it will send the `subscribed` response shown above. If he refused, his client would send an `unsubscribed` response. It is also common for clients to ask the user if they would like to subscribe to the requestor at the same time to form a mutual presence subscription.

Presence is used throughout the Jabber system for a variety of purposes, of which the most visible and important is maintaining user presence to let other Jabber users know when you are available for chatting. Jabber user presence involves the IQ protocols and user accounts, which are topics that we haven't covered yet. We'll defer discussion of user presence until chapter 8 when we will have all the protocols in place.

Luckily for us, the basic groupchat messaging protocol uses presence in a simple way. This protocol is a great introduction to using presence. Let's take a look at how presence and groupchat messages work together to create group chats (chatrooms) and then add groupchat support to the Jabber server and client software.

5.3 Adding groupchat support

Our discussion in chapter 4 explained the format for groupchat `<message>` packets, but did not explain how groupchats groups are formed, how to join them, and how to leave them. The reason is these groupchat housekeeping chores are all performing using the Jabber presence update protocol. Now that we know how Jabber presence operates and have a working `Packet` class, let's take a look at how you join a groupchat group.

5.3.1 Groupchat protocols

There are four critical things we need to be able to do in groupchat:

- *Join the group*—Send an `available` `<presence>` to the groupchat group Jabber ID.
- *Send messages to everyone in the group (broadcast messages)*—Send a `groupchat` `<message>` to the groupchat group Jabber ID.

- *Send messages to one person in the group (private messages)*—Send a `groupchat` `<message>` to the person's group Jabber ID using their group nickname. Sending private groupchat messages is often called "whispering".

- *Leave the group*—Send an `unavailable` `<presence>` to the groupchat group Jabber ID.

As you can see, two tasks use the presence update protocol, the other two the groupchat message protocol.

Groupchat groups are organized using a clever naming scheme. A normal user Jabber ID is of the form:

```
[user name]@[Jabber server]/[resource]
```

The groupchat protocol discussed here is groupchat 1.0 or more commonly referred to as *basic groupchat*. (The conference protocols are being developed as an advanced groupchat protocol that replaces basic groupchat. However, servers will probably support basic groupchat for a long time to come.)

A groupchat group Jabber ID takes the form:

```
[group name]@[groupchat server]/[nickname]
```

To join a group, use the presence update protocol to send an `available` presence to the groupchat group, specifying your desired nickname. For example, figure 5.2 shows a sequence diagram of the group joining process. In order to subscribe to the "java-users" group on the groupchat server `groups.shigeoka.com` using the nickname "smirk," I would send:

```
<presence to='java-users@groups.shigeoka.com/smirk'
          from='iain@shigeoka.com/work'/>
```

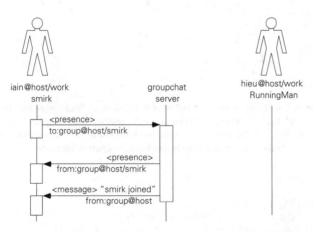

Figure 5.2   **The user "iain" joins a group named "group" on the "host" Jabber server by sending a** `<presence>` **packet with the desired group nickname of "smirk." The server responds with a confirming** `<presence>` **from the new group nickname and a welcome message.**

The groupchat server associates my Jabber ID with the nickname "smirk" in its own internal group list. It then propagates the presence status of all group members to all group members. Since I'm now a group member the server will send me this update:

```
<presence to='iain@shigeoka.com/work'
          from='java-users@groups.shigeoka.com/smirk'/>
```

The server will typically also send a welcome message to the group:

```
<message to='iain@shigeoka.com/work'
         from='java-users@groups.shigeoka.com'
         type='groupchat'>
 <body>smirk has joined java-users</body>
</message>
```

Notice that the sender is the groupchat server, not a groupchat participant.

Now let's say my friend Hieu also joins java-users (figure 5.3) by sending:

```
<presence from='hieu@vanillanet.com/work'
          to='java-users@groups.shigeoka.com/RunningMan'/>
```

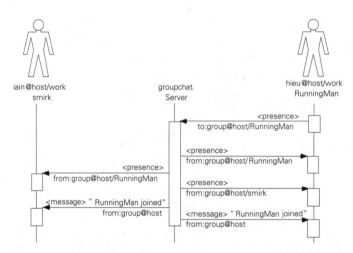

Figure 5.3 The user "hieu" joins the group named "group" with the nickname "RunningMan." The server must ensure that both "hieu" and "iain" are informed of the new list member "RunningMan." In addition, "hieu" is sent a <presence> packet from list member "smirk" so he is aware of the presence of all list members. Notice all <presence> and <message> packets are from groupchat addresses.

Hieu receives from the server:

```
<presence to='hieu@vanillanet.com/work'
          from='java-users@groups.shigeoka.com/smirk'/>
<presence to='hieu@vanillanet.com/work'
          from='java-users@groups.shigeoka.com/RunningMan'/>

<message to='hieu@vanillanet.com/work'
```

```
         from='java-users@groups.shigeoka.com'
         type='groupchat'>
 <body>RunningMan has joined java-users</body>
</message>
```

I also receive the presence update (my status doesn't change so the server doesn't have to update my presence):

```
<presence to='iain@shigeoka.com/work'
          from='java-users@groups.shigeoka.com/RunningMan'/>


<message to='iain@shigeoka.com/work'
         from='java-users@groups.shigeoka.com'
         type='groupchat'>
  <body>RunningMan has joined java-users</body>
</message>
```

I don't know RunningMan is Hieu, nor does Hieu know that I'm smirk. The groupchat server keeps track of the group member nicknames and hides our real identities. I can send messages directly to RunningMan without knowing Hieu's real Jabber ID:

```
<message to='java-users@groups.shigeoka.com/RunningMan'
         from='iain@shigeoka.com/work'
         type='groupchat'>
  <body>Hi RunningMan!</body>
</message>
```

The message goes to the groupchat server (figure 5.4) The server looks up the "RunningMan" nickname to find Hieu's Jabber ID and my Jabber ID to find the "smirk" nickname. The server rewrites the addresses in the message packet and sends it to Hieu. Hieu receives:

```
<message to='hieu@vanillanet.com/work'
         from='java-users@groups.shigeoka.com/smirk'
         type='groupchat'>
  <body>Hi RunningMan!</body>
</message>
```

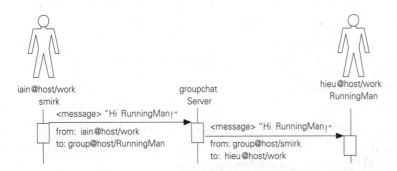

Figure 5.4 User "iain" sends a private groupchat message to list member "RunningMan." Notice how the groupchat server adjusts the sender and recipient addresses of the message.

Hieu can send a message to the entire group (figure 5.5) by addressing it to the group's Jabber ID:

```
<message to='java-users@groups.shigeoka.com'
         from='hieu@vanillanet.com/work'
         type='groupchat'>
  <body>Anyone there?</body>
</message>
```

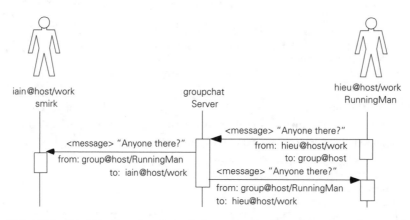

Figure 5.5   User "hieu" sends a groupchat message to all group members. Once again, notice how the groupchat server adjusts sender and recipient addresses of the message.

The server will forward the message to everyone in the group, rewriting the sender address to use Hieu's group nickname. Hieu is part of the group so he will receive the response:

```
<message to='hieu@vanillanet.com/work'
         from='java-users@groups.shigeoka.com/RunningMan'
         type='groupchat'>
  <body>Anyone there?</body>
</message>
```

I'm also in the group so I get a copy:

```
<message to='iain@shigeoka.com/work'
         from='java-users@groups.shigeoka.com/RunningMan'
         type='groupchat'>
  <body>Anyone there?</body>
</message>
```

Hieu realizes this is a boring group with only one other person in it and decides to leave (figure 5.6). To leave a group, the user's presence is changed to unavailable. Hieu can do this by sending the following packet:

```
<presence to='java-users@groups.shigeoka.com/RunningMan'
          from='hieu@vanillanet.com/work'
          type='unavailable'/>
```

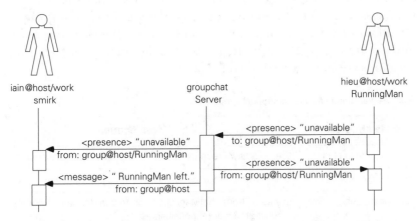

Figure 5.6   User "hieu" leaves the group by sending an "unavailable" <presence> packet to the groupchat server. The server updates all list members with the change in presence, and sends a "goodbye" message to remaining list members.

Hieu receives a confirmation from the groupchat server:

```
<presence to='hieu@vanillanet.com/work'
          from='java-users@groups.shigeoka.com/RunningMan'
          type='unavailable'/>
```

I receive the presence update packet and a message packet from the groupchat server:

```
<presence to='iain@shigeoka.com/work'
          from='java-users@groups.shigeoka.com/RunningMan'
          type='unavailable'/>

<message to='iain@shigeoka.com/work'
         from='java-users@groups.shigeoka.com'
  <body>RunningMan has left</body>
</message>
```

Knowing how Jabber message routing works, there are ways to implement a groupchat server as a client chatbot application with minimal help from the server. The approach is very attractive for creating a Jabber server that runs on different machines, distributed across a network. However, to keep things simple and efficient,[6] we'll modify our server to support groupchat. Embedding groupchat on the server is the most common approach for adding groupchat support to a server.

5.3.2 *Server modifications*

To support groupchat and presence, we will create a message packet handler to replace the generic `PacketHandler` class from chapter 3. This class must route normal message packets, but send groupchat messages to a new groupchat manager. In addition, we must add a new presence packet handler for presence packets, and create a groupchat manager to manage groupchat sessions. These modifications are summarized in table 5.2.

Table 5.2 Server modifications to support groupchat.

Module affected	Modification
New packet handler classes	Create a new PresenceHandler and a MessageHandler class.
Remove Delivery Handler	DeliveryHandler will be replaced by MessageHandler.
New Groupchat subsystem	Create a GroupChatManager class to coordinate and handle groupchat server responsibilities.

We'll start with the packet handler classes.

The new packet handlers

In our original server, all packets were routed as best as possible by the `PacketHandler` class. Now that our server is becoming more sophisticated, we need to start differentiating between the incoming Jabber packets and begin server-side processing of packets.

The first thing to change is the way packets are handled. First, we need to discard the old `DeliveryHandler` class. Its behavior of blindly forwarding all packets to their recipient will cause problems now that groupchat message packets must be diverted to a new `GroupChatManager` class. We'll replace the `DeliveryHandler` class with the `MessageHandler` class that will be able to recognize groupchat messages and handle them appropriately.

---

[6] Servers with *monolithic* designs (implemented as a single, tightly integrated application) are more efficient for processing messages than distributed designs with external chatbots. To support an external chatbot, messages travel from the client to the server, are parsed in the server, reserialized as XML packets, sent to the chatbot, parsed in the chatbot, processed in the chatbot, reserialized as XML packets, sent to the server, parsed in the server, reserialized as XML packets, and sent to the client. That's two extra serialization and parsing steps that are eliminated when the chatbot functionality is implemented directly in the server. However, monolithic designs can only handle larger loads by running them on faster hardware which gets expensive. Distributed designs allow you to spread processing across multiple, less expensive machines. This is important when your Jabber server must handle hundreds of thousands of users.

You may be wondering, "Why not cover the GroupChatManager first?" My answer is, "I don't know what it needs to do yet." We know that it will manage groupchat messages, but what the interfaces should look like is still a mystery. Once we see what the handler classes require from the GroupChatManager and what they can provide we'll have a better idea of what should be built into the GroupChatManager. With that in mind, let's take a look at the new MessageHandler class.

The MessageHandler class shown in listing 5.2 receives incoming <message> packets from the QueueThread. Handling them ends up being relatively simple. If the message's type is groupchat we send it to the GroupChatManager. If not, it is delivered to its recipient.[7]

Listing 5.2   The MessageHandler class

```
public class MessageHandler implements PacketListener {

  static SessionIndex sessionIndex;
  GroupChatManager chatMan = GroupChatManager.getManager();
  public MessageHandler(SessionIndex index) { sessionIndex = index; }

  public void notify(Packet packet){
    String recipient = packet.getTo();
    if (recipient.equalsIgnoreCase(Server.SERVER_NAME)){
      //Packet dropped
      return;
    }

    if (packet.getType().equals("groupchat")){
      if (chatMan.isChatPacket(packet)){
        chatMan.handleChatMessage((MessagePacket)packet);
      } else {
      }
          return;
    }

    deliverPacket(packet);
  }

  static public void deliverPacket(Packet packet){
    try {
      Session session = sessionIndex.getSession(packet.getTo());
      if (session != null){
        packet.writeXML(session.getWriter());
```

---

[7] Messages are still dropped if the recipient is offline. This flaw will be addressed in the next chapter when we add user account support to the server.

```
      } else {
      }
    } catch (Exception ex){
      Log.error("MessageHandler: " + ex.getMessage());
    }
  }
}
```

The implementation is straightforward and follows closely from the old `DeliveryHandler` class. The major modification is the handling of groupchat messages, and the addition of a static `deliverPacket()` method for delivering packets to recipients. Other classes like the new `GroupChatManager` will use `deliverPacket()` for consistent and generic packet delivery.

The `PresenceHandler` class (listing 5.3) similar in design to the `Message Handler` except it sends all incoming `<presence>` `Packets` to the `GroupChatManager`. We don't need to distinguish between `Packet` types yet because all `<presence>` `Packets` should be groupchat-related.

Listing 5.3   The PresenceHandler class

```
public class PresenceHandler implements PacketListener {

  SessionIndex sessionIndex;
  GroupChatManager chatMan = GroupChatManager.getManager();
  public PresenceHandler(SessionIndex index) { sessionIndex = index; }

  public void notify(Packet packet){
    if (chatMan.isChatPacket(packet)){
      chatMan.handleChatPresence((PresencePacket)packet);
    } else {
    //Packet dropped
    }
  }
}
```

Once again, you can see how we rely on the `GroupChatManager` to know what to do with this packet. Now that we've seen that the external interface to `GroupChatManager` should be `handlerChatMessage()`, let's take a look at this mysterious `GroupChatManager` class.

The groupchat manager

The `GroupChatManager` receives all of the server's `<message>` packets of type groupchat, and all `<presence>` packets. We know from the groupchat protocol discussed in section 5.3.1 that it must do a few basic things:

- Receive presence packets from new users. These packets allow users to join a group. Upon accepting the new user, the server:
  - Updates all group members with member presence.
  - Sends a welcome server message to all group members.

- Receive presence packets from existing users and
  - Update all group members with presence.
  - If the user presence is of type `unavailable`:
    - Remove member from group.
    - Send an exit server message to all remaining members.
- Receive groupchat group message packets and forward it to all group members.
- Receive groupchat group nickname message packets and forward it to that member.

To enable this behavior, the `GroupChatManager` must:

- Maintain a list of groups. For each group:
  - Maintain a mapping of user Jabber ID's to group nicknames.
  - Maintain a mapping of group nicknames to user Jabber ID's.
  - Maintain a mapping of user Jabber ID's to user group presence status.
  - Determine if a user is a member of the group.
  - Add users to the group.
  - Remove users from the group.
- Create groups if needed.
- Remove groups if needed.
- Use the incoming packets to manage the groups and their membership.

The list of requirements may seem large but our existing Jabber classes and the standard Java classes help a lot. Let's take a look at the `GroupChatManager` class, beginning with the constructor and its one data field.

The GroupChatManager class constructor, and data field

```java
public class GroupChatManager {

  private GroupChatManager(){}

  static GroupChatManager man;

  static public GroupChatManager getManager(){
    if (man == null){
      man = new GroupChatManager();
    }
    return man;
  }


  Hashtable groups = new Hashtable();
```

We created an empty, private constructor to prevent anything from creating an instance of GroupChatManager except for the class itself. If you need an instance of the class, you use getManager(). The getManager() method enforces a Singleton design pattern: only one instance of the GroupChatManager will exist in the server. We don't want different modules to be working with different GroupChatManagers. The single instance of GroupChatManager must be a single point of groupchat information for the entire server.

The GroupChatManager manages a set of groupchat groups. Each in turn manages its members and their presence. To handle this, we use a java.util.Hashtable of groups called "groups." The group Hashtable maps the full name of each group to a Group object (listing 5.4).

> **Listing 5.4   The GroupChatManager class Group inner-class and group access method**

```java
class Group {
  String jid;
  Group(String jabberID){ jid = jabberID; }

  String getJabberID() {return jid;}

  Hashtable nick2jid = new Hashtable();
  Hashtable jid2presence = new Hashtable();
  Hashtable jid2nick = new Hashtable();
}

Group getGroup(String name){
  if (groups.containsKey(name)){
    return (Group)groups.get(name);
  } else {
    //Create group
    Group activeGroup = new Group(name + "@" + Server.SERVER_NAME);
```

```
        groups.put(name,activeGroup);
        return activeGroup;
    }
}
```

Each `Group` object contains the Jabber ID for the group and three `Hashtables`. The three `Hashtables` are described in the table 5.3:

Table 5.3   The Group class's `Hashtable` fields.

Table	Key	Value	Comment
Nick2jid	Member nickname	Member Jabber ID	Used to convert group nicknames to real Jabber IDs.
Jid2nick	Member Jabber ID	Member nickname	Used to convert real Jabber ID's to group nicknames.
Jid2presence	Member Jabber ID	Presence Packet	The list of each group member's current presence (as a Presence-Packet).

I decided to expose the three `Hashtables` directly to `GroupChatManager` rather than provide access methods. My reasoning is twofold. First, there is a tight coupling between `GroupChatManager` and its `Group` objects and I can't think of any immediate benefits that would result from isolating them from each other. Second, only the `GroupChatManager` will ever work with `Group` objects.

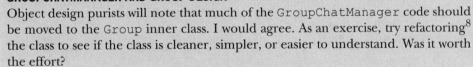

GROUPCHATMANAGER AND GROUP DESIGN
Object design purists will note that much of the `GroupChatManager` code should be moved to the `Group` inner class. I would agree. As an exercise, try refactoring[8] the class to see if the class is cleaner, simpler, or easier to understand. Was it worth the effort?

The server needs to be able to tell if a Jabber ID is a group address or a user address. Presence packets sent to groupchat addresses create or act on the group; presence packets sent to user addresses update your user presence status.

---

[8] *Refactoring* describes a process of systematically reorganizing and rewriting source code. The goal of refactoring is to maintain a clean, understandable, and well-designed code base despite code modifications, changes, or additions.

Normally Jabber servers use a different server name for groupchat groups to make this differentiation. For example, users have accounts on `jabber.org` and groupchats are carried out on `conference.jabber.org`. You can configure a DNS server to point both server names to the same server machine. In such setups, one server application will handle both server names but use the packet addresses to differentiate user traffic from chatbot traffic.

I have found this configuration is difficult to support in smaller networks, a situation where the server will probably be used. Instead of different server names, I use a naming convention for usernames to tell user and group addresses apart. In the server, usernames that end in .group indicate a group address. So groups on my server have addresses of the form[9]:

```
[group name].group@[server name]/[nickname]
```

We can create a method in `GroupChatManager` to detect group addresses:

The GroupChatManager class isChatPacket() method

```
public boolean isChatPacket(Packet packet){
  JabberID recipient = new JabberID(packet.getTo());
  return recipient.getUser().endsWith(".group")
         && recipient.equalsDomain(Server.SERVER_NAME);
}
```

The `isChatPacket()` method is used in the `handleChatPresence()` method to make sure the presence update is being used for groupchat. The remainder of `handleChatPresence()` decides how to treat incoming presence `Packet`s. The `handleChatPresence()` method (listing 5.5) is called from the server's `Presence-Handler` class.

Listing 5.5   The GroupChatManager class handleChatPresence() method

```
public void handleChatPresence(PresencePacket packet){
  JabberID recipient = new JabberID(packet.getTo());
  if (!isChatPacket(packet)){
    return;
  }

  Group group = getGroup(recipient.getUser());
  String nick = recipient.getResource();

  //The nickname exists for the group
  if (group.jid2nick.containsKey(nick)){
    //The nickname matches the sender's Jabber ID
    if (group.nick2jid.get(nick).equals(packet.getFrom())){
```

---

[9]   A majority of Jabber servers use this format: `[group name]@conferences.[server name]/nickname`.

```
      updatePresence(group, packet);
  } else {
      sendConflictingNicknameError(packet);
  }
} else {
    joinGroup(group,packet);
  }
}
```

Groupchat <presence> packets are used for two things: updating a group member's presence or joining a group. If the nickname doesn't exist in the group, the packet is being used to join the group and handleChatPresence() calls joinGroup() shown in listing 5.6.

Listing 5.6   The GroupChatManager class joinGroup() method

```
void joinGroup(Group group, PresencePacket packet){

  //The packet is sent to the group/nickname
  JabberID gid = new JabberID(packet.getTo());
  //The nickname will be registered to the sender's Jabber ID
  String sender = packet.getFrom();
  //Update the group Hashtables
  group.jid2nick.put(sender,gid.getResource());
  group.nick2jid.put(gid.getResource(),sender);
  //Update the presence for all group members (also updates
  //jid2presence Hashtable)
  updatePresence(group,packet);

   //Send the new member presence updates for all other members of the group
   Iterator presencePackets = group.jid2presence.values().iterator();
   while (presencePackets.hasNext()){
      Packet p = (Packet)presencePackets.next();
      p.setTo(packet.getFrom());
      MessageHandler.deliverPacket(p);
   }
   //Send a server welcome message
   serverMessage(group, gid.getResource() + " has joined the group");
}
```

The joinGroup() method adds a user to the group by:

- Updating all of the group's Hashtables
- Updating the user's presence in the group using updatePresence()

- Sending the joining member the presence of all existing group members in the group's jid2presence table
- Delivering a welcome server message

The process is primarily group membership housekeeping.

The updatePresence() method is called from joinGroup() or from handlePacket(). The handlePacket() method uses updatePresence() when an incoming <presence> packet updates a nickname that exists in the group and the sender is already a member of the group (the sender's Jabber ID matches the one registered with the nickname in nick2jid).

Updating presence involves changing the sender address to their group/nickname address, and forwarding the packet to all group members.

```
void updatePresence(Group group, PresencePacket packet){

    String sender = packet.getFrom();

    //Convert sender address to group/nickname
    packet.setFrom(group.getJabberID()
                   + "/"
                   + (String)group.jid2nick.get(packet.getFrom()));

    //Deliver packet to all group members
    deliverToGroup(group,packet);
    //Update their presence record
    group.jid2presence.put(sender,packet);

    //If an unavailable packet, remove the user from the group
    if (packet.getType() == null){
      return;
    }

    if (packet.getType().equals("unavailable")){
      removeUser(group,sender);
    }
}
```

The sendConflictingNicknameError() method is the last major presence-handling method of GroupChatManager. The handlePacket() method calls sendConflictingNicknameError() if the incoming <presence> packet nickname exists in the group, but doesn't match the member who joined under that nickname. In this case, we have to assume that the <presence> packet sender is a new user trying to join under a nickname already in use. If this is the case, we send a <presence> packet error using the sendConflictingNicknameError() method.

The GroupChatManager class sendConflictingNicknameError method

```
void sendConflictingNicknameError(Packet packet){
    try {
        Writer out = packet.getSession().getWriter();
        ErrorPacket ePacket = new ErrorPacket(packet.getSession());
        out.write("<presence to='");
        out.write(packet.getFrom());
        out.write("' from='");
        out.write(packet.getTo());
        out.write("'>");
        ePacket.setCode(409);
        ePacket.setMessage("Conflict: nickname taken");
        ePacket.writeXML();
        out.write("</presence>");
    }catch (Exception ex){
        Log.error("GroupChatManager: " + ex.getMessage());
    }
}
```

The method is a bit crude as we generate the error packet manually[10] rather than use the presence `Packet` object.

As you can see, handling incoming presence `Packets` is primarily an exercise in membership bookkeeping. Handling groupchat message `Packets` is simpler. The server's `MessageHandler` class calls the `handleChatMesasge()` method (listing 5.7) on the `GroupChatManager` for all groupchat messages:

Listing 5.7   The GroupChatManager class handleChatMessage() method

```
public void handleChatMessage(MessagePacket packet) {

    JabberID recipient = new JabberID(packet.getTo());
    Group group = getGroup(recipient.getUser());

    //Convert sender address to group/nickname
    packet.setFrom(group.getJabberID()
                + "/"
                + (String)group.jid2nick.get(packet.getFrom()));

    //Addressed to entire group
    if (recipient.getResource() == null){
        deliverToGroup(group,packet);
    } else {
        //Addressed to group member
```

---

[10] In a refactoring pass through the code, a `Packet` object should be used to generate the XML.

```
        packet.setTo((String)group.nick2jid.get(recipient.getResource()));
        MessageHandler.deliverPacket(packet);
    }
}
```

The `handleChatMessage()` method converts the sender's address to their group/nickname address, and sends the message. If the message was addressed to the group, the message is sent to each member using the `deliverToGroup()` method (listing 5.8), otherwise, it is sent only to the intended recipient.[11]

`GroupChatManager` has four utility methods that you have already seen used in the `handleChat*()` methods. The first set (listing 5.8) deals with delivering group messages: `serverMessage()` sends messages from the server, while `deliverToGroup()` forwards packets to all group members.

Listing 5.8 The GroupChatManager class message sending convenience methods

```
void serverMessage(Group group, String msg){
    MessagePacket packet = new MessagePacket(null);
    packet.setFrom(group.getJabberID());
    packet.setType("groupchat");
    packet.setBody(msg);
    deliverToGroup(group,packet);
}

  void deliverToGroup(Group group, Packet packet){

    Enumeration members = group.jid2nick.keys();
    while(members.hasMoreElements()){
      packet.setTo((String)members.nextElement());
      MessageHandler.deliverPacket(packet);
    }
  }
```

The second set of convenience methods allows you to easily remove users from groups. The basic procedure involves cleaning up the group `Hashtables` and sending a server message to all remaining group members. The second `removeUser()` method shown in listing 5.9 allows you to remove a user from all

---

[11] There is one critical shortcoming in my implementation. The `handleChatMessage()` method does not check whether the sender is a member of the group. Although this is not a requirement of the standard, I think that only group members should be able to send groupchat messages to the group or group members. I will leave the task of adding this feature to you if you feel it is important.

groups. The server packet handling `CloseStreamHandler` class removes a disconnected user from all groupchatgroups using this method.

Listing 5.9   The GroupChatManager removeUser() method

```
public void removeUser(Group group, String jabberID){

    String nick = (String)group.jid2nick.get(jabberID);

    //Can't remove a user that doesn't exist
    if (nick == null){
      return;
    }

    //Clean up the group Hashtables
    group.jid2nick.remove(jabberID);
    group.jid2presence.remove(jabberID);
    group.nick2jid.remove(nick);

    //Remove group if it has no members left
    if (group.jid2nick.size() == 0){
      groups.remove(group.getJabberID());
    //Otherwise, send server message to remaining members
    } else {
      serverMessage(group,nick + " has left");
    }
  }

  public void removeUser(String jabberID){
    Iterator grps = groups.values().iterator();
    while (grps.hasNext()){
      removeUser((Group)grps.next(),jabberID);
    }
  }
}
```

Let's take a look at the `CloseStreamHandler` to see the `GroupChatManager`
`.removeUser()` method in action.

The modified CloseStreamHandler class
The `CloseStreamHandler` requires a minor modification in order to ensure
groupchat membership is cleaned up when a user leaves. I have highlighted the
change in bold.

The modified CloseStreamHandler class

```
public class CloseStreamHandler implements PacketListener {

  SessionIndex sessionIndex;
  public CloseStreamHandler(SessionIndex index) { sessionIndex = index; }

  public void notify(Packet packet){
    try {
      Session session = packet.getSession();

      GroupChatManager.getManager().removeUser(
                        packet.getSession().getJID().toString());
      session.getSocket().close();
      sessionIndex.removeSession(session);

    } catch (Exception ex){
      sessionIndex.removeSession(packet.getSession());
    }
  }
}
```

The final change we need is to modify the Server class to install the new packet handler classes in the QueueThread.

The modified Server class

The modifications to the Server class are isolated to the configuration of the QueueThread's packet handlers. We can move the QueueThread creation procedure to a separate method, createQueueThread() shown in listing 5.10. The method will be called at the beginning of the Server class's constructor.

Listing 5.10   The modified Server class createQueueThread() method

```
void createQueueThread(){

    QueueThread qThread = new QueueThread(packetQueue);
    qThread.setDaemon(true);
    qThread.addPacketListener(new OpenStreamHandler(index),
                          "stream:stream");
    qThread.addPacketListener(new CloseStreamHandler(index),
                          "/stream:stream");
    qThread.addPacketListener(new MessageHandler(index),
                          "message");
    qThread.addPacketListener(new PresenceHandler(index),
                          "presence");
    qThread.start();
}
```

These changes wrap up the server support for basic presence and groupchat in the server. Now we need to modify the Jabber client to exercise these features so we can test both the client and server.

5.3.3 Client modifications

We need to build a new test client to test the groupchat capabilities of our server. We can reuse our basic test client classes with minor modifications to create our new client. The client modifications involve three changes:

- Add a <presence> packet sending support to the JabberModel.
- Add a <presence> packet handler class.
- Modify the client to test groupchat.

These changes begin with the JabberModel. The only new Jabber client feature the server supports is sending and receiving <presence> packets. In order to send <presence> packets we can add a sendPresence() method that mimics our existing sendMessage() method.

The modified JabberModel class sendPresence() method

```
public void sendPresence(String recipient,
                         String type,
                         String show,
                         String status,
                         String priority) throws IOException {

    Packet packet = new Packet("presence");

    if (recipient != null){
      packet.setTo(recipient);
    }
    if (type != null){
      packet.setType(type);
    }
    if (show != null){
      packet.getChildren().add(new Packet("show",show));
    }
    if (status != null){
      packet.getChildren().add(new Packet("status",status));
    }
    if (priority != null){
      packet.getChildren().add(new Packet("priority",priority));
    }
    packet.writeXML(session.getWriter());
  }
```

As you can see, sendPresence() is really a convenience method to protect JabberModel users from the internal details of the Packet class and the <presence> packet structure. High-performance clients such as automated chatbots will probably need to optimize JabberModel convenience methods like sendPresence() and sendMessage() for better efficiency and resource usage.[12]

Our client will respond to <presence> packets just as we did to <message> packets: we will print a short summary of the packet information. For <presence> packets, we're interested in the packet's addresses and the type of presence sent.

The Client PresenceHandler Class

```
public class PresenceHandler implements PacketListener {

  public void notify(Packet packet){
    System.out.println("Received presence: " + packet.getType());
    System.out.println("    To: " + packet.getTo());
    System.out.println("  From: " + packet.getFrom());
  }
```

The PresenceHandler class is registered with the QueueThread as a handler of <pres­ence> packets in the JabberModel's constructor. Now we'll be able to see what <pres­ence> and <message> packets are received on the client, and in what order.

The final order of business is to test groupchat on the server using our client. We'll do this by implementing the conversation example we used earlier to explain how groupchat works. The conversation proceeds as follows:

Table 5.4 The test client's groupchat conversation

"Iain" client	"Hieu" client
Connect and create Jabber stream	Connect and create Jabber stream
Send presence type=available to=java-users.group@server/smirk	
	Send presence type=available to=java-users.group@server/RunningMan
Send "private" message "Hi RunningMan!" type=groupchat to=java-users.group@server/RunningMan	

---

[12] For example, JabberModel.sendPresence() creates many temporary objects that are used once and discarded. If this method is called frequently, it is more efficient to reuse these objects.

Table 5.4   The test client's groupchat conversation (continued)

	Send group message "Anyone there?" type=groupchat to=java-users.group@server
	Send presence type=unavailable to=java-users.groups@server/RunningMan
Disconnect	Disconnect

We can simulate the groupchat conversation using two `TestThread` subclasses like we did in chapter 4. In this example, we'll use a `GroupChatClient` class to initialize the `TestThread` subclasses in the same manner as `SimpleMessageClient` so I won't repeat the code here. The actual test is carried out in the new `TestThread` subclasses `IainTestThread` (listing 5.11) and `HieuTestThread` (listing 5.12).

Listing 5.11   The IainTestThread inner-class of GroupChatClient

```
public class IainTestThread extends TestThread {

  public void run(){
    try {
      model.connect();
      waitFor("stream:stream",null);
      String groupName = "java-users.group@" + model.getServerName();

      model.sendPresence(groupName + "/smirk",  ⟵——| Group nickname
                    null,   ⟵——| Type | Show
                    null,   ⟵
                    null,   ⟵——| Status | Priority
                    null);  ⟵
      for (Packet packet = waitFor("presence",null);
            !packet.getFrom().endsWith("RunningMan");
            packet = waitFor("presence",null)){
      }
      model.sendMessage(groupName + "/RunningMan",  ⟵——| Group nickname

                    null,   ⟵——| Subject | Thread
                    null,   ⟵
                    "groupchat",  ⟵——| Type | Packet ID
                    null,   ⟵
                    "Hi RunningMan!");  ⟵——| Body
```

```
        waitFor("presence","unavailable");
        model.disconnect();
      } catch (Exception ex){
        ex.printStackTrace();
      }
    }
  }
```

We implement the `HieuTestThread` class in the same way as the `IainTestThread`.

Listing 5.12   The HieuTestThread inner-class of GroupChatClient

```
public class HieuTestThread extends TestThread {

    public void run(){
      try {
        model.connect();
        waitFor("stream:stream",null);
        String groupName = "java-users.group@" + model.getServerName();
        model.sendPresence(groupName + "/RunningMan",        ◁——————┐ Group nickname
                      null,   ◁————┐ Type      │ Show
                      null,   ◁————┘           │
                      null,   ◁————┐ Status    │ Priority
                      null);  ◁————┘           │
      for (Packet packet = waitFor("message",null);
           packet.getFrom().endsWith("smirk");
           packet = waitFor("message",null)){
        model.sendMessage(groupName,         ◁————————┐ Group Jid
                      null,   ◁————┐ Subject  │ Thread
                      null,   ◁————┘          │
                      "groupchat",  ◁————┐ Type  │ Packet ID
                      null,   ◁————┘          │
                      "Anyone there?");  ◁————┐ Body
        sleep(1000)
        model.sendPresence(groupName + "/RunningMan",  ◁————┐ Group nickname
                      "unavailable",  ◁————┐ Type  │ Show
                      null,   ◁————┘          │
                      null,   ◁————┐ Status  │ Priority
                      null);  ◁————┘          │
        sleep(1000);
        model.disconnect();
      } catch (Exception ex){
        ex.printStackTrace();
      }
    }
  }
}
```

Watch the packets printed by the client's packet handlers to follow the conversation. Normally a user will be watching incoming packets as lines on their line-by-line groupchat display. They will see server messages welcoming new members, and be able to respond to other group members' messages with their own. Properly simulating this conversational flow in a test client can be difficult. However, when you're testing your software, these automated test clients ease the burden of repeatedly running the same client-side tests. If tests are easier to run they will be run more often, increasing the quality of your code.

Robust protocol implementations relying on user input can be the most difficult pieces of software to write. I personally find it is hard to force myself to automate software when a manual method of running tests is available. It is very tempting to fall back to the "user agent client" with its nice GUI rather than writing test software. However automated tests pay off with big dividends in software quality and faster development as the project grows. So stick with it!

5.4   *Shortcomings of our server and basic groupchat*

There are several serious shortcomings to the groupchat support software presented here. First, there is only a limited amount of error-checking in both the client and server. In just a few minutes of testing the server with telnet I'm sure you can uncover many situations where the server fails to properly respond to errors in packets sent to it. In most cases, the results are to drop the packet or close the connection. However, there are several situations where its behavior is unpredictable. (Try logging in with multiple clients using the same username and resource.)

Error checking and error handling are crucial elements of all good software. In these examples, a lot of standard error checking code has been omitted to make the examples compact and easier to read. For example, in many places, references should be checked for null values and default values provided. This is a crucial difference in software designed for explanation versus software designed for use. If you intend to use this software in the real world, please revisit it and add error-checking code as needed.

Finally, groupchat provides very little control over group membership. Typical chatroom functionality such as restricting membership to invited members, kicking people off a group, and so forth, is simply not present with basic groupchat. Advanced groupchat, referred to as conferencing in Jabber, is handled through additional standards in the `jabber:iq:conference` IQ extension protocol.[13]

5.5 Conclusions

Presence is a powerful IM tool that is used with all of the Jabber protocols to manage the online presence status of a client. In this chapter we have seen how it is used with the message protocol to support groupchat. The minimal amount of code needed to support groupchat presence, and the power of such a feature, is clearly demonstrated by our simple server and client.

The IQ protocols provide access to all Jabber functionality that is neither messaging nor presence updates. This functionality includes Jabber rosters, another IQ extension protocol. Rosters enable us to finish the Jabber presence support that we began to add in this chapter. With rosters, and complete presence support, we'll have a fully functional IM system.

---

[13] You can read about the jabber:iq:conference protocol in appendix A. The conference protocols are under development and their implementation is fragmentary in servers and clients. When the specification settles down, I expect most servers and clients to add conference support. However, most clients today only support plain groupchat.

Info/Query and client registration

6

For many applications, the simple foundation of Jabber messaging and chat is adequate. However, a full-featured instant messaging system must add one more crucial feature to the mix: the concept of a user.

A Jabber user represents one person. Clients act on behalf of a user and a particular user may have multiple clients active at any time. As discussed in chapter 2, clients and other entities acting on behalf of a user are called resources and are indicated by a resource identifier at the end of a Jabber ID.

A user is represented in the Jabber system by a user account stored and maintained on the user's Jabber server. Clients authenticate (i.e., login) with the user's Jabber server using the user's authentication information. Once authenticated, the client can download and update user account information stored on the Jabber server; such as the user's registered email address, and act on the user's behalf (typically by sending messages for the user).

This chapter focuses on the protocols and procedures required to create and manage a user account on a Jabber server. All administrative protocols rely on the last core Jabber protocol: Info/Query[1].

6.1 Info/Query: the catch-all protocol

Although the majority of Jabber IM traffic is composed of message and presence packets, most of the work in implementing an IM client or server lies in supporting a variety of administrative and management protocols that support messaging and presence. Jabber has exposed all of these features using a generic query protocol called IQ (Figure 6.1).

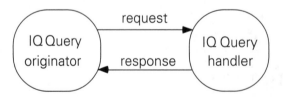

Figure 6.1
Info/Query is a simple request-response protocol carried out between a query originator and a query handler.

IQ is a simple, extensible request-response protocol that allows participants to probe,[2] query, or set data using a generic basic protocol. IQ itself is a basic framework for conducting these query operations while allowing IQ extension

---

[1] There are only three *core* Jabber protocols: <message>, <presence>, and <iq>. We've covered <message> and <presence> and will tackle <iq> here. Implementing these core Jabber protocols allows you to operate in Jabber networks in a standard way. Many recommended Jabber protocols exist to guide developers in enhancing Jabber systems by building on top of the core protocols. In particular, the majority of standard recommended Jabber protocols are IQ extension protocols that extend the IQ core protocol.

protocols to specify exactly what data is exchanged according to their particular needs. This allows the basic IQ query mechanism to remain relatively static, while supporting a diverse and rapidly evolving set of services.

The IQ protocol exploits the extensible namespace feature of the XML.[3] XML namespaces allow designers to create valid, independent XML subdocuments within a larger XML document. Namespaces allow new XML tag sets to be developed independently without worrying about clashing element names.

The IQ protocol relies on each IQ extension protocol to define a new namespace. A Jabber server and client that support an IQ extension will handle the XML in each namespace according to the rules spelled out in the IQ extension protocol.

The majority of IQ queries are conducted between a client and server. However, there are several IQ protocols that are carried out strictly between clients, such as the client version query protocol. Jabber servers must decode IQ requests, and respond to server IQ extensions while passing client-to-client IQ queries to the appropriate client.

To understand the IQ protocol, let's examine the details of the IQ protocol, and then show example code used in standard Jabber IQ extension protocols.

6.1.1 *The IQ protocol*

The IQ protocol has two primary participants: a query originator and a query handler. In most situations, the originator is a Jabber client.[4] The query handler can be either a client or a server.

The protocol begins with a query originator sending an IQ query packet to the query handler. The IQ query packet travels between the query originator and the query handler using normal Jabber packet relaying. In other words, the packet is sent to the originator's Jabber server. The server then handles the query if it is the recipient, or delivers it to its recipient as it would a Jabber message.

Unlike a Jabber message, the IQ packet is not stored for later delivery if the recipient is unreachable. In addition, the IQ packet must be addressed to a specific recipient. You can't address an IQ packet to a user like iain@shigeoka.com. It

---

[2] I use the term "probe" to indicate the exploration of client/server capabilities while "querying" is using a particular capability to obtain specific information. For example, I may *probe* a server to see if it supports a directory service. I can then *query* the directory service to get information on a particular user.

[3] See http://www.w3c.org/xml for more information on the XML namespace specification.

[4] The most common exception to this rule is a *roster push* generated in the server and sent to clients in response to presence updates. We'll cover roster pushes in chapter 8.

must be sent to a resource like iain@shigekoa.com/work. The one exception is IQ packets sent to the server where you can omit the recipient Jabber ID entirely.

IQ query packets will either set or get data from the query handler. The query handler either successfully handles the IQ query and generates an IQ result packet, or fails and generates an IQ error packet. The IQ result or error packet is then relayed back to the query originator.

A basic IQ packet follows the format shown in listing 6.1

Listing 6.1   Basic format of an IQ packet.

```
<iq type='set|get|result|error'
    to='handler_jid'
    from='originator_jid'
    id='unique'>
  <query xmlns='iq extension namespace'>
    <query_field1/>
    <query_field2/>
  </query>
</iq>
```

The IQ "type" attribute indicates the type of query packet(s) being sent. These are detailed in table 6.1.

Table 6.1   The IQ packet types and their usage.

IQ type	Message sent from	Description
get	originator–to–handler	Originator wishes to obtain information from handler.
set	originator–to–handler [a]	Originator wishes to update information maintained by handler.
result	handler–to–originator	Handler returns the results of the originator's get/set request.
error	handler–to–originator	Handler encountered an error carrying out get/set request.

a. Occasionally IQ set queries are sent from handler to originator when many replies to a single query are batched. The series of set queries is terminated by a final result <iq> packet. Results of a jabber:iq:search protocol (see appendix) query may return several **set** replies containing results, and a final result reply to mark the end of the search.

Despite the fact that multiple <query> packets can occur within a single <iq> packet, there can only be a single logical query occurring at once.[5] Multiple <query> packets are normally used to return multiple matching results, similar to the return of multiple records in an SQL result.

---

[5] In other words, all <query> packets must use the same namespace and must relate to the same logical query.

It is also important to point out that the `<iq>` packet doesn't have to contain a `<query>` subpacket. Result `<iq>` packets often don't contain any subpackets. In addition, the `<iq>` packet can contain other subpackets like `<vCard>`. We won't be covering any of the `<iq>` protocols that use subpackets other than `<query>` but you can learn more about them in appendix A.

IQ query originators do not have to wait for a reply before sending other IQ query packets, nor should they expect the order of IQ results or errors to come in the same order as they sent them. In order for query originators to match an IQ query to an IQ result each should contain the standard Jabber `id` attribute. This is a query-originator generated identifier that the IQ query handler will copy into its IQ result or error packet. The query originator can inspect the `id` on IQ results and errors to match responses to queries.

As you can see from the example, the `<iq>` element itself is a simple wrapper tag that contains one or more `<query>` tags (figure 6.2). This design allows Jabber servers to generically handle IQ packets without inspecting or having any knowledge about the specific queries being performed. This is important: nonstandard queries in standard IQ packets can be sent between clients without compromising Jabber standards compliance. This opens up an entire world of extensibility to Jabber systems while relying on a single, standard Jabber messaging infrastructure.

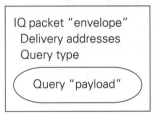

Figure 6.2
IQ packets act as generic "envelopes" decorated with delivery addresses and the type of query it contains. The actual query is carried out in an "opaque" query payload.

Since the IQ packet and protocols don't define anything beyond a generic envelope the details of specific IQ protocols must be handled somewhere else. These details are defined as IQ extensions.

6.1.2 *IQ extensions*

The `<query>` packet(s) within an `<iq>` packet establish a default XML namespace using the `xmlns` attribute. Each namespace defines an IQ extension with its own tags and protocol to handle them. The namespace keeps query-specific tags from clashing with other tags in other Jabber protocols. In addition, the IQ extension protocol name is defined by its namespace. In other words, if the IQ extension is defined as tags in the `jabber:iq:foobar` namespace, then the corresponding protocol is formally referred to as the `jabber:iq:foobar` protocol. In order to participate in that query, you must follow the protocol established for that namespace.

Typically the `<query>` packet contains simple child elements representing fields of data. In queries with a type attribute of `get`, a populated field is used as a matching key, and an empty field element indicates data that the client is requesting (or a wildcard).

For example, I have an imaginary query defined in the `my:query:` namespace IQ extension protocol. The query is designed to query people's contact information. Here is an example of a query to find all users with the first name of "Bob" and return their last name and email address:

Example name IQ query

```
<iq type='get' to='directory@manning.com' from='me@manning.com'>
  <query xmlns="my:query:namespace">
    <name-first>Bob</name-first>
    <name-last/>
    <email/>
  </query>
</iq>
```

The IQ handler might reply with two different users named Bob.

Example name IQ result

```
<iq type='result' to='me@manning.com' from='directory@manning.com'>
  <query xmlns='my:query:namespace'>
    <name-first>Bob</name-first>
    <name-last>Smith</name-last>
    <email>bob.smith@manning.com</email>
  </query>
  <query xmlns='my:query:namespace'>
    <name-first>Bob</name-first>
    <name-last>Doe</name-last>
    <email>bob.doe@manning.com</email>
  </query>
</iq>
```

Most IQ extensions follow this basic request-response pattern. The main difference between most IQ extension protocols is the expected query fields and their meaning to the query originator and handler. The Jabber protocols organize the IQ extension protocols functionally according to application-specific needs.

The IQ protocol design allows you quickly and efficiently to add your own custom IQ protocols. As long as both the originator and handler understand the custom IQ extension protocol, they can operate in standardized Jabber networks without disrupting any other Jabber entity. Customizing the Jabber IQ protocol through IQ extensions exploits the existing Jabber network as a high-level XML transport system for your IQ requests and results.

There are ten standard Jabber IQ extensions and approximately ten other proposed extensions on their way to becoming standards. The exact status of the extension protocols will probably change between the time I'm writing this and the time you read this. The Jabber community is working toward reorganizing the standards and adopting the proposed extensions as standard parts of the Jabber protocol.

This state of flux can be disconcerting for people used to standards with more stability. However, the design of the IQ protocols and the ease of using XML allow these changes to be easily incorporated into both clients and servers as they occur. The best way to stay abreast of the state of Jabber is to monitor the Jabber Software Foundation website (foundation.jabber.org) or the Jabber mailing lists.

6.2 *Registration creates and manages accounts*

The first step in supporting user accounts is to enable people to create them on a Jabber server. The first Jabber IQ extension protocol I will cover in this book is the `jabber:iq:register`, commonly referred to as the register protocol. In general, the register protocol is used in three scenarios:

- Creating new user accounts
- Updating user account information, usually by changing:
  - authentication credentials
  - account contact information
- Removing user accounts

The protocol is especially useful on open Jabber servers that provide Jabber IM to the public. Obviously, there are many situations where a Jabber server administrator will not want to allow people to create accounts on the server without explicit permission. The situation is analogous to the creation of email accounts on email servers. In some cases, you want to allow anyone to create an account on the server as is done with popular open email services like Yahoo! Mail.

However, the majority of mail servers require you to have the server administrator create an account on the server, or pay a fee before an account is created. In a situation where controlling who can create an account on the server is important, you should make sure that you disable user account creation capabilities in the register protocol. You will still need to support the register protocol for authenticated users if you want them to update their own account information, such as their passwords. In some cases, even this task must be controlled by the Jabber administrator and you can remove support for the register protocol entirely.

6.2.1 *User accounts*

In its purest form, a Jabber user account simply stores the authentication credentials (a username and password) that clients and other user resources employ to authenticate with the server. Beyond this basic requirement, most Jabber servers will associate other data with a user account. This information may include email addresses, a user's real name, and other information the server wishes to track about the user.

In addition, the server will usually store other Jabber support information as part of the user's account. For example, most Jabber servers allow you to attach XML vCards to a user account. vCards are like business cards, in XML format, that contain contact information about a person. Jabber client applications may also store configuration information on the Jabber server rather than local files or system registries. Application settings will follow users around as they use clients on different devices.

There are many ways for a Jabber server to store user account information. The details of how you implement user accounts on the server and the storage of these user accounts is beyond the scope of the Jabber standards. A common method is to employ user account files. For example, the reference Jabber server implementation (jabberd) uses XML files to store user information in a spool directory. Other implementations may wish to use a directory service or database to store user account information.

If the server does not support the account creation feature of the register protocol, custom tools must be developed to create and manage user accounts. Custom administration tools will almost certainly rely on directly manipulating the server's user account storage system. For example, with jabberd's XML user files, to create a user account, you can copy an empty XML user template file, edit its information using a normal text editor, and copy it into the spool directory.

We'll take the simplest approach and store user accounts as Java objects in `java.util.Hashtable`. User accounts are lost when the server shuts down. Accounts must be created every time the server is started. You can easily extend the implementation to save the `Hashtable` to a file, and load it when the server restarts or serialize it to XML files like those used in jabberd.

Although the implementation of user accounts can vary widely and involves complicated programming, the register protocol itself is simple and straightforward.

6.2.2 *The register protocol*

The register protocol, defined in the `jabber:iq:register` namespace, is carried out directly between the client and its Jabber server. The register protocol is often the only protocol that Jabber servers allow a client to conduct before they are authenticated.[6] If you disable the register protocol's ability to create new accounts, you will only be able to use the register protocol after you are authenticated.

In general, the register protocol involves sending a register get query to probe the server's capabilities and then setting registration information using a set query.[7] Figure 6.3 shows a sequence diagram of this process. Probing the server prior to setting is not required but will let you know what registration fields the server supports. The result of sending unsupported fields to the server is not specified by the register protocol.

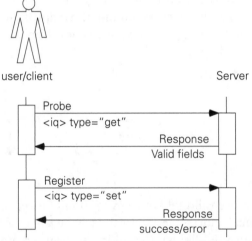

user/client   Server

Probe
<iq> type="get"

Response
Valid fields

Register
<iq> type="set"

Response
success/error

Figure 6.3
The register protocol typically
involves probing the server for
register support followed by account
creation/update using a set
packet.

The server will usually either drop the unsupported fields or store them without using them. In the former case, the client is wasting bandwidth, in the latter, there is another IQ extension protocol, `jabber:iq:private`,[8] that is specifically

---

[6] For example, the message and presence packets are almost never accepted from an unauthenticated client.

[7] One of the toughest aspects of discussing jabber is making sure everyone is using a common vocabulary. In this case, we are talking about a groupchat message packes that is written in XML code as: <message type="groupchat">message content</message>.

[8] See appendix A for more information about this protocol.

designed to store arbitrary client data on the server. For these reasons it is recommended that you probe the server for register protocol support prior to using the protocol.

A register probe involves sending an empty register `get` query packet to the server:

```
<iq type='get' id='register_get_id'>
  <query xmlns='jabber:iq:register'/>
</iq>
```

Notice the lack of sender or recipient addresses in the `<iq>` packet. Prior to authentication, you may only address messages to the server so setting a recipient address is irrelevant. In addition, the client has no authenticated Jabber ID. This makes it incorrect to set either the `to` or `from` attributes of the `<iq>` packet. Since the `<query>` tag contains no subpackets, the server treats the query as a probe of its register protocol support to see what registration fields it handles.

The server responds with an IQ result query containing the empty fields it supports, or an IQ error indicating that the register protocol is not supported.[9] The typical response looks like the following:

```
<iq type='result' id='register_get_id'>
  <query xmlns='jabber:iq:register'>
    <username/>
    <password/>
    <hash/>
    <email/>
    <phone/>
  </query>
</iq>
```

The server can indicate zero or more valid Jabber registration fields representing name, address, phone number, email address, and so forth (see the jabber:iq:register reference page in the appendix for valid fields). Clients will typically create a form with a text field next to a label containing the name of the field. For example, in response to the probe example shown earlier the typical client would present a form that looks like:

```
Username:
Password (hidden):
E-mail:
Phone number:
```

---

[9] You'll typically encounter this behavior if you try to register using an unauthenticated client on a server that does not allow you to use register to create new user accounts. However the error may also indicate that register is entirely unsupported on the server.

Notice that three of the fields, <username>, <password>, and <hash>, are not handled as generic registration fields. Clients should recognize them as standard Jabber register protocol fields that have special significance as shown in table 6.2.

Table 6.2   Standard register fields and their significance.

Field	Meaning
username	Will be used as the "user" part of the Jabber ID associated with this account. In addition, "username" identifies the account to authenticate with (see chapter 7 on authentication).
password	Used as the "password" credential in plain and digest authentication. The presence of the password element indicates that the server supports either plain or digest authentication (see chapter 7 on authentication).
hash	Used as the "hash" credential in zero-knowledge authentication. The presence of the hash element indicates the server supports zero-knowledge authentication. The server expects register packets to contain <hash>, <sequence>, and <token> fields in a "set" register query when setting up zero-knowledge authentication credentials.

I'll cover the authentication protocols in the next chapter so we'll skip the details of how they work. The only thing you need to be aware of is that users must select a username and password to register a new account.[10] The client will use the password to generate the authentication credentials that go into the <password>, <hash>, <sequence>, and <token>.

The client obtains the user's registration information, fills in the appropriate register fields, and sends them in a set query to the server. There are two basic types of set register queries depending on whether the client and server will be using plain/digest or zero-knowledge authentication.[11] In the case of plain or digest authentication, the register set query sends the password as plain text in the <password> field:

```
<iq type='set' id='register_set_id'>
  <query xmlns='jabber:iq:register'>
```

---

[10] Modifying or removing accounts requires the client to be authenticated. In this case, the username and password need to be sent only if they are being modified. Normally, usernames are not changeable but there is nothing in the standards restricting you from doing this.

[11] The server will indicate to the client which register authentication methods it supports by sending either a <password/>, <hash/>, or both in the register probe result packet. Plain, digest, and zero-knowledge are the three authentication protocols supported by the Jabber standards. We'll discuss them in depth in chapter 7.

```
    <username>myName</username>
    <password>myPassword</password>
    <email>myName@server.com</email>
    <phone>760-555-1234</phone>
  </query>
</iq>
```

User names are case-insensitive.

In the case of zero-knowledge authentication support in the register proto-col, the client must generate the zero-knowledge authentication credentials <hash>, <sequence>, and <token> from the user's password. Usernames are case-insen-sitive. Once the client generates these credentials, it sends them in the register set query.[12]

```
<iq type='set' id='register_set_id'>
  <query xmlns='jabber:iq:register'>
    <username>myName</username>
    <hash>23ea323be3231</hash>
    <sequence>100</sequence>
    <token>9823cd2323fa</token>
    <email>myName@server.com</email>
    <phone>760-555-1234</phone>
  </query>
</iq>
```

Successfully setting the user account values with the register protocol will result in the server returning an empty result packet:

```
<iq type='result' id='register_set_id'/>
```

Otherwise the server returns a normal IQ error packet indicating why the register set query failed. Typically, this is due to the username being taken in the case of new user registration, or the client needing to be authenticated to change an existing user account.

Finally, if your server allows it, the register protocol supports the automatic removal of accounts. In order to do so, authenticate with the server and send a register removal packet:

```
<iq type='set' id='register_remove_id'>
  <query xmlns='jabber:iq:register'>
    <remove/>
  </query>
</iq>
```

---

[12] One of the main benefits of zero-knowledge authentication is that the client never shares the user's password with the server. This eliminates the possibility that an attacker can intercept the password when it is being sent across the network, and prevents server break-ins from compro-mising a user's password.

The server will respond with either an empty result packet indicating success, or an error packet explaining what is wrong. As with automatic account creation, automatic removal is a feature that administrators should carefully consider before they enable it on their servers.

Now that we've covered the register protocol used to support user accounts, let's take a look at the code modifications to the Jabber server and client needed to support them.

6.3   *The Jabber server modifications*

This chapter introduces user accounts to the server. This is a major departure from our previous design where we only kept track of the active sessions on the server. User accounts signal the first of many server-managed responsibilities that should be supported by a complete Jabber server.

Once we add user account support to the server, we'll be ready to implement the register protocol. Following our packet-handling pattern, we'll create a `RegisterHandler` class. Let's begin by looking at the new user accounts.

6.3.1 *Adding user accounts*

Server-managed user accounts represent the start of the server's role as a centralized, domain repository for Jabber information (figure 6.4). User account management involves keeping information for each user, and associating sessions (Jabber resources) with each account. In addition, accounts must store other data such as "store and forward" messages for user accounts with no active sessions.

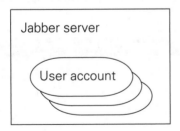

Figure 6.4
The server maintains a set of user accounts.

We'll create a `User` class to represent each user account on the server.

The User class

Each user account has one or more credentials (e.g., a password or a combination of sequence, token, and hash)[13] used to authenticate the user. In addition, each user account keeps track of the active sessions for that user. In this way, the User class fills part of the role of the old SessionIndex class (figure 6.5).

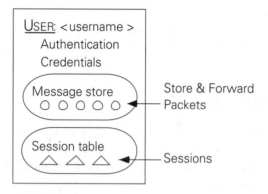

Figure 6.5 The User class represents a user account on the server. It maintains account information such as authentication credentials, stores messages for later delivery, and tracks Session objects that have authenticated with this user account.

Each user account is identified by a unique username and stores authentication credentials.

We will store password, hash, sequence, and token authentication credentials in the user account as simple strings as shown in listing 6.2. Certain types of authentication require different credentials. By storing all four, we can cover all of the standard Jabber authentication standards. In many cases, a server will only support one type of authentication and you can remove the unnecessary authentication credentials for each user account.

Listing 6.2   The User class constructor, member variables, and access methods

```
public class User {

    String username;
    public User(String name) { username = name; }

    String pass;
    public void setPassword(String password){ pass = password; }
    public String getPassword(){ return pass;}
```

---

[13] The type of authentication credential associated with a user account depends on what the server supports. The standard Jabber client/server authentication protocols will require either a password, or a combination of sequence, token, and hash values. The meaning and usage of these credentials will be explained in chapter 7.

```
String hash;
public void    setHash(String value) { hash = value; }
public String getHash()              { return hash;  }

String sequence;
public void    setSequence(String value) { sequence = value;}
public String getSequence()              { return sequence; }

String token;
public void    setToken(String value){ token = value;}
public String getToken() {return token;}
```

Each user account can receive messages while no active sessions exist (no resources are available). The `User` class stores these messages in a simple `java.util.LinkedList`. Two methods, `storeMessage()` and `deliverMessages()` shown in listing 6.3, are provided to store messages for later delivery and deliver them respectively.

Listing 6.3   The User class "store and forward" message store

```
LinkedList messageStore = new LinkedList();

  public void storeMessage(Packet msg) {
    messageStore.add(msg);
  }

  public void deliverMessages(){
    while (messageStore.size() > 0){
      Packet storedMsg = (Packet)messageStore.removeFirst();
      storedMsg.setSession(activeSession);
      storedMsg.setTo(null);
      MessageHandler.deliverPacket(storedMsg);
    }
  }
```

When a client authenticates with the server, it adds a session to the user account. At that point, all stored messages should be sent to that client. The `deliverMessages()` method allows us to send all messages in the `messageStore` to the `activeSession` for the user account. The `deliver Messages()` method is called in the `addSession()` method covered next.

User sessions are stored in a simple `java.util.Hashtable` object. Unlike the first come, first served `SessionIndex` method for selecting the default session for user packet routing, we'll use a simple integer to indicate the priority of each `Session`. The `Session` with the highest priority is the primary or default session. I'll keep track of this primary session in the `activeSession` member variable (listing 6.4).

Listing 6.4   The User class Session management methods

```
Session activeSession;  ◄──────────────────┐ Primary
                                            │ Session
  Hashtable resources = new Hashtable();  ◄─────┐ key:resource (String), value:Session

  public Iterator getSessions(){
    return resources.values().iterator();
  }

  public void changePriority(Session session){          Check on active
    if (activeSession.getPriority() < session.getPriority()){   Session
      activeSession = session;
    }
  }

  public void addSession(Session session){
    resources.put(session.getJID().getResource(),session);
    if (activeSession == null){
      activeSession = session;
    } else if (activeSession.getPriority() < session.getPriority()){
      activeSession = session;
    }
    deliverMessages();  ◄──────────────┐ Check on
  }                                     │ delivery

  public void removeSession(Session session){
    resources.remove(session.getJID().getResource());
    activeSession = null;

    Iterator sessionIterator = resources.values().iterator();
    if (sessionIterator.hasNext()){
      activeSession = (Session)sessionIterator.next();
      while (sessionIterator.hasNext()){
        Session sess = (Session)sessionIterator.next();
        if (sess.getPriority() > activeSession.getPriority()){
          activeSession = sess;
        }
      }
    }
  }
}
```

The most complex part of managing the Sessions is properly updating the activeSession when removing Sessions in the removeSession() method. Although it is possible to store the Sessions in an ordered list, this simple way of tracking the highest-ranking session works well. In addition, most user accounts will have zero or one session at any time. Even users with multiple simultaneous resources will usually have only two or three sessions. In all cases, the manual search of the list on each session removal is usually trivial.

The primary reason for maintaining the list of resources for a particular user is to deliver packets to the correct client (Jabber resource). Since the Packet class can write itself to a java.io.Writer object, all we need is a way of getting the correct Writer given a resource name. Passing a null resource to getWriter() gives you the Writer for the primary Session.

The User class getWriter() method

```
public Writer getWriter(String resource) throws IOException
  Session session;
  if (resource == null){
    session = activeSession;
  } else if (resource.length() == 0){
    session = activeSession;
  } else {
    session = (Session)resources.get(resource);
  }
  if (session == null){
    return null;
  }
  return session.getWriter();
}
}
```

The User class only manages the sessions that have authenticated with that account. The server needs to be able to locate user accounts based on the user's name. A new UserIndex class fills that role.

The UserIndex replaces SessionIndex

The new UserIndex class replaces SessionIndex. It fills the SessionIndex's primary role of managing sessions as shown in figure 6.6. In addition, it provides a simple way for the Server to locate Writer objects for servers based on a username and resource. The UserIndex also adds a capability of looking up a user account for a given Session.

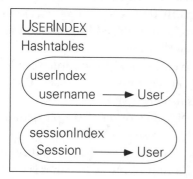

Figure 6.6
The `UserIndex` provides server objects a central table for looking up `User` objects by username or `Session`.

Two `Hashtable` objects are used to store the class's indexing information. We provide the normal set of access methods to add, get, and remove users from the `UserIndex` as shown in listing 6.5.

Listing 6.5   The UserIndex member variables and user management methods

```
public class UserIndex {

  //User table, key: username (String), value: User
  Hashtable userIndex = new Hashtable();

  //Session table, key: Session, value: User
  Hashtable sessionIndex = new Hashtable();

  public User addUser(String name){
    User user = getUser(name);
    if (user == null){
      user = new User(name);
    }
    userIndex.put(name,user);
    return user;
  }

  public User getUser(String name){
    return (User)userIndex.get(name);
  }

  public User getUser(Session session){
    return (User)sessionIndex.get(session);
  }

  public void removeUser(String name){
    userIndex.remove(name);
  }
```

The Server typically uses the UserIndex to locate a Writer object (listing 6.6) with a given Jabber ID. Two convenience methods make locating Writers by Jabber ID simple by conducting the user and session writer lookup in one step.

The UserIndex getWriter() convenience methods

```
public Writer getWriter(String jabberID) throws IOException {
   return getWriter(new JabberID(jabberID));
}

public Writer getWriter(JabberID jabberID) throws IOException {
   return getUser(jabberID.getUser()).getWriter(jabberID.getResource());
}
```

The UserIndex manages sessions as well as users (listing 6.7). Fortunately all the work is done in the User class. So the UserIndex methods only need to do some basic error checking.

The UserIndex session management methods

```
public void addSession(Session session){
   User user = getUser(session.getJID().getUser());
   user.addSession(session);
   sessionIndex.put(session,user);
}

public void removeSession(Session session){
   sessionIndex.remove(session);
   if (session.getJID() == null){
      return;
   }
   getUser(session.getJID().getUser()).removeSession(session);
}
}
```

I'll skip showing the very minor changes to other classes needed to support the new user account system. These include changes to the Session class to support session priorities and changes to the OpenStreamHandler and CloseStreamHandler classes that must now use the UserIndex rather than the SessionIndex to obtain session Writer objects for packet delivery. These minor changes are straightforward and included in the full source code available online.

The one interesting helper class change is the new MessageHandler class.

A user-aware MessageHandler class

The MessageHandler class must be modified to use the new UserIndex instead of the SessionIndex. In addition, its packet delivery algorithm is changed in two important ways. First, I have added a method deliverPacketToAll() (listing 6.6) that delivers a packet to every session for a user. This is important for packets that alert all clients to user account updates. In addition, the normal deliverPacket()

method has been updated to store messages in user accounts when no resources are available.

Listing 6.6   The MessageHandler class delivery methods

```
static public void deliverPacketToAll(String username, Packet packet){
    packet.setTo(null);  ◁──────────────────────┐  Clear
    User user = userIndex.getUser(username);     │  recipients
    Iterator sessions = user.getSessions();
    while (sessions.hasNext()){
      Session session = (Session)sessions.next();
      if (session.getPriority() >= 0){
        packet.setSession(session);
        deliverPacket(packet);
      }
    }
  }

  static public void deliverPacket(Packet packet){
    try {
      String recipient = packet.getTo();
      Writer out;

      if (recipient == null){
        out = packet.getSession().getWriter();
        if (out == null){
          Log.info("Undeliverable packet " + packet.toString());
          //
          return;  ◁──────────────────┐  Undeliverable
        }                              │  packet
      } else {
        out = userIndex.getWriter(recipient);  ◁──────────┐  Use the
      }                                                    │  UserIndex
      if (out != null){
        packet.writeXML(out);
      } else {
        //Store messages for offline users
        User user = userIndex.getUser(new JabberID(recipient).getUser());
        user.storeMessage(packet);
      }
    } catch (Exception ex){
    }
  }
}
```

REFACTORING MESSAGEHANDLER

The expanding responsibilities of `MessageHandler` are typical of software that grows as it accommodates new features. In our early server code developed in chapter 3, `MessageHandler` only delivered packets it received. The `deliverPacket()` method was a simple, logical way of breaking the delivery logic out of the main event handler method. In chapter 5, we made `deliverPacket()` static so that any class could use it to send packets.

In this latest incarnation, the `deliverPacket()` has been expanded to use `User` and `UserIndex`. We've added `deliverPacket ToAll()` to handle situations where packets must be delivered to all resources logged into a user account. The new `deliverPacketToAll()` and `deliverPacket()` methods have taken over the `MessageHandler` class and aren't necessarily related to its original purpose of handling incoming <message> packets. Developers often refer to this situation as lava flows or spaghetti code (and they often use more colorful terms when the situation is discussed over beers or when writing source code comments).

The solution is *refactoring*. Refactoring is the methodical reorganization of source to maintain a simple, clean, and well-designed codebase. This is especially important in developing and maintaining code that must change or evolve rapidly.

Refactoring begins with identifying "ugly" code, redesigning it, making appropriate changes, and testing the changes to ensure proper code operation. In the case of `MessageHandler`, we have seen that the `deliverPacket*` methods really belong in a separate utility class. To refactor `MessageHandler`, we could create a `PacketDeliverer` class, and move the two deliver methods to that class. The real work would then be in locating all uses of the `MessageHandler.deliverPacket*` methods and replacing them with the new `PacketDeliverer.deliver*` methods.

It is important to maintain the same functionality of the code while refactoring. In addition, many refactoring efforts stall or are ineffective because developers are reluctant to change code with many dependencies. This is especially critical because refactoring commonly used code often bestows the greatest benefits. This is true with the `deliverPacket*` methods as they are scattered throughout our codebase.

Fortunately there are refactoring tools to avoid the tedium of search and replace when moving methods and classes. In addition, automated unit testing using tools like JUnit (www.junit.org) or JTest (www.parasoft.com) can help you to ensure that your program continues to function the same between refactoring changes. For example, the latest version of JBuilder from Borland adds a lot of refactoring tools.

Refactoring is a valuable process that will help you keep your source code healthy and your developers happy.

With user account support in place, we're ready to add our implementation of the register protocol.

6.3.7 *Adding registration support*

As discussed earlier, the Jabber registration protocol allows users to create user accounts on open servers and modify existing user accounts when authenticated.

Our server will be an open server allowing anyone to create accounts on the server. This makes supporting the registration protocol primarily a matter of user account bookkeeping.

The RegisterHandler class

The `RegisterHandler` class handles all registration IQ packets. The simple nature of the registration protocol allows us to implement the entire registration protocol within the `notify()` event handler method. The class needs just a little preparation work in its constructor.

The RegisterHandler class constructor

```
public class RegisterHandler implements PacketListener {

    static UserIndex userIndex;
    Packet required;

    public RegisterHandler(UserIndex index) {
        userIndex = index;
        required = new Packet("iq");
        required.setFrom(Server.SERVER_NAME);
        required.setType("result");
        new Packet("username").setParent(required);
        new Packet("password").setParent(required);
        new Packet("hash").setParent(required);
    }
```

The constructor saves a reference to the server's `UserIndex` and creates a prefabricated IQ result packet to send to clients that are probing the server's registration protocol support. This is used in the `notify()` packet handler method during get IQ queries (listing 6.7).

Listing 6.7 The RegisterHandler class notify() packet handling method

```
public void notify(Packet packet){

    String type = packet.getType();
    Packet query = packet.getFirstChild("query");

    if (type.equals("get")){
        required.setSession(packet.getSession());
        required.setID(packet.getID());
        MessageHandler.deliverPacket(required);
        return;
```

Set IQ queries will create or update a user account. The first thing to do with a set query is to extract the query's <username> field and obtain the server's User object for that user account. There are three possible situations to handle:

- The user account exists and we're authenticated: we update the account
- The user account exists and we're not authenticated: send an error
- The user account doesn't exist: create account

The code to handle set queries is shown in listing 6.8.

Listing 6.8   The RegisterHandler class notify() packet handling method (continued)

```
} else if (type.equals("set")) {
String username = query.getChildValue("username");
User user = userIndex.getUser(username);
if (user != null){
  if (packet.getSession().getStatus() != Session.AUTHENTICATED ||
      !username.equals(packet.getSession().getJID().getUser())){
    Packet iq = new Packet("iq");
    iq.setSession(packet.getSession());
    iq.setID(packet.getID());
    ErrorTool.setError(iq,401,"User account already exists");
    MessageHandler.deliverPacket(iq);
    return;
  }
} else {
  user = userIndex.addUser(username);
}
```

Once we have the user account, we simply update it with the values from the register query packet and send an empty result IQ packet to the sender indicating success. There are two small complications to the basic update process to support one of the standard Jabber authentication algorithms known as zero-knowledge authentication.

Zero-knowledge authentication requires a sequence number that is decremented on every successful login attempt. The server stores the password corresponding to the current sequence number. However, the server must ask the client send it the password corresponding to the next lower sequence number (sequence − 1). To make this simple, our server will store the (sequence - 1) value rather than the sequence number itself so it easier for us to generate authentication get query results.

```
user.setPassword(query.getChildValue("password"));

int setSequence = Integer.parseInt(query.getChildValue("sequence"));
user.setHash(query.getChildValue("hash"));
//Ready for next get request
user.setSequence(Integer.toString(setSequence - 1));
user.setToken(query.getChildValue("token"));
```

```
Packet iq = new Packet("iq");
iq.setSession(packet.getSession());
iq.setID(packet.getID());
//Success
iq.setType("result");
MessageHandler.deliverPacket(iq);
//Drop the packet, it's of unknown type (not set or get)
} else {
}
}
}
```

The `RegisterHandler` packet handling class adds register protocol support to our server. To complete the upgrade, add these packet handler classes as `QueueThread` packet listeners and restart the server. With register support, our server is able to handle the normal client startup procedure of connecting, streaming, optionally registering, and messaging.

We'll defer modifying the client until the next chapter when we have completed support for user accounts by adding account authentication to the server. For now, use telnet to test our Java Jabber server. Create user accounts and make sure the server responds with the proper error messages when you attempt to create accounts that already exist.

6.4 Conclusions

The Jabber IQ protocol provides a general mechanism for us to interact with Jabber servers and clients. It is specialized for particular situations by using the `<query>` nested element and the Jabber IQ extension protocols. This design allows the generic handling of Jabber IQ messages, while providing targeted standards and flexibility in defining new queries in the future.

Although the protocol is most commonly used for simple configuration and information retrieval, the IQ protocol can be applied to practically any task. I anticipate that many exciting uses of IM will emerge from the creation of custom IQ extension protocols to enable Jabber clients and servers to provide many services beyond simple IM.

One important thing is missing from the implementation of user accounts in the `User` class and their management in `UserIndex`. User accounts are never saved to a file, nor are they ever read in from a file. This means that the server always starts with no user accounts. When the server is shut down, it loses all of its user account information.

Obviously this result is not acceptable for most servers. The reference Jabber server stores user account information in simple XML files. Other developers have modified that server to attach to databases or directory servers to store and retrieve account information. Expanding our Java server to support some form of user account storage will probably be essential for anyone wishing to use the Java server for serious applications.

"Do-it-yourself" Jabber user account creation, supported by the register protocol, is an important but optional feature of Jabber servers. However, the most important feature of user accounts is in client authentication. We can't complete our support for user accounts until we get to chapter 7 where we'll add authentication support.

Client authentication

7

189

In the previous chapter we introduced the general-purpose IQ protocols and added support for user account registration to the server. We are missing support for one of the primary features of the user account: client authentication to regulate access to resources.

In this chapter, we'll add support for the standard Jabber authentication protocols and put those authentication credentials to work. Authentication is the first line of Jabber security[1] so it's important that we understand how Jabber authentication works, what it does for us, and, just as importantly, what it can't do for us.

7.1   *Authentication controls account access*

The Jabber authentication protocol is an IQ extension protocol. It is currently the only Jabber standard that addresses security.[2] The Jabber authentication protocol allows clients to prove to the server that they are who they claim to be. The client normally has no similar assurance that the server is who it claims to be.[3]

The Jabber authentication and access model is simple: unauthenticated users have a certain set of rights (usually permission to use the registration and authentication protocols) and authenticated users have full access to the Jabber system. This is handy because security often adds complexity that is difficult to understand and implement.

Unfortunately, this simplistic authentication model is also very limiting. There is no standard way of restricting access to groups of users, creating finer grained access levels, or communicating these security models to Jabber clients. For example, as a server administrator, you may want to restrict messaging to certain Jabber domains, and limit the amount of data sent, the size of messages, and so forth through the Jabber server. Creating these sophisticated Jabber security systems are beyond the scope of the current Jabber standards.

Jabber authentication is tied directly to a user account. You authenticate yourself as a Jabber user and log into a user account. Your security authorization to act on the system is directly linked to your user account. User authorization essentially makes authentication and authorization equivalent in Jabber systems. Most security systems separate the concepts so that you can authenticate as a user, and are given authorization based on that authentication. For example, I may authenticate as user

---

[1] We'll discuss Jabber security beyond authentication in chapter 10.

[2] Work is underway in the Jabber community to craft a complete security system for Jabber. See the security Jabber Interest Group (JIG) at foundation.jabber.org.

[3] This limitation can be easily overcome (see "Security through SSL" in chapter 10).

"iain" but should be authorized to act as the user iain as well as the user administrator in order to carry out my duties.

The limited nature of Jabber security makes it difficult to create more sophisticated access models. For example, we may wish to create a guest account with basic messaging rights that users without accounts can use for limited messaging (e.g., only sending messages to a "sponsor feedback" address). In addition, a superuser account should perhaps allow you to use the register protocol to change any other user account, not just the superuser's. Normal user accounts have full messaging rights, but can only edit their own account information using the register protocol.

Despite these minor drawbacks, the Jabber authentication protocol provides sufficient access control for most IM tasks. It accomplishes this with three different algorithms for client authentication: plain, digest, and zero-knowledge. Each offers a tradeoff in ease of implementation versus authentication safety. Plain authentication is the simplest and least secure, and zero-knowledge is the most complex and provides the highest level of security.

7.1.1 *The authentication protocol*

The Jabber authentication protocol, defined in the `jabber:iq:auth` namespace, consists of two phases shown in figure 7.1. The first is a probe phase to determine the authentication methods supported on the server. In addition, the probe will return essential authentication data used in the zero-knowledge authentication method if it is supported. The second phase is to attempt authentication by sending an authentication `set` query containing the proper authentication credentials.

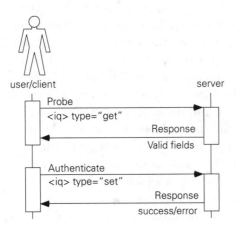

Figure 7.1
Authentication usually requires two steps:
probe and authenticate. Probing is required
by zero-knowledge authentication in order
to obtain the current authentication tokens
for the user.

Authentication probing uses an authentication get query. You must specify the username for the Jabber user account you wish to authenticate in a <username> field of the get query. The server will return the supported authentication methods and authentication information for that particular user. Most Jabber servers do not support multiple types of authentication based on user accounts so the results of the probe will typically be the same.

```
<iq type='get' id='auth_get_id'>
  <query xmlns='jabber:iq:auth'>
    <username>iain</username>
  </query>
</iq>
```

The server responds with the authentication fields it requires. The presence or absence of some of the fields indicates the authentication methods supported:

```
<iq type='result' id='auth_get_id'>
  <query xmlns='jabber:iq:auth'>
    <username>iain</username>
    <resource/>
    <password/>
    <digest/>
    <token>33ab323</token>
    <sequence>99</sequence>
  </query>
</iq>
```

The presence of a <password> field indicates that plain authentication is supported. The <digest> field indicates that the server supports digest authentication. Finally, if the <token> and <sequence> fields are present, they contain the token and sequence values for use in zero-knowledge authentication with the server. It is possible to receive a result that includes none of these fields. These servers may only support anonymous authentication or may use an authentication technique not covered by the Jabber standard protocols.

Once your client knows the authentication capabilities of the Jabber server, it must select an authentication method to use. It is important that you send the authentication credentials for only one authentication method in your set query. The results of sending multiple credentials (like plain and zero-knowledge credentials) in the same authentication packet are not specified by the Jabber standard. The authentication protocols allow you to log in to the server, but don't provide a method for logging out. To log out of a Jabber server, you must end the Jabber session using the closing XML stream tag </stream:stream>.

The simplest but least commonly used method is anonymous authentication.

Anonymous authentication

The simplest authentication technique, anonymous, allows you to log into a server without a user account. There is no way to detect anonymous authentication from an authentication probe so the client has to try an anonymous authentication and watch the response for success or failure.

To anonymously authenticate (figure 7.2), simply send an empty `set` query:

```
<iq type='set' id='auth_set_id'>
  <query xmlns='jabber:iq:auth'/>
    </iq>
```

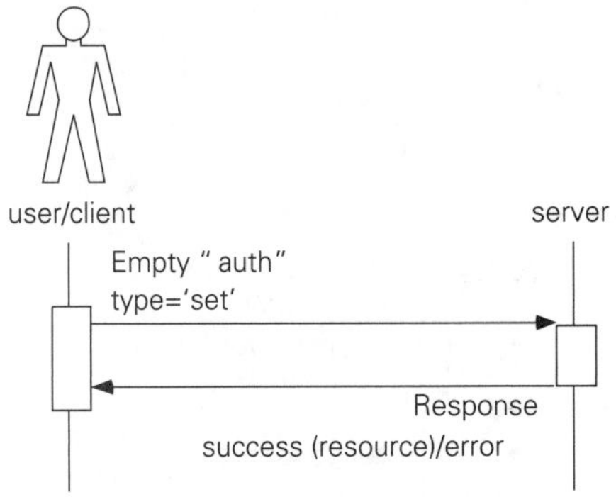

user/client   server

Empty " auth"
type='set'

Response
success (resource)/error

Figure 7.2
Anonymous authentication occurs when the client sends an empty `set` authentication query. The server will respond with a resource for the anonymous connection if successful, or a standard IQ error packet.

The server will respond with an error if it does not support anonymous authentication. If it does support anonymous authentication, it will return a result query containing your assigned resource:

```
<iq type='result' id='auth_set_id'>
  <query xmlns='jabber:iq:auth'>
    <resource>randomResourceName</resource>
  </query>
</iq>
```

Your client may now send and receive messages using a Jabber ID of the form server.name/resource where "server.name" is the name of the Jabber server domain, and "resource" is the resource returned in the result packet. It is extremely rare to find Jabber servers that allow anonymous authentication.

Plain authentication

Plain is the first authentication method that provides some level of security. Its primary advantage is the extreme simplicity of implementing it. Plain authentication works by sending a plain text copy of the user's password to the server in the authentication set query:

```
<iq type='set' id='auth_set_id'>
  <query xmlns='jabber:iq:auth'>
    <username>iain</username>
    <resource>work</resource>
    <password>myPass</password>
  </query>
</iq>
```

The server directly compares the password to the one stored in the user's account (figure 7.3). If they match, the server sends the client an empty result query packet indicating the client has been authenticated with the server. If it doesn't match, the server sends a standard error IQ packet.

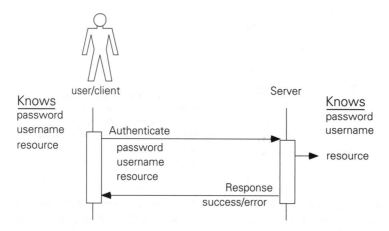

Figure 7.3 Plain authentication simply compares the client's password with the server's password for a given username. Success results in authentication and the server accepting the client's chosen resource name for the session.

The primary problem with plain authentication is that the password is sent in the open to the server. It is easy for eavesdroppers to watch the data on the network going to the Jabber server and steal users' passwords as they're being sent. For this reason, it is highly recommended that clients avoid using plain authentication if at all possible.

Digest authentication

To avoid sending passwords as plain text, the digest authentication adds an extra step to the process (figure 7.4). Recall from chapter 3 that all Jabber protocols occur within an XML stream. The server starts its stream using the `<stream:stream>` packet containing a random session ID string in the packet's `id` attribute.

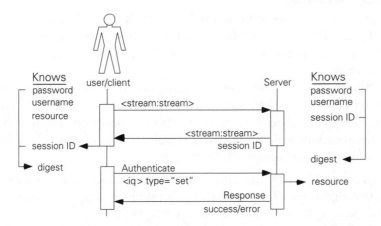

Figure 7.4 Digest authentication uses the `<stream:stream>` packet's session ID and user password to generate a digest. The digest is generated on both client and server and compared during the authentication process.

To generate a digest authentication credential, you take the session ID from the server's initial `<stream:stream>` tag and concatenate it with the user's password. The resulting string is then hashed using the SHA-1 message digest algorithm. The lowercase hexadecimal text (UTF-8/ASCII) representation of the resulting hash is then sent in the `<digest>` field of the authentication set query:

```
<iq type='set' id='auth_set_id'>
  <query xmlns='jabber:iq:auth'>
    <username>iain</username>
    <resource>work</resource>
    <digest>139ab93c13f31</digest>
  </query>
</iq>
```

Java makes compliance with the Jabber authentication algorithm simple to implement using the `java.security.MessageDigest` class. The code that does this is shown later in this chapter.

The drawback to digest authentication is that the user's password must be sent to the server during the register protocol as plain text (discussed in chapter 6). In addition, the server must store the user's password as plain text. A compromise of the server's security could compromise all of its users' passwords. The zero-knowledge authentication method was developed to eliminate these problems.

Zero-knowledge authentication

The most secure, and most complex method supported by the Jabber protocols is zero-knowledge authentication, often written as "0k." The zero-knowledge authentication method is complex and its adoption in servers and clients has been slow because of this.

Zero-knowledge authentication removes the requirement for servers to store the user's password. In fact, the authentication information the server stores is a throw-away credential that can be used to authenticate the user only once. Successful zero-knowledge authentications generate a new, one-time use, authentication credential.

The technique uses four pieces of information:

- *User's password*—Used by the client along with a token to generate valid zero-knowledge keys. The password is stored on the client (or entered by the user) and never sent to the server. A zero-knowledge key set is defined by the combination of password and token.

- *Token*—A randomly generated piece of information used to create a set of zero-knowledge keys. The token is stored on the server. Splitting the password and token between client and server respectively makes the key set created from them unique to the client/server pair.

- *Sequence*—A constantly decrementing number indicating which key in the key set is being used.

- *Hash*—A particular key in the key set identified by sequence number.

Initially the client must generate all of these pieces of information for use in the register protocol. To do this, the client:

1. Creates an SHA-1 message digest of the user's password to create $hashA$. The digest (a series of bytes) is then converted to the lower-case hexadecimal text (UTF-8/ASCII) representation of the digest we'll call $hashA^{asciihex}$.

2. Generates a random token string.

3. Creates a digest of the concatenation of $hashA^{asciihex}$ and the token string to create $hash_0$. The $hash_0$ digest is converted to its lower-case hexadecimal text representation $hash_0^{asciihex}$.

4. Selects an arbitrary sequence number M (e.g., 500).

5. Digests $hash_n^{asciihex}$ to create $hash_{n+1}$ and converts it to a hexadecimal text representation $hash_{n+1}^{asciihex}$ until it generates $hash_m^{asciihex}$ where M is the sequence number from the previous step.

The client sends the token, sequence (M), and hash ($hash_m{}^{asciihex}$) to the server in the register protocol if it support zero-knowledge authentication.[4] To authenticate, the client follows a two-step authentication process shown in figure 7.5. In the first step, the client sends an authentication probe query and the server will return the token, and sequence number minus one (M-1). The server's reply tells the client, "Take this token, and this sequence number, and generate a new hash." The client follows the same procedures as described previously except it uses the given token and sequence numbers to generate $hash_{m-1}{}^{asciihex}$. It sends this value to the server in the authentication set query:

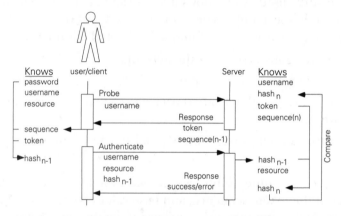

Figure 7.5 Zero-knowledge authentication begins with the client probing (auth get query) the server for the user's token and sequence number. The client uses these to generate hashn-1. It authenticates (auth set query) by sending the username, resource, and hash. The server uses hashn-1 and the token to generate hashn-1 which it compares with its stored hashn. If authentication is successful, the server replaces hashn with the new hashn-1 and decrements the sequence number.

```
<iq type=m'set' id='auth_set_id'>
  <query xmlns='jabber:iq:auth'>
    <username>iain</username>
    <resource>work</resource>
    <hash>139ab93c13f31ee97</hash>
  </query>
</iq>
```

The server takes $hash_{m-1}{}^{asciihex}$ and generates $hash_m{}^{asciihex}$ from it by simply hashing it once using the SHA-1 message digest. It compares this new $hash_m{}^{asciihex}$ to the one the client sent during the register protocol. If they don't match, the client failed to properly authenticate and the server sends a standard IQ error response.

---

[4] If a client uses the register protocol to register with a server that supports zero-knowledge authentication, the server can generate the token, sequence, and hash values from the password just like the client does here. However, the server must keep the password as well so it can support the client if it authenticates using plain or digest authentication.

If they do match, the client is authenticated. The server then decrements the user account's sequence number to M-1 and stores $hash_{m-1}^{asciihex}$. The next time a client authenticates, the server will send the token and M-2 to the client. The process can continue until the sequence number reaches zero. The client must use the register protocol before the sequence number reaches zero to reset the zero-knowledge credentials using a new token and sequence number.

Notice that the server cannot predict what $hash_{n-1}^{asciihex}$ is from $hash_n^{asciihex}$. It truly is a one-time use key. If an eavesdropper steals a copy of $hash_n^{asciihex}$ and sees that it was successfully used (so it knows it has a valid $hash_n^{asciihex}$) the credential it has just stolen has instantly become obsolete and useless.

The zero-knowledge authentication technique has several advantages:

- Passwords are never transferred over the network.
- Passwords are never stored on the server.
- Passwords stolen during authentication packet exchanges become useless as soon as they are used.
- The majority of processing load is transferred to the client aiding Jabber server scalability.

The one significant security vulnerability with zero-knowledge authentication is supporting the reset of the token, sequence, and hash values before the sequence number reaches zero. The reset process occurs using the register protocol (covered in chapter 6) and should only be allowed by authenticated clients.

I strongly suggest that only clients on secure Jabber connections (see chapter 9) be allowed to access the register protocols and reset the zero-knowledge authentication credentials. If you do not, an attacker can execute a *man in the middle attack*, relaying information between the client and server while they authenticate with each other. Once the client is authenticated, the attacker can send a reset with new authentication credentials to the server, effectively hijacking the account. A secure connection prevents these attacks.

As you can see, the extra work is well worth the effort for most clients and servers to support. Zero-knowledge authentication is a relatively new Jabber standard so support for it is not as pervasive as for other techniques. However, I believe that soon the majority of Jabber clients and servers will support zero-knowledge authentication.

Now let's take a look at the code modifications to the Jabber server and client needed to support user authentication protocols.

7.2 The Jabber server modifications

Authentication involves adding two important classes to the server. The first is the `Authenticator` class. It implements the Jabber authentication algorithms and will be used in the server and client for authentication tasks. In addition, we will need an `AuthHandler` class to handle IQ `jabber:iq:auth` queries.

The real authentication work is conducted in the `Authenticator` class.

The Authenticator class

The `Authenticator`[5] class implements the digest and zero-knowledge authentication algorithms. In addition, it provides a method for generating random numbers. Random number generation is an important tool for most cryptographic algorithms. We'll use the `java.security.SecureRandom`[6] class and the SHA1PRNG algorithm[7] to generate these numbers (listing 7.1).

Listing 7.1   The Authenticator class and its random number generator

```
public class Authenticator {

  static SecureRandom random;
  static {
    try {
      random = SecureRandom.getInstance("SHA1PRNG");
    } catch (Exception ex){
      Log.error("Could not create SecureRandom ", ex);
      System.exit(-1);
    }
  }

  static public String randomToken(){
    return Integer.toHexString(random.nextInt());
  }
```

---

[5] You need to be careful when using this class. There is another `Authenticator` class in java.net. If you must import both `java.net.Authenticator` (usually when you do an `import java.net.*`) and this `Authenticator` class, you will need to specify the full class name including package name to differentiate the two for the compiler.

[6] Initiating `SecureRandom` can take a long time resulting in significant startup delays. The class runs through some computationally intensive operations in order to generate a well-behaved pseudo-random number. On my computer it adds about a 3–5 second startup delay. I have heard of extreme cases where it takes 30–60 seconds. If you don't need the level of security provided by `SecureRandom` (for example during testing or on some clients), you can switch to a less expensive random number generator or random number algorithm.

[7] The SHA1PRNG random number algorithm ships as a standard part of the Sun Java libraries. It is secure but computationally intensive algorithm.

We only need one instance of `SecureRandom` for the application so it is best to create a static instance of it for the entire class. Random numbers are generated and converted into text tokens using the `randomToken()` method. The method is static so anyone can generate a random token by calling `Authenticator.randomToken()`.

On the other hand, each time we create an `Authenticator` object, we need a separate SHA-1 message digest. Message digests generate a unique, reproducible digest for a set of data. We can't share a message digest between authenticators because the data we send to each must be hashed separately. The `java.security.MessageDigest` takes care of all the details of the SHA-1 digest algorithm.

The Authenticator class constructor

```
MessageDigest sha;

public Authenticator() {
  try {
    sha = MessageDigest.getInstance("SHA");
  } catch (Exception ex){
    Log.error("Could not create SHA MessageDigest ", ex);
    System.exit(-1);
  }
}
```

The `Authenticator` can create Jabber digests using the Jabber digest authentication algorithm. It must have a stream ID and password in order to generate the digest (listing 7.2).

Listing 7.2   The Authenticator class digest algorithms

```
public String getDigest(String streamID, String password){
  sha.update(streamID.getBytes());
  return HexString.toString(sha.digest(password.getBytes()));
}

public boolean isDigestAuthenticated(String streamID,
                                     String password,
                                     String digest) {
  return digest.equals(getDigest(streamID,password));
}
```

The `isDigestAuthenticated()` method checks a digest against a given stream ID and password by creating a digest for the stream ID and password and then checking it against the given digest.

It is important to note that the comparison is between lowercase hexadecimal string representations of the digest. The HexString class used in getDigest() generates such a representation given any byte array. It is a common mistake to have the correct hexadecimal value for the digest but to use uppercase hexademical numbers (e.g., characters A-F) rather than lowercase. Since the Jabber reference server is case-sensitive, all other compliant Jabber servers and clients should use lowercase only.

Despite the apparent complexity of the zero-knowledge authentication algorithm, it is very simple when implemented in Java as shown in listing 7.3.

Listing 7.3   The Authenticator class zero-knowledge authentication algorithms

```
public String getZeroKHash(int sequence, byte[] token, byte[] password){

  //Running hash is hash(A)
  byte[] runningHash = sha.digest(password);

  //Running hash is hash0
  sha.update(HexString.toString(runningHash).getBytes());
  runningHash = sha.digest(token);

  //Increment (sequence - 1) times to get hash(sequence)
  for (int i = 0; i < sequence; i++) {
    //Make sure to hash lower case, hexadecimal string
    String hashI = HexString.toString(runningHash).getBytes();
    runningHash = sha.digest();
  }
  return HexString.toString(runningHash);
}

public boolean isHashAuthenticated(String userHash, String testHash){
  testHash = HexString.toString(sha.digest(testHash.getBytes()));
  return testHash.equals(userHash);
}
}
```

It is easy to see how much more computationally intensive getZeroKHash() is than isHashAuthenticated(), especially for large sequence numbers. Fortunately for Jabber system scalability, getZeroKHash() is called on the client, while isHashAuthenticated() is used on the server. This puts the burden of zero-knowledge authentication on the client. Clients only need to authenticate once per session so the one-time cost of conducting zero-knowledge is not an issue in most situations.

Our Jabber server uses the Authenticator class to handle authentication packets in the AuthHandler class.

The AuthHandler class

The `AuthHandler` class is responsible for handling two authentication requests. The first is a `get` IQ query requesting authentication information for a particular user. The second is a `set` IQ query attempting to authenticate a client (Jabber resource) with a user account.

In both cases, the incoming packet will identify the user account we're dealing with in the <username> field of the query. To organize the class, we'll split the handling of both scenarios into a set of helper methods. Each method will need to access a common set of information about the query. This information is stored as class member variables.

The AuthHandler class constructor and member variables

```
static UserIndex userIndex;
  public AuthHandler(UserIndex index) { userIndex = index; }

  Packet iq = new Packet("iq");
  User user;
  String username;
  String resource;
  Session session;
  Authenticator auth = new Authenticator();
```

The names of the member variables should be self-explanatory. Their initial values are set up in the `notify()` method. In addition, the `notify()` method shown in listing 7.4 implements the basic authentication-handling logic.

Listing 7.4   The AuthHandler class notify() packet handling method

```
public void notify(Packet packet){

    String type = packet.getType();
    Packet query = packet.getFirstChild("query");

    username = query.getChildValue("username");

    iq.setID(packet.getID());              Set up reply
    iq.setSession(packet.getSession());    IQ packet
    iq.getChildren().clear();
    iq.setType("result");  ◁──────────────     Probably
                                               be a result
    user = userIndex.getUser(username);
    if (user == null){  ◁──────────────────    Invalid user
      sendErrorPacket(404,"User not found");
      return;
    }
```

```
  if (type.equals("get")){
    sendGetPacket();
    return;
  } else if (type.equals("set")){
    session = packet.getSession();
    resource = query.getChildValue("resource");
    if (resource == null){
      sendErrorPacket(400,"You must send a resource");
      return;
    }
    handleSetPacket(query);
  } else {   | Dropping
  }          | packet
}
```

The real meat of the class lies in its `handleSetPacket()` and `send*Packet()` methods. The `send*Packet()` methods are simpler so let's take a look at them first.

The AuthHandler class send*Packet() methods

```
void sendErrorPacket(int code, String msg){
  ErrorTool.setError(iq,code,msg);
  MessageHandler.deliverPacket(iq);
}

void sendGetPacket () {
  Packet reply = new Packet("query");
  reply.setAttribute("xmlns","jabber:iq:auth");
  reply.setParent(iq);
  new Packet("username",username).setParent(reply);
  new Packet("resource").setParent(reply);
  new Packet("password").setParent(reply);
  new Packet("digest").setParent(reply);
  new Packet("sequence",user.getSequence()).setParent(reply);
  new Packet("token",user.getToken()).setParent(reply);
  MessageHandler.deliverPacket(iq);
}
```

The `sendErrorPacket()` method is a convenience method for sending an error message back to the client. The `sendGetPacket()` method creates a standardized `get` query response and sends it back to the sender. The information in the response is obtained from the user account we looked up in the `notify()` method.

The handleSetPacket() method (listing 7.5) is where the authentication of clients takes place.

Listing 7.5   The AuthHandler class handleSetPacket() method

```
void handleSetPacket(Packet query){

    String password = query.getChildValue("password");
    String digest = query.getChildValue("digest");
    String hash = query.getChildValue("hash");

    if (password != null){
      if (user.getPassword().equals(password)){
        authenticated();
        return;
      }
    } else if (digest != null){
      if (auth.isDigestAuthenticated(session.getStreamID(),password,digest)){
        authenticated();
        return;
      }
    } else if (hash != null){
      if (auth.isHashAuthenticated(user.getHash(),hash)){
        user.setHash(hash);
        int newSeq = Integer.parseInt(user.getSequence()) - 1;
        user.setSequence(Integer.toString(newSeq));
        authenticated();
        return;
      }
    }
    sendErrorPacket(401,"Bad user name or password");
  }
```

The authentication method is determined by the presence of a <password>, <digest> or <hash> field. In each case, we use the Authenticator object auth to verify the authentication credentials in the set query. If the authentication passes we call the authenticated() method and return. Otherwise, we use sendErrorPacket() to inform the client they sent a bad user name or password.[8] Notice that we must update the user account with a new sequence and hash value when using zero-knowledge authentication.

Once a client is authenticated, we use the authenticated() method to send the empty result IQ response indicating success, and set up the session with its authenticated Jabber ID and set its status to Session.AUTHENTICATED. Finally, the session is added to the UserIndex.

---

[8] A production server should also make sure the resource is not already in use.

The AuthHandler class authenticated() method

```
void authenticated(){

    MessageHandler.deliverPacket(iq);
    session.setJID(new JabberID(username,Server.SERVER_NAME,resource));
    session.setStatus(Session.AUTHENTICATED);
    userIndex.addSession(session);
  }
}
```

The relatively complex authentication features are implemented by a small amount of code. Most of the work is being carried out in our helper classes like `User`, `UserIndex`, `Authenticator`, and `MessageHandler`. Isn't it good to see that hard work pay off? By encapsulating functionality into our core classes, logic classes like our packet handlers remain clean. This allows us to concentrate on the logic processes in the packet handlers without worrying about the details of data formatting or account management.

To complete the upgrade, add `AuthHandler` to the `QueueThread` packet listeners and restart the server. With register and authentication support, our server is now able to handle the normal client startup procedure of connecting, streaming, optionally registering, authenticating, and messaging.

The most significant consequence of our server modifications to support authentication is that you can start using normal Jabber clients to test the server. Try downloading a Jabber client from the web (start with the ones at www.jabber.org) and see how well the server can handle third-party Jabber clients. Remember that many Jabber clients are themselves under heavy development so you may get better results by using the more stable Jabber clients such as those being used for commercial purposes.[9]

7.3 *The Jabber client modifications*

Adding IQ, register, and authentication support to Jabber clients is far simpler than for servers. For starters, clients don't have to maintain user account information beyond storing their own user's authentication credentials. In addition, the client must register or authenticate only once when it first connects with the server. From that point forward, it need no longer worry about further authentication or registration needs.

---

[9] I suggest using the Jabber Instant Messenger client from Jabber Inc. (www.jabber.com) or the Disney Instant Messenger client from the Disney Go Network (www.go.com)

On the other hand, clients have their own unique bookkeeping responsibilities, especially with the IQ protocols. Recall that in the server, we can create IQ handlers that respond to IQ extension protocols by looking at the namespace of the <query> packets within it. However, IQ responses, especially the successful IQ result packet, lack this information. Here is a typical response packet:

```
<iq type='result' id='iq_id'/>
```

There is no way to tell what IQ extension protocol the result packet belongs to. This is where packet IDs come into play. When you send a packet, you can set the ID to any value. The Jabber server always returns its replies with the same ID. The client can examine the ID on response packets to determine what IQ conversation the result belongs to.

Implementing this in the client's `JabberModel` class is not as difficult as it may seem.

7.3.1 Modifying the JabberModel

The `JabberModel` class must be modified to handle the new IQ extensions introduced in this chapter. These changes are centered on three functional areas:

- Registering the new client packet handler classes
- Matching IQ responses to IQ requests using packet IDs
- Adding methods for sending registration and authentication packets to the server

The modifications begin in the constructor where the `QueueThread` has its new packet handlers registered. Changes are indicated in bold in listing 7.6.

Listing 7.6   The JabberModel class constructor and new member variables

```
public class JabberModel {

  JabberModel(TestThread qThread) {
    PacketQueue = qThread.getQueue();
    qThread.addListener(new OpenStreamHandler(),"stream:stream");
    qThread.addListener(new CloseStreamHandler(),"/stream:stream");
    qThread.addListener(new MessageHandler(),"message");
    //Registers as an iq extension
    qThread.addListener(authHandler,"jabber:iq:auth");
    qThread.addListener(new IQHandler(),"iq");
  }

  Authenticator authenticator = new Authenticator();

  //plain, digest, or 0k
  String auth;
```

```
public String getAuthMode() {return auth;}
public void    setAuthMode(String mode) { auth = mode; }

String password;
public String getPassword() {return password;}
public void    setPassword(String pass) {password = pass;}
```

A significant new development is the registration of the `AuthHandler` packet handler to handle the `jabber:iq:auth` packet type. Previously both the `QueueThread` and `TestThread` classes only match a packet registration to the packet element name. However, for IQ packets, we'll look at the namespace of the `<query>` subelement of any `<iq>` packet to determine appropriate packet handlers. The code fragment that follows will do the trick in both the `QueueThread` and `TestThread` classes:

TestThread and QueueThread now match IQ extension names for `<iq>` packets

```
String matchString;
    if (packet.getElement().equals("iq")){
    child = packet.getFirstChild("query");
    if (child == null){
      matchString = "iq";
    } else {
      matchString = child.getNamespace();
    }
    } else {
    matchString = packet.getElement();
    }
```

This minor change allows us to add packet handlers for the large number of IQ extensions that a fully featured Jabber server will support.

In order to matching incoming packets to ongoing IQ conversations, we'll create a `java.util.Hashtable` containing packet handler classes indexed by packet ID as shown in figure 7.6. The `IQHandler` will look up packet IDs in this `Hashtable` and send the packet to the correct packet handler:

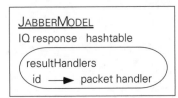

Figure 7.6
`Hashtable` **is used to temporarily match IQ packet IDs to appropriate packet handlers.**

The JabberModel class IQ packet handler support methods and variables

```
PacketListener authHandler = new AuthHandler();
Hashtable resultHandlers = new Hashtable();

public void addResultHandler(String id_code,PacketListener listener){
  resultHandlers.put(id_code,listener);
}

public PacketListener removeResultHandler(String id_code){
  return (PacketListener)resultHandlers.remove(id_code);
}
```

The last modifications to JabberModel involve the new register and authentication protocols. To keep things general, JabberModel has two general purpose methods, register() and authenticate(). These start the registration or authentication process respectively. Each method uses the system parameter jab.user.auth stored in member variable auth to determine whether it should use zero-knowledge (0k), digest (digest), or plain authentication. The register methods are shown in listing 7.7.

Listing 7.7 The JabberModel class register() methods

```
public void register() throws IOException {
  if (auth.equals("0k")){
    register0k();
  } else {
    registerPlain();
  }
}

void registerPlain() throws IOException {
  Writer out = session.getWriter();
  out.write("<iq type='set' id='reg_id'><query xmlns='jabber:iq:register'>");
  out.write("<username>");
  out.write(this.user);
  out.write("</username><password>");
  out.write(this.password);
  out.write("</password></query></iq>");
  out.flush();
  addResultHandler("reg_id",new RegisterHandler());
}

void register0k() throws IOException {
  String token = authenticator.randomToken();
  String hash = authenticator.getZeroKHash(100,
                                    token.getBytes(),
                                    password.getBytes());
  Writer out = session.getWriter();
  out.write("<iq type='set' id='reg_id'><query xmlns='jabber:iq:register'>");
```

```
    out.write("<username>");
    out.write(this.user);
    out.write("</username><sequence>");
    out.write("100");
    out.write("</sequence><token>");
    out.write(token);
    out.write("</token><hash>");
    out.write(hash);
    out.write("</hash></query></iq>");
    out.flush();
    addResultHandler("reg_id",new RegisterHandler());
}
```

The registration methods send hard-coded IQ packets to the server. In addition, each uses the IQ packet handler support methods to register the client's `RegisterHandler` class to receive responses with the same packet ID as it has sent.

Authentication support follows the same basic pattern as registration (listing 7.8).

Listing 7.8   The JabberModel class authenticate() methods

```
//Used to generate auth ids
int counter;
public void authenticate() throws IOException {
  if (auth.equals("0k")){
    authenticate0k();
  } else if (auth.equals("digest")){
    authenticateDigest();
  } else {
    authenticatePlain();
  }
}

void authenticatePlain() throws IOException {
  addResultHandler("plain_auth_" + Integer.toString(counter),authHandler);
  Writer out = session.getWriter();
  out.write("<iq type='set' id='plain_auth_");
  out.write(Integer.toString(counter++));
  out.write("'><query xmlns='jabber:iq:auth'><username>");
  out.write(this.user);
  out.write("</username><resource>");
  out.write(this.resource);
  out.write("</resource><password>");
  out.write(this.password);
  out.write("</password></query></iq>");
  out.flush();
}
```

```
void authenticateDigest() throws IOException {
    addResultHandler("digest_auth_" + Integer.toString(counter),authHandler);
    Writer out = session.getWriter();
    out.write("<iq type='set' id='digest_auth_");
    out.write(Integer.toString(counter++));
    out.write("'><query xmlns='jabber:iq:auth'><username>");
    out.write(this.user);
    out.write("</username><resource>");
    out.write(this.resource);
    out.write("</resource><digest>");
    out.write(authenticator.getDigest(session.getStreamID(),password));
    out.write("</digest></query></iq>");
    out.flush();
}
```

The exception to the client's normal IQ pattern of registering an IQ result handler and sending a packet is found in our implementation of client zero-knowledge authentication. To begin authentication following the zero-knowledge protocol, we have to ask the server for the current sequence and token using a get query. The client then uses the Authenticator to generate the appropriate hash value.

The JabberModel class authenticateOk() method

```
void authenticateOk() throws IOException {
    Writer out = session.getWriter();
    out.write("<iq type='get' id='auth_get_");
    out.write(Integer.toString(counter++));
    out.write("'><query xmlns='jabber:iq:auth'><username>");
    out.write(this.user);
    out.write("</username></query></iq>");
    out.flush();
  }
}
```

The glaring change is the lack of a call to addResultHandler(). Recall from our earlier discussions of the authentication protocol, that a get IQ authentication query results in a response containing a <query> element filled with the user's <token> and <sequence> for zero-knowledge. Since the result will contain a <query> element with a corresponding jabber:iq:auth namespace, we can use the normal QueueThread packet listener registration to handle these packets.

As with our earlier versions of the client code, the real protocol implementation occurs in the packet handler classes.

7.3.9 The client IQ packet handlers

There are three new client packet handler classes to add support for IQ, register, and authentication. Although we added support for server IQ handling in chapter 6, our client does not yet support IQ packets. However, we can reuse much of the server code from chapter 6 in the client. Let's begin with the simplest of our new client packet handlers, the IQHandler class, that adds generic support for IQ result packets.

The IQHandler class

The TestThread in JabberModel has an IQHandler class registered as a packet handler instead of the RegisterHandler. The IQHandler will use the IQ packet handling support features of our new JabberModel to properly route IQ result packets to their final handlers. The sequence diagram showing how the IQHandler uses the JabberModel's ResultHandler when it receives Packet objects from the TestThread is shown in figure 7.7.

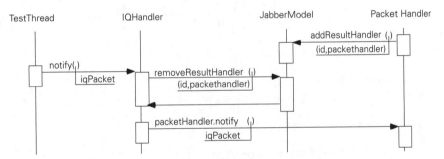

Figure 7.7 The IQHandler uses the JabberModel's new result handler Hashtable to map incoming <iq> packet IDs to appropriate packet handler objects.

For each incoming IQ packet, the IQHandler (listing 7.9) attempts to locate the IQ result handler for the packet using the packet's ID. If the IQHandler finds a registered PacketListener, IQHandler calls its PacketListener.notify() method with the Packet. If a result handler is not found, the packet is silently dropped.

Listing 7.9   The IQHandler class

```
public class IQHandler implements PacketListener {

  JabberModel jabberModel;

  public void notify(Packet packet) {
    if (jabberModel == null){
```

```
      jabberModel = JabberModel.getModel();
    }
  if (packet.getID() != null){
    PacketListener listener =
                    jabberModel.removeResultHandler(packet.getID());
    if (listener != null){
      listener.notify(packet);
      return;
    }
  }
 }
}
}
```

The `IQHandler` is used to route all register IQ responses to the `Register Handler` class.

The RegisterHandler class

The `RegisterHandler` class responds to register result packets. Only two rather trivial results are possible:

- *Success*—The client will attempt to automatically authenticate after registration.

- *Failure*—The result will contain the server's error message.

The RegisterHandler class

```
public class RegisterHandler implements PacketListener {

  public void notify(Packet packet){
    try {
      if (packet.getType().equals("result")){
        JabberModel.getModel().authenticate();
      } else {
        String message = "Failed to register";
        if (packet.getType().equals("error")){
          message = message + ": " + packet.getChildValue("error");
        }
        System.err.println(message);
      }
    } catch (Exception ex){
      ex.printStackTrace();
    }
  }
}
```

The `AuthHandler` class is a bit more complex than `RegisterHandler`.

The AuthHandler class

The AuthHandler class (listing 7.10) resembles a combination of the authenticate methods of the JabberModel class and the result handler of the RegisterHandler class. The JabberModel authenticateOk() method causes this dual nature because it must use an authentication get query to get user information in order to carry out zero-knowledge authentication. If we get a response from this get query, we need to send the authentication set query.

Listing 7.10   The AuthHandler class notify () method (zero-knowledge)

```
public class AuthHandler implements PacketListener {

  JabberModel jabberModel;
  Authenticator auth = new Authenticator();
  int counter;

  public void notify(Packet packet) {
    if (jabberModel == null){
      jabberModel = JabberModel.getModel();
    }
    try {
      if (packet.getID().startsWith("auth_get")){

        Packet query = packet.getFirstChild("query");
        String token = query.getChildValue("token");
        int sequence = Integer.parseInt(query.getChildValue("sequence"));
        String hash = auth.getZeroKHash(sequence,
                                  token.getBytes(),
                                  jabberModel.getPassword().getBytes());

        jabberModel.addResultHandler("0k_auth_"
                    + Integer.toString(counter),
                    this);
        Writer out = packet.getSession().getWriter();
        out.write("<iq type='set' id='0k_auth_");
        out.write(Integer.toString(counter++));
        out.write("'><query xmlns='jabber:iq:auth'><username>");
        out.write(jabberModel.getUser());
        out.write("</username><resource>");
        out.write(jabberModel.getResource());
        out.write("</resource><hash>");
        out.write(hash);
        out.write("</hash></query></iq>");
        out.flush();
```

Notice that this time, the zero-knowledge authentication query is registered as a result handler. We could have avoided the dual nature of the `AuthHandler` class by using a separate authenticate result handler class as the result handler. I would certainly consider doing so in a future refactoring of the client. The reduced implementation complexity may be worth the increased design complexity.

If the incoming packet is not the result of a `get` request, it's the final authentication result from the server. Once again, this is either a successful result or an error. If we successfully authenticate with the server, we'll change the session status to `Session.AUTHENTICATED`.

The AuthHandler class notify() method (continued)

```
      } else if (packet.getType().equals("result")){
        packet.getSession().setStatus(Session.AUTHENTICATED);
      } else if (packet.getType().equals("error")){
        System.err.println("Failed to authenticate: "
                           + packet.getChildValue("error"));
      } else {
        System.err.println("Unknown auth result: " + packet.toString());
      }
    } catch (Exception ex){
      ex.printStackTrace();
    }
  }
}
```

With the help of the `Authenticator` class, implementing authentication and registration support in the client is a relatively trivial exercise.

We don't need to do much to support authentication in our Java client. We simply call `JabberModel.authenticate()` after making a connection.[10] For example, we can modify the `SimpleMessageClient` from chapter 4 to wait for a session status change to `Session.AUTHENTICATED` instead of detecting the opening `<stream:stream>` packet as shown in the following code fragment.

```
do {
  notifyHandlers(packetQueue.pull());
} while (model.getSessionStatus() != Session.AUTHENTICATED);
```

Rerun the client against the server to see how both work together. Try using the client to register and authenticate against other Jabber servers.

---

[10] Optionally, you may call `JabberModel.register()` prior to `authenticate()` to create a user account.

7.4 *Conclusions*

Client authentication allows the server to protect server resources. If you relied on the honor system, sooner or later the IM equivalent to email spam would start to overwhelm your server. In addition, *spoofing* IM messages would be trivial.

Spoofing involves sending messages as if you were another user. This can be a costly problem. For example, imagine the damage a disgruntled employee could do by sending messages that claimed to be from the boss that said, "You're fired!" Jabber authentication provides you with some assurances that a message was sent by the user in the `from` attribute of the packet.[11]

Finally, now that you have authentication to link users to user accounts, you can start to explore more advanced Jabber server features that aren't part of the Jabber standard but provide great benefits to customers. For example, many companies are required by internal policy or the law to keep records of all communications, including email and instant messages. Your custom Java Jabber server can log packets that it sends and receives to the company auditing system and can verify that they were sent using a given user account.

In addition, Jabber authentication is the first step in creating advanced security systems based on IM. We'll cover advanced security features in chapter 10 that can fill out security within Jabber. In addition to these security features, however, sophisticated users and administrators will demand greater control over access. Your next-generation servers can add these without violating the Jabber authentication standards.

For example, imagine that your business is using IM as a main communication tool. You may wish to allow users to have full IM access. However when IM abuse is detected, those particular users can be restricted from sending instant messages outside of the company's Jabber domain during business hours. A similar policy may be in place to restrict users from sending instant messages to certain addresses during work time, or limit bandwidth usage during the busiest times of the day.

In chapter 5 we covered the basics of presence and how it applied to groupchat. However we couldn't discuss user presence properly because we had not yet covered user accounts. In addition, user presence works closely with another IM concept, the roster (also called the buddy list).

---

[11] This is actually enforced by the server when it forces the sender `to` address to be the same as the Session's authenticated user name.

Rosters rely on a combination of the presence protocols and the roster IQ extension protocol defined in the namespace `jabber:iq:roster`. In the next chapter, we'll cover the roster protocol and explain how presence and rosters work together to form the Jabber framework for user presence, the last major piece of the Jabber puzzle.

Roster and user presence

217

The last major protocols for our Jabber IM system are rosters and user presence. Our tour begins by describing what rosters are, and how they work with the presence protocols to maintain a systemwide user presence. We'll cover the roster protocol in detail and finish with the modified Java Jabber server and client software that supports rosters and user presence.

8.1 *Roster protocol: presence's missing piece*

The story of the Jabber roster began in chapter 5 with the presence protocols. The presence protocols allow us to do two things: update a user's presence status and manage presence subscriptions. Presence updates are straightforward, and they are covered in chapter 5 where presence is used to manage groupchat group membership. Presence updates can also be used to update the user's presence status.

The major difference in updating a user's presence status versus groupchat is controlling where the presence updates go. In groupchat, presence updates are sent to the groupchat server, and from there, to group members.

It is possible for every user to send their presence to all other users. However, if we sent the presence updates between every user on the Jabber system, servers and clients would quickly be swamped, leaving no resources for messaging! In addition, users need to control access to their presence updates for privacy and ease of use.

To address these issues, Jabber has a concept of a presence subscription. As the name implies, a presence subscription determines the subscribers who wish to receive presence updates from presence publishers. Subscribers must request a subscription from the publisher, and the publisher has the option of accepting or refusing a subscription. Each user must manage both their publisher and subscriber presence relationships.

To organize and manage subscriptions for each user, Jabber has defined a standard data structure known as the Jabber roster. The Jabber roster[1] is a list of other users identified by their Jabber ID. We'll call these users *roster subscribers* even though their presence subscription relationship can be as presence subscribers, publishers, or both for the roster owner. Storing all subscription information for each user in their roster helps to simplify the job of the client developer and in some cases the server developer.

For the client developer, having every subscription relationship described in the roster provides them with a single, authoritative source of presence information. For the server developer, when carrying out presence related tasks, you only

---

[1] The Jabber roster is better known by its AOL name, the "buddy list."

need to work with the presence publisher's roster in order to properly deliver presence packets. The cost of this system is a slightly more complicated roster management task for the server, and the duplication of presence subscription information in different user's rosters.

However, since the Jabber architecture uses distributed servers operating different Jabber domains, synchronizing presence subscription information between user accounts is a task that needs to be carried out by a standard Jabber protocol. The Jabber presence subscription protocols allow users to subscribe to the presence of other users even those in other Jabber domains. Servers use the presence subscription protocol support to synchronize rosters for users both inside and outside of their own Jabber domain. We'll see how this is done in our Java server later in this chapter.

The particular type of subscription relationship is tracked in the roster and categorized by subscription types summarized in table 8.1.

Table 8.1 Presence subscription relationships.

Subscription	Description
to	The user is interested in receiving presence updates from the subscriber.
from	The subscriber is interested in receiving presence updates from the user.
both	The user and subscriber have a mutual interest in each other's presence.
none	The user and subscriber have no interest in each other's presence.

In addition to basic subscription information, the roster allows the user to store standard user interface information about each subscriber as (figure 8.1). This information includes a user-friendly roster nickname to display instead of the Jabber ID, and group tags that will allow the client to display subscribers by groups (typically in a tree or tab sheet display).

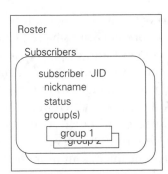

Figure 8.1
A Jabber roster contains a list of subscriber items. Each subscriber is identified by a Jabber ID, and can have an optional nickname and status. User client applications can also add optional groups to the subscriber item to aid in grouping roster items for user display.

The interesting Jabber twist on rosters is that all of this information is stored and managed by the server. This greatly simplifies the client implementation and allows the roster information to automatically be used whenever a user logs in to their same account. A change made to the roster in one client will be automatically pushed to other clients logged into the same account. The roster protocols were developed to allow clients to manage these server-side rosters.

Despite the close relationship between the roster and presence, the roster is a separate concept from presence. I like to think of the roster as one of those walls of letter-sized holes often used in hotels to store keys and messages for guests. Just as a hotel's box holes have room numbers on them, each hole in the Jabber roster represents a subscription and has a user's Jabber ID underneath it.

Using the roster protocols, we can put nickname labels over each hole so they are easier to work with. In addition, we can add different lights to each hole indicating a group. That way, if we want to see holes for a group, we simply turn on the light for that group, making it even easier to find subscriber holes. Finally, each hole represents a certain type of Jabber subscription. This is akin to how a hotel's boxes have different types according to the types of rooms the hotel has: smoking, nonsmoking, deluxe suite, and so forth. Different actions will be taken depending on what type of box is being accessed (if someone checks out of a smoking room, a new set of matches is thrown into his room box, while a non-smoking room gets a fresh flower).

In this analogy, the roster protocols are used to manage this set of boxes. You can change the group lights and manipulate the nickname labels for each hole. However, managing the boxes is separate from determining what goes into the boxes.

For rosters, each subscription hole is used by the presence protocols. So for example, sending a presence update to the server causes the server to look at the user's roster, find all items that are of subscription type both or from, and send a copy of the presence packet to them. This is just like sending a box of ashtrays to the front desk, and having the attendant automatically place the ashtrays into holes if they are for smoking rooms.

The versatility of the roster and presence protocols can lead to confusion. Don't let it. At the most important level, both roster and presence are simple to master.

The basic client algorithm for roster management and display is to begin by obtaining the server roster using a *roster reset* (empty get query). The client displays the returned roster. If the user wishes to make changes to the roster (nicknames or groups), the client sends a *roster update* (set query). However, the client does not directly update the displayed roster. Instead, the client sends the update information to the server and waits for a *roster push* from the server.

A roster push is simply an asynchronous roster set query sent from the server to all of a user's authenticated, available clients whenever a roster change is made.

Changes to the roster can occur at any time so clients must always be ready to receive a roster push from the server and update their displays. Roster pushes occur when:

- A roster update (set query) changes decorations for the roster (e.g., nicknames and groups).
- A presence subscription exchange causes:
  - A roster entry to be created.
  - The subscription type of a roster entry to change.
  - A roster entry to be removed.

As you can see, the presence subscription protocols described in chapter 5 have a huge effect on the roster and the two protocols work together to manage a user's presence.

The server is in charge of managing the roster and its subscriptions. Clients can only set the roster nicknames and group settings using the roster protocol. In addition, they can indirectly affect the roster via presence subscriptions. However, it is important to note, that it is the server that reads presence subscription packets and roster updates and manages the roster.

The design of Jabber presence subscriptions and rosters greatly eases the client's job. Most importantly, clients can send presence updates to the server without worrying about who must be notified. The server will automatically forward the presence update to presence subscribers using the roster. The server also makes sure that when a client is disconnected, all presence recipients receive an unavailable presence update.

Clients are still free to send presence updates directly to subscribers in order to send different presence updates to different subscribers. However, if you do this, the client must make sure to manually update all of its subscribers, as the server will not manage presence packets with recipient addresses.

The presence protocol and packets are described in chapter 5 so we only need to cover the roster protocol to complete the Jabber protocols needed to support user presence.

8.1.1 *The roster protocol*

The roster protocol is an IQ extension protocol defined in the jabber:iq: roster namespace. There are three basic roster protocols:

- *Roster reset*—Used by clients to obtain a copy of the roster stored on the server.
- *Roster update*—Used by clients to update the roster stored on the server.
- *Roster push*—Asynchronous roster updates sent from the server to clients.

We'll cover all three in the following sections beginning with roster reset.

Roster reset

A roster reset allows a client to obtain a complete copy of the roster. You obtain a roster reset by sending an empty `get` query:

```
<iq type='get' id='roster_get_id'>
  <query xmlns='jabber:iq:roster'/>
</iq>
```

The roster replies with a complete copy of the roster:

```
<iq type='result' id='roster_get_id'>
  <query xmlns='jabber:iq:roster'>
    <item jid='sub1ID' name='nickname1' subscription='both'>
      <group>Personal</group>
      <group>Backpacking</group>
    </item>
    <item jid='sub2ID' name='nickname2' subscription='from'>
      <group>Work</group>
      <group>Marketing</group>
      <group>Company Softball</group>
    </item>
  </query>
</iq>
```

Notice that the roster `<query>` packet can contain zero or more `<item>` packets. Each `<item>` packet represents a single subscriber entry with zero or more `<group>` fields. The item attributes are outlined in table 8.2.

Table 8.2   Roster `<item>` packet attributes.

Attribute	Required	Meaning
jid	Yes	The subscriber's Jabber ID.
name	Optional	The subscriber's roster nickname.
subscription	Yes	Indicates the subscription relationship the user has with this subscriber. Can be: • "none" (no subscription) • "to" (user has subscription with subscriber) • "from" (subscriber has subscription with user) • "both" (user and subscriber have a mutual subscription)
ask	Optional	Indicates the subscription status if a change request is pending. Can be: • "subscribe" (request to subscribe) • "unsubscribe" (request to unsubscribe)

Roster update

Clients can perform a roster update by sending a roster set query containing the <item> packet with updated information. Roster updates cannot change the subscription or the value of the ask attribute of the roster item and the server ignores their values if they are set.

```
<iq type='set' id='roster_set_id'>
  <query xmlns='jabber:iq:roster'>
    <item jid='sub1ID' name='shandy'>
      <group>Personal</group>
      <group>Backpacking</group>
    <group>Bicycling</group>
    </item>
  </query>
</iq>
```

The server responds with either an empty result packet indicating success or a standard IQ error packet. The server will send the roster changes to all authenticated clients using a roster push.

Roster push

The roster push is simply a server-initiated roster set query containing the complete <item> packet(s) for any roster item that has changed. Roster pushes are one-way from the server to clients so the client should not send an IQ result packet back to the server. A roster push for the previous update example would look like:

```
<iq type='set'>
  <query xmlns='jabber:iq:roster'>
    <item jid='sub1ID' name='shandy' subscription='both'>
      <group>Personal</group>
      <group>Backpacking</group>
      <group>Bicycling</group>
    </item>
  </query>
</iq>
```

If a client unsubscribes from a roster using the presence subscription protocol, the roster item for that subscription will be removed on the server. The server will send a roster push to all clients to indicate this by using a subscription attribute set to the value remove. The client would then remove that item from its roster display.

For example, if I unsubscribed from sub1ID and they unsubscribed from me (no subscriptions),[2] I would get the following roster push from the server:

---

[2] Unsubscribing from another user's presence only removes your subscriber subscription to them (a subscription of type to). If you wish to remove their subscription to you (a subscription of type from) you must send a presence packet with type set to unsubscribed in order to forcibly unsubscribe them.

```
<iq type='set'>
  <query xmlns='jabber:iq:roster'>
    <item jid='sub1ID' subscription='remove'/>
  </query>
</iq>
```

User presence is primarily handled by the Jabber server. Let's take a look at the work needed to support it in our Java Jabber server.

8.2   *The Jabber server modifications*

Jabber roster and presence protocols create a user presence system for Jabber IM. Jabber relies on user presence for determining the message routing and "store and forward" delivery of packets. For the server, roster and presence support are aspects of the server's overall user account support.

We began to create the user account subsystem of the server in the previous chapter beginning with the User class. This class stores authentication credentials for the account and manages the Session objects belonging to that account. In this chapter, we need to add presence support to the User class.

8.2.1 *Representing user presence*

User presence is a two-faced beast. Presence describes the state of a resource and is associated with a Session on the server. Roster describes the presence subscriptions for the user and is associated with the user account. Thus, a user has one roster, but can have as many presences as authenticated sessions (figure 8.2).

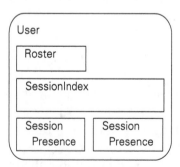

Figure 8.2
A user account has one roster, but many sessions, each with its own presence status.

Things are complicated because the Jabber messaging model tries to hide the details of multiple sessions from other users. In other words, you may have multiple clients attached to the server at the same time, say one for your cell phone and another on your PC. However, other users should only see you as a single user entity, and send messages to your user address.

Unfortunately, each client has its own presence (your PC may be unavailable while your cell phone is available). Other users will see that you are available and unavailable at the same time. Clients can hide these details by displaying the most available presence. In general, this is the most satisfying solution. Most users only care if they can send a message to another; as long as there is an available resource, they can send messages and they are happy.[3]

To reflect the dual nature of user presence, we'll create two classes: Presence and Roster. The Presence class keeps track of the presence status for a Session, and the Roster class tracks the user's roster. The Presence class (see listing 8.1) is simple to implement, as it is primarily a data structure class.

Listing 8.1   The Presence class

```
public class Presence {

    boolean available;
    public boolean isAvailable(){return available;}
    public void    setAvailable(boolean isAvailable){ available = isAvailable;}

    static public final String SHOW_CHAT = "chat";
    static public final String SHOW_AWAY = "away";
    static public final String SHOW_XA   = "xa";
    static public final String SHOW_DND  = "dnd";

    String show;
    public String getShow()                    { return show;     }
    public void    setShow(String newShow) { show = newShow; }

    String status;
    public String getStatus()                        { return status;     }
    public void    setStatus(String newStatus) { status = newStatus; }

    String priority;
    public String getPriority()                          { return priority;     }
    public void    setPriority(String newPriority) { priority = newPriority; }
}
```

Our Session class has a Presence member variable to track the presence status for each session. Our packet routing classes like MessageHandler will use the Presence object of the Session class to determine packet delivery behavior.

---

[3]   Sophisticated users, may have different preferences. They may want to know as much about other user's resources as possible or may want information regarding specific resources. For example, users may want to know when you are at your PC because they need to chat about a document they placed on a file server accessible from your PC. They don't care about your presence on other resources.

Rosters are a little more complicated to manage.

8.2.2 Adding a roster subsystem

Supporting rosters on the server requires a moderate amount of work. From the server's perspective, roster management is an exercise in bookkeeping. We need to maintain the roster data structure on the server, and update it using incoming IQ roster packets and <presence> packets. Since both IQ roster and <presence> packets will influence the roster, we'll need to make sure that the packet handling classes are modified to support the roster subsystem.

Rosters are tightly linked to their corresponding user account (figure 8.3). Each user account contains one roster, even if the roster itself is empty. A user account can have multiple sessions representing simultaneous resources, but the account shares one global roster.

Figure 8.3
Each user account has one, and only one, roster.

In our Java server, the User class represents a user account. We will add a Roster class to the User class to represent a user's roster. The Roster class in turn stores a list of subscriber items as shown in figure 8.4 (each item acts as one of the slots in the hotel key box analogy).

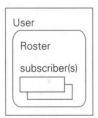

Figure 8.4
Each roster contains zero or more roster subscriber items.

Subscriber items are mainly data classes storing the subscription type (from, to, both, or none), and optional ask status of the subscription. The ask status is present when the subscriber is in the process of asking for a change in subscription status. For example, imagine a situation where "iain" and "hieu" don't have a subscription. Iain sends a presence packet requesting permission to subscribe to hieu's presence:

```
<presence to='hieu@server' type='subscribe'/>
```

Iain's roster subscription item after this reaches the server will be:

```
<item jid='hieu@server' type='none' ask='subscribe'/>
```

The server will send a roster push containing the updated roster item to all resources connected to the server. On the other hand, the roster for "hieu" will be empty. Hieu only receives the `<presence>` subscription request. Hieu's client can approve the subscription request by sending

```
<presence to='iain@server' type='subscribed'/>
```

Hieu's roster is updated by his server to contain the following roster subscriber item:

```
<item jid='iain@server' type='from'/>
```

Iain's roster is updated by his server to contain the following roster subscriber item:

```
<item jid='hieu@server' type='to'/>
```

The clients can then update their roster entry, assigning a nickname and adding one or more groups to the item using the roster IQ extension protocol. The server only cares about each subscriber item's subscription Jabber ID, the type of subscription, and the optional `ask` status of the item. The roster entry's nickname and optional group subitems are information the server must store for clients to use.

Since the server must only store roster metainformation like groups without understanding it, we can simplify the server by only storing the information we need to understand (e.g., type and `ask` status) in a `Subscriber` class, and storing a separate raw text copy of the packet containing the full contents of the item (figure 8.5). When the server is manipulating the roster, it only looks at the `Subscriber` information. When the server needs to send a copy of a roster item to a client, it can send the raw packet text without worrying about what it contains.

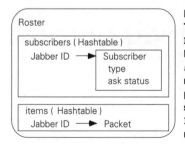

Figure 8.5
The `Roster`'s subscriber items are stored in two `Hashtables`, indexed by the subscriber item's Jabber ID. The `subscribers` `Hashtable` maps subscriber objects storing information the server needs to maintain the roster and to properly route user presence updates. The `items` `Hashtable` maps subscribers `Packets` storing the raw roster item `Packet` object that can be sent to clients during roster pushes.

`Subscriber` is an inner class of the `Roster` class. The `Roster` class will use it internally.

The Roster constructor, subscriber Hashtables, Subscriber Inner-class

```
public class Roster {

  //User's username used for presence updates
  String user;
  public Roster(String username) { user = username; }

  Hashtable items = new Hashtable();

  //The Subscriber inner-class
  Hashtable subscribers = new Hashtable();

  class Subscriber {
    String subscription;
    String ask;
  }

  //Simplify delivery by maintaining list of current presence subscribers
  LinkedList presenceRecipients = new LinkedList();
```

The most common task that the Roster will face is forwarding copies of presence update packets to presence subscribers. With this in mind, we'll use a separate java.util.LinkedList to maintain a copy of presence subscribers so that we can quickly forward updates without working our way through the Hashtables looking for to or both subscribers. The slight overhead in maintaining a redundant list of subscribers pays off in more efficient presence updates. The two Hashtables and one LinkedList are really all that the Roster class must manage.

Handling <presence> updates is the most involved part of roster management. The difficulty is not in any complexity in the presence packets. Unfortunately, like many programming tasks, handling presence updates is simply tedious work. Every incoming presence packet[4] requires us to examine the packet and determine what to do with it. This process is handled in the updatePresence() method shown in listing 8.2.

Listing 8.2   The Roster class UpdatePresence(): packet examination

```
public void updatePresence(Packet presence){
  String type = presence.getType();
  Session session = presence.getSession();
  Presence sessionPresence = session.getPresence();
  String recipient = presence.getTo();
  JabberID recipientID;
  boolean isUserSent;
  if (recipient == null){
```

---

[4] Every presence packet except those addressed to the groupchat server is handled by calling this method.

```
    recipientID = new JabberID(Server.SERVER_NAME);
    isUserSent = true;
} else {
    recipientID = new JabberID(recipient);
    if (user.equals(recipientID.getUser())){
      isUserSent = false;
    } else {
      isUserSent = true;
    }
}
String sender = presence.getFrom();
JabberID senderID;
if (sender == null){
  senderID = session.getJID();
} else {
  senderID = new JabberID(sender);
}
String subscriber = isUserSent ? recipientID.toString() :
                                 senderID.toString();

if (type == null) {
  type = "available";
}
```

In the first part of update we unpack the `Packet` filling in any implied fields that were left blank. We also begin the sorting process by determining if the packet is user-managed or server-managed. User-managed presence packets are addressed to another Jabber user. The server forwards these directly to their recipient.

The server does not automatically update the user's other presence subscribers. That is reserved for server-managed updates. Server-managed presence updates are addressed to the server or have no recipient (`to`) address. The server automatically forwards these updates to all of the user's presence subscribers.

In both cases, we can determine if a packet is a presence update if its type is available or `unavailable` (listing 8.3).

Listing 8.3   The Roster class UpdatePresence(): presence updates

```
if (type.equals("available") || type.equals("unavailable")){

  //User-managed presence updates are delivered untouched
  if (!isUserSent){
    MessageHandler.deliverPacket(presence);
    return;
  }

  //Server-managed presence updates are forwarded to all subscribers
```

```
    //Update the Session's presence status
    sessionPresence.setAvailable(type.equals("available"));
    sessionPresence.setShow(presence.getChildValue("show"));
    sessionPresence.setStatus(presence.getChildValue("status");
    String priority = presence.getChildValue("priority");
    sessionPresence.setPriority(priority);
    if (priority != null){
      session.setPriority(Integer.parseInt(priority));
    }

    //Deliver to all user's presence subscribers
    updateSubscribers(presence);
    return;
}
```

The presence update handling part of updatePresence() relies on the MessageHandler to deliver user managed packets directly to a recipient. For server-managed updates, the method updateSubscribers() is used to send the presence update to all of the user's presence subscribers. In addition, we must update the Presence object in the sender's session.

Normally, presence updates originate from the client. However, servers will sometimes need to know the presence status of users on other servers and can't wait for an update. Servers can request the presence of another user using a <presence> packet with type set to the value probe. We won't handle these packets in our Jabber server but we'll check for these probe packets and drop them:

The Roster class updatePresence() method: handling presence probes

```
if (type.equals("probe")) {
   System.out.println("Roster: We don't handle probes yet " +
                       presence.toString());
   return;
}
```

The last set of presence packets we handle are those with types of subscribe, unsubscribe, subscribed, and unsubscribed. The subscribe and unsubscribe packets create a roster item (if one doesn't exist) and set the subscription ask status appropriately.

A subscribed or unsubscribed packet is sent to confirm the subscription request. When we get a subscription packet, we clear the ask status for the subscription item and change the subscription type appropriately (listing 8.4).

Listing 8.4   Roster class UpdatePresence(): presence subscription

```
Subscriber sub = (Subscriber)subscribers.get(subscriber);
    if (sub == null){
        sub = new Subscriber();                    Create
        sub.subscription = "none";                 subscription
        subscribers.put(recipient,sub);            item
    }
    if (type.equals("subscribe") || type.equals("unsubscribe")){
        sub.ask = type;  ◁─────────────────────────────    Set up subscription
    } else if (type.equals("subscribed")){ ◁───────────    request status
        sub.ask = null;
        if (isUserSent){                                   Subscription
            if (sub.subscription.equals("from")){          accepted
                sub.subscription = "both";
            } else if (sub.subscription.equals("none")){
                sub.subscription = "to";
            }
        } else {
            if (sub.subscription.equals("to")){
                sub.subscription = "both";
            } else if (sub.subscription.equals("none")){
                sub.subscription = "from";
            }
        }
    } else if (type.equals("unsubscribed")){   ◁───────    Subscription
        sub.ask = null;                                    revoked/refused
        if (isUserSent){
            if (sub.subscription.equals("from")){
                sub.subscription = "none";
            } else if (sub.subscription.equals("both")){
                sub.subscription = "to";
            }
        } else {
            if (sub.subscription.equals("to")){
                sub.subscription = "none";
            } else if (sub.subscription.equals("both")){
                sub.subscription = "from";
            }
        }
    }
    Packet item = (Packet)items.get(subscriber);  ◁─────    Update for
    if (item != null){                                     roster push
        item.setAttribute("subscription",sub.subscription);
        item.setAttribute("ask",sub.ask);
        Packet iq = new Packet("iq");
        iq.setType("set");
        Packet query = new Packet("query");
        query.setAttribute("xmlns","jabber:iq:roster");
        query.setParent(iq);
        item.setParent(query);
```

```
      MessageHandler.deliverPacketToAll(user,iq);  ◁────── Forward the
    }                                                       subscription
      MessageHandler.deliverPacket(presence);               packet to
  }                                                          recipient

  void updateSubscribers(Packet packet){  ◁────── Send updated
    Enumeration subs = subscribers.keys();            presence to
    while (subs.hasMoreElements()){                    subscribers
      packet.setTo((String)subs.nextElement());
      MessageHandler.deliverPacket(packet);
    }
  }
}
```

Handling presence updates is the most difficult part of roster management. The easiest is responding to a roster reset (roster get IQ query). A roster reset simply is a request from a client for the server to send a copy of the complete roster. Clients usually send roster resets and then authenticate with the server in to generate their roster user displays. Since the roster items are stored as Packet objects in the items Hashtable sending a Roster snapshot is as easy as iterating through the table and attaching the roster item Packets to a parent <query> packet.

The Roster class getPacket() method

```
public Packet getPacket(){
  Packet packet = new Packet("query");
  packet.setAttribute("xmlns","jabber:iq:roster");
  Iterator itemIterator = items.values().iterator();
  while (itemIterator.hasNext()){
    ((Packet)itemIterator.next()).setParent(packet);
  }
  return packet;
}
```

Roster updates (roster set IQ queries) are only slightly more complex. To handle the update, we need to store a copy of the new item in our items Hashtable and send a roster push to all resources currently logged in to that user account.

Listing 8.5 The Roster class updateRoster() method

```
public void updateRoster(Packet packet){

  //Extract the query packet
  Packet rosterQuery = packet.getFirstChild("query");
  rosterQuery.setAttribute("xmlns","jabber:iq:roster");
  Iterator rosterItems = rosterQuery.getChildren().iterator();
  while (rosterItems.hasNext()){
```

```
    //For each <item> packet in the query
    Object child = rosterItems.next();
    if (child instanceof Packet){
      Packet itemPacket = (Packet)child;

      String subJID = itemPacket.getAttribute("jid");
      //Create Subscriber object for <item> if needed
      Subscriber sub = (Subscriber)subscribers.get(subJID);
      if (sub == null){
        sub = new Subscriber();
        sub.subscription = "none";
        sub.ask = null;
        subscribers.put(subJID,sub);
      }
      //Update <item> with subscriber info for roster push
      itemPacket.setAttribute("subscription",sub.subscription);
      itemPacket.setAttribute("ask",sub.ask);
      //Store updated <item> packet
      items.put(subJID,itemPacket);
    }
  }

  //Roster push
  packet.setType("set");
  MessageHandler.deliverPacketToAll(packet);
}
```

It is ironic that when managing the roster, the roster protocols are easy to handle and the presence protocols require the most work.[5] Now that we see how the Roster class manages the roster, let's take a look at the server's packet handlers that will route the roster-related packets to the Roster class.

8.2.6 *The roster packet handlers*

Two packet handlers will handle roster-related packets: RosterHandler and PresenceHandler. From their names, it is obvious that the RosterHandler class handles IQ packets belonging to the jabber:iq:roster namespace, while our existing PresenceHandler will continue to handle <presence> packets but is now roster-aware.

---

[5] I would have preferred if the presence subscription protocols were moved into the roster protocols to keep presence out of roster management. This arrangement seems cleaner. However, it makes sense to keep all presence-related tasks together in the presence protocols and that is the case for Jabber's standard user presence protocols. In addition, with this division of labor, roster becomes an exclusively client/server protocol, leaving presence to handle anything that must pass through intervening servers.

The PresenceHandler class must differentiate between groupchat packets and user presence packets. The former are routed to the GroupchatManager discussed in chapter 5, while the latter are resent to the Roster member of the appropriate User object.

The PresenceHandler class

```
public class PresenceHandler implements PacketListener {

  UserIndex userIndex;
  GroupChatManager chatMan = GroupChatManager.getManager();
  public PresenceHandler(UserIndex index) { userIndex = index; }

  public void notify(Packet packet){
    if (packet.getSession().getStatus() != Session.AUTHENTICATED){

      packet.setTo(null);
      packet.setFrom(null);
      ErrorTool.setError(packet,401,
                         "Authentication required to send presence");
      MessageHandler.deliverPacket(packet);

    } else if (chatMan.isChatPacket(packet)){
      chatMan.handleChatPresence(packet);

    } else {
      User user = userIndex.getUser(packet.getSession().getJID().getUser());
      user.getRoster().updatePresence(packet);
    }
  }
}
```

The RosterHandler class is even simpler since it routes all packets directly to the appropriate User class's Roster object.

The RosterHandler class

```
public class RosterHandler implements PacketListener {

  UserIndex userIndex;
  public RosterHandler(UserIndex index) { userIndex = index; }

  public void notify(Packet packet) {
    packet.setTo(null);
    packet.setFrom(null);

    if (packet.getSession().getStatus() != Session.AUTHENTICATED){

      ErrorTool.setError(packet,401,
                         "Authentication required to send roster updates");
      MessageHandler.deliverPacket(packet);
      return;
```

```
      }

    User user = userIndex.getUser(packet.getSession());
    if (packet.getType().equals("set")){
      user.getRoster().updateRoster(packet);
      return;
    }

    if (packet.getType().equals("get")){

      packet.setType("result");
      packet.getChildren().clear();
      user.getRoster().getPacket().setParent(packet);
      MessageHandler.deliverPacket(packet);
      return;
    }

    ErrorTool.setError(packet,400,"What kind of IQ is this?");
    MessageHandler.deliverPacket(packet);
  }
}
```

The packet handling classes finish up the last significant addition to the Jabber server we'll cover in this book. The server now supports the core Jabber protocols and provides a fully functional, basic IM platform.

There are a few minor code changes not shown here that are required to support these new classes. They're scattered about and relatively minor, so I'll leave it to you to read the server code itself if you want the full details. These changes include:

- Registering the two new packet handlers with the `QueueThread` object in the Server's constructor.
- Sending a `<presence>` update with a type of `unavailable` when a client closes its XML streams.
- Limiting delivery of `<message>` packets to `available` resources.[6]

We've seen these changes done in previous chapters to support new server features so we won't cover the subject again.

As our Jabber server is now relatively complete, you can freely test it with any Jabber client to ensure that presence, rosters, and messaging support are functioning correctly. Try adding other users to your roster, changing your presence,

---

[6] Our original server code delivers messages when clients are authenticated. We need to add an AVAILABLE session status so that `MessageHandler` can deliver messages or store them for later delivery.

and sending messages. Testing the server using different clients is very useful in ensuring that the server behaves as expected.

Manual testing, especially when relying on other people's Jabber clients, can be tedious. Let's expand our Jabber client code to test user presence and rosters.

8.3 The Jabber client modifications

There is little to add to our Jabber client to test the server's new user presence and roster support. The client's JabberModel class already allows us to send <presence> packets. We only need to add the ability to send roster updates to the server using the JabberModel. In addition, we will need to create a RosterHandler class to handle incoming roster packets, and modify the Client class to test our new features.

8.3.1 Adding minimal roster support

The client's roster support requires a simple way to send roster updates using the JabberModel class, and handling incoming roster packets using a RosterHandler class. Both tasks are straightforward. Let's begin with the JabberModel modifications.

In order to make Jabber interactions simple for the client, we'll add three new methods to the JabberModel:

- sendRosterGet()—Sends a roster reset packet (get query) to the server, requesting a full roster snapshot be sent.
- sendRosterSet()—Sends a roster update packet (set query) to the server to modify a roster item.
- sendRosterRemove()—Sends a roster update packet (set query) to the server to remove a roster item.

In these three methods shown in listing 8.6, we create a roster packet and send it to the server. As with most <iq> protocols, the server will respond to roster queries with an empty successful result packet. Clients should assign unique packet IDs to the requests so they can match it to responses.

Listing 8.6   The JabberModel class roster methods

```
public void sendRosterGet()
  throws IOException {
    Packet packet = new Packet("iq");
    packet.setType("get");
    packet.setID("roster_get");
    Packet query = new Packet("query");
    query.setAttribute("xmlns","jabber:iq:roster");
    query.setParent(packet);
    packet.writeXML(session.getWriter());
```

```
    }

    public void sendRosterRemove(String jid)
    throws IOException {
      Packet packet = new Packet("iq");
      packet.setType("set");
      packet.setID("roster_remove");
      Packet query = new Packet("query");
      query.setAttribute("xmlns","jabber:iq:roster");
      query.setParent(packet);
      Packet item = new Packet("item");
      item.setAttribute("subscription","remove");
      item.setAttribute("jid",jid);
      item.setParent(query);
      packet.writeXML(session.getWriter());
    }

    public void sendRosterSet(String jid,
                              String name,
                              Iterator groups)
    throws IOException {
      Packet packet = new Packet("iq");
      packet.setType("set");
      packet.setID("roster_set");
      Packet query = new Packet("query");
      query.setAttribute("xmlns","jabber:iq:roster");
      query.setParent(packet);
      Packet item = new Packet("item");
      item.setAttribute("jid",jid);
      item.setAttribute("name",name);
      item.setParent(query);
      while (groups.hasNext()){
        new Packet("group",(String)groups.next()).setParent(item);
      }
      packet.writeXML(session.getWriter());
    }
```

The server will send the client roster pushes. A Jabber user agent client with a GUI would use these roster pushes to update the roster display. Our test client has no such display. We will simply print out the roster push to standard output (System.out). As your test client needs become more sophisticated, you may want to examine the roster push contents and keep statistics on your roster's behavior.

The RosterHandler class

```
public class RosterHandler implements PacketListener {

  public void notify(Packet packet) {
    System.out.print("roster: ");
    System.out.println(packet.toString());
  }
}
```

With the basics of roster handling now in place, it's time to update the client application to test the server's new user presence and roster capabilities.

8.3.7 *Testing the server*

To test user presence support, we will first use the presence protocols to subscribe to a user's presence updates, approve the subscription of another client, and update the presence of our client. Since our tests run best if we test presence between two users, we have two options for creating our test client. The first is to automate one side of the conversation and use a standard Jabber client for the other. That way we know that other Jabber clients, interacting through the server with our client, behave properly. This is important for ensuring interoperability when communicating with users employing other Jabber clients.

Our main concern is testing our server, which brings us to the second option. To make testing simple, automated, and more controllable, we will once again run two client sessions within our Jabber client (figure 8.6).

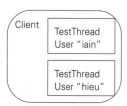

Figure 8.6
The client contains two `TestThreads` that control two separate client sessions.

With this in mind, let's create an `IainTestThread` and `HieuTestThread` class within a new `RosterClient` class. The `TestThread` subclasses will each conduct a server test of user presence support by carrying out the steps listed in table 8.3.

Table 8.3   The sequence of tasks carried out by the two test threads in our client application.

IainTestThread	HieuTestThread
Connect to the server. Authenticate with the server as user "iain." Send presence "available".	Connect to the server. Authenticate with the server as user "hieu." Send presence "available".
Subscribe to the presence of user "hieu."	
	Accept subscription from user "iain."
Update roster to place hieu in group "friends" with the nickname "RunningMan."	
Send presence "unavailable".	
Disconnect.	Disconnect.

Let's begin by examining the code for `IainTestThread` (listing 8.7).

Listing 8.7   The IainTestThread class

```
public class IainTestThread extends TestThread {

  public void run(){
    try {
      model.connect();
      model.authenticate();
      do {
        notifyHandlers(packetQueue.pull());
      } while (model.getSessionStatus() != Session.AUTHENTICATED);

      model.sendPresence(null,null,null,null,null);

      String hieuName = "hieu@" + model.getServerName();
      model.sendPresence(hieuName,
                  "subscribe",
                  null,
                  null,
                  null);

      waitFor("presence","subscribed");

      LinkedList groups = new LinkedList();
      groups.add("friends");
      model.sendRosterSet(hieuName,
                  "RunningMan",
                  groups.iterator());

      waitFor("iq","set");

      model.sendPresence(null,
                  "unavailable",
                  null,
                  null,
                  null);
      model.disconnect();
    } catch (Exception ex){
      ex.printStackTrace();
    }
  }
}
```

Annotations:
- `} while (model.getSessionStatus() != Session.AUTHENTICATED);` — **Wait until authenticated**
- `model.sendPresence(null,null,null,null,null);` — **Set "available" presence**
- `String hieuName = "hieu@" + model.getServerName();` — **Subscribe to "hieu"**
- `waitFor("presence","subscribed");` — **Wait for confirmation**
- `model.sendRosterSet(hieuName,` — **Update roster**
- `waitFor("iq","set");` — **Roster push**
- `model.sendPresence(null,` — **Signal "unavailable" presence**

It's pretty amazing what we can do with our simple `TestThread` class in just a few lines of code. I've noticed that the `JabberModel.sendPresence()` method typically uses the recipient and type parameters and ignores the others. This would signal to me that we should add some convenience methods to the `JabberModel` to make working with presence simpler. Overall, the design of the JabberModel and its use in the TestThread subclasses makes for a pleasant client coding experience.

The HieuTestThread in listing 8.8 also extends the TestThread and carries out the other side of the roster test.

Listing 8.8   The HieuTestThread class

```
public class HieuTestThread extends TestThread {

    public void run(){
      try {
        model.connect();
        model.authenticate();
        do {
          notifyHandlers(packetQueue.pull());
        } while (model.getSessionStatus() != Session.AUTHENTICATED);
        model.sendPresence(null,null,null,null,null);

        waitFor("presense","subscribe");
        String iainName = "iain@" + model.getServerName();
        model.sendPresence(iainName,
                     "subscribed",
                     null,
                     null,
                     null);
        waitFor("presence","unavailable");
        model.disconnect();
      } catch (Exception ex){
        ex.printStackTrace();
      }
    }
  }
}
```

Try running the test on our Java Jabber server to see how it behaves. Notice how the presence subscription request and approval cause spontaneous server roster pushes. Is the server's behavior what you expect? Try running the test against another Jabber server (e.g., the open source reference Jabber server). Is the test behavior the same between our server and others?

8.4   *Conclusions*

The Jabber user presence and roster protocols round out the core Jabber protocols, creating a basic, functional IM system. User presence and rosters are what set IM apart from other Internet communication systems and it's taken us three chapters to cover it. As we've seen, both user presence and roster rely on other systems that need to be in place before we could properly address them.

Although user presence and roster support are the most complex parts of the server, supporting user presence and the Jabber roster is primarily a bookkeeping implementation exercise. Sophisticated Jabber systems will inevitably use a database and other data management tools to allow these user-account-related operations to scale smoothly to large numbers of users and provide reliable service.

The Java server we've been working on is now capable of supporting most Jabber IM clients. In addition, our client software has all the features you need to turn it into a graphical user agent or automated chatbot. Next we examine where we can take the software, and what you would need to do to turn it into commercial-grade products.

Creating a complete Jabber system

243

The chapter provides an overview of the significant tasks facing anyone wishing to create a complete Jabber server or client. These problems exist whether you are extending the server and client software developed in this book or writing your own from scratch. To focus the discussion on the generic issues facing developers, we'll skip looking at more source code and concentrate on the problems and possible solutions available.

To begin, we'll take a generic look at additional protocol issues that we have not yet covered. From a technical standpoint, supporting the remaining standard Jabber protocols in our Java Jabber server and client is a straightforward exercise in adding more packet handlers that follow the specification. The real difficulty lies in selecting which protocols you should implement. The first part of this chapter will discuss these issues and provide guidance in this decision-making process.

9.1   *Creating Jabber-compliant implementations*

In the previous chapters, we've taken a look at the core Jabber protocols which protocols are fundamental to building a complete IM system. Using this knowledge, we have implemented a Jabber client and server in Java that provides the IM capabilities found in all Jabber systems. A scan through appendix A of this will show that there are many other support protocols and other features available as part of the Jabber specification.

In most cases, these additional protocols are straightforward to understand and to implement. Even if you have an unlimited budget (or no deadlines), there may be some support protocols defined in the Jabber protocols that you don't want to implement for business, security, or policy reasons.

Suppose your company wants to implement a small Jabber client that will run on a wireless personal digital assistant (PDA) like a Palm Pilot. Sending messages and simple presence is all you want this client to do. Other protocols won't increase the value of the client software and can lead to poor performance and excessive memory consumption on these limited devices.

These issues bring to light the problem of defining a coherent, interoperable Jabber standard while providing developers the flexibility to target Jabber technology in a variety of applications.

Jabber is attacking this problem on three fronts:

- Formal standards
- Powered by Jabber logo campaign
- Jabber environments

9.1.1 *Setting standards: the Jabber Software Foundation*

The first steps in controlling the Jabber standards have been taken by the Jabber Software Foundation. The Foundation is primarily funded and administered by Jabber.com Inc., a commercial company composed of most of the open source Jabber project's original developers including Jeremie Miller, the Jabber inventor. The Foundation is modeled after the popular and Apache Software Foundation and is tasked with maintaining the Jabber community and creating Jabber standards. It is split into a number of Jabber Interest Groups (JIGs), each forming a committee focused on a particular area of Jabber technology.

One of the main goals of JIGs is to produce next-generation Jabber standards to replace the original ones, never a primary source of information concerning the Jabber protocols. They are inconsistent and incomplete and cannot be used, by themselves, to create a "clean room" implementation of the Jabber standards. Instead, you are forced to examine the behavior of the Jabber server reference implementation (jabberd) to obtain the definitive behavior of the Jabber protocols. This is not an unusual situation for standards being developed in parallel with an implementation.

However, the Jabber standards are maturing enough that a more formal standards process can be put into place to define them. This process is under way and I hope that by the time you read this some of the Jabber Software Foundation standards are in place. In the meantime, I have provided my own reference to the existing Jabber standards in the appendix of this book. I anticipate that the eventual Foundation standards should closely follow the existing Jabber standards outlined in this book.

9.1.2 *Enforcing standards: Jabber Powered applications*

The Jabber standards are important because they enable any Jabber-compliant client to reliably communicate with a Jabber-compliant server. If client and server developers begin to implement their own versions of the Jabber standards, we'll run into problems where only certain features work on certain clients or servers and isolated "Jabber islands" will begin to form within the Jabber network. Similar problems plagued the web during the "browser wars" when web browsers started implementing custom tags and you had to have a particular web browser (Netscape or Internet Explorer) in order to view a web page.

To encourage standards compliance and spread the news about Jabber, the Jabber Software Foundation has begun a Jabber Powered logo campaign (www.jabberpowered.org). This effort allows clients or servers that use Jabber technology to advertise the fact using a Jabber Powered logo (figure 9.1) maintained by the Jabber Software Foundation. Java developers will be familiar with this tactic as Sun has used a similar program to promote pure Java programming with their 100% Pure Java logo campaign. The requirements for using the Jabber Powered logo are extremely limited at this time.

 **Figure 9.1**
The Jabber Powered logo.

When the formal Jabber Software Foundation standards are released clients and servers may be required to pass standards compliance tests prior to being able to display the logo (figure 9.1). This will be a major breakthrough because at this point, there are no Jabber compliance tests or formal techniques for determining what does and what does not follow the standards.

9.1.3 *Organizing standards: Jabber environments*

Finally, like Java, the Jabber community recognizes that one standard cannot fit all situations. The Java community has addressed this issue by creating Java configurations and profiles, beginning with Java 2 Micro Edition (J2ME). In the Java system, configurations are used to define the basic computing resources of a particular device such as its basic computing capabilities, RAM and storage, user interfaces, and so forth.

For example, the Java Connected Limited Device Configuration (CLDC) defines a configuration for small embedded devices such as cell phones and PDAs with very minimal computing resources. The Connected Device Configuration (CDC) defines the next step up in computing power and covers slightly bigger devices such as set top boxes, Internet appliances, and so forth.

The Java system then defines profiles for each configuration that tailors Java technology (primarily the Java libraries available) to specific applications. So there is a Mobile Information Device Profile (MIDP) that defines additional libraries on the CLDC foundation for PDAs. A TV Profile is being proposed for CDC devices to support generic TV controls such as electronic programming guides and channel selection.

Jabber standards are facing the same problems as the Java standards had: one solution will not fit every problem domain. Resource-limited environments have very different requirements from enterprise servers. There is currently a proposal in the Jabber Software Foundation to create a similar set of configurations and profiles for the Jabber standards. The idea is to establish a limited set of Jabber environments that define subsets of the Jabber standards that must be implemented for a Jabber server or client to meet a particular environment's standards compliance (figure 9.2). This helps to identify which Jabber protocols should be present on either clients or servers and helps to enforce a more uniform user experience with Jabber.

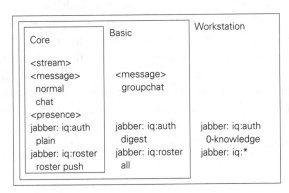

Figure 9.2
There are many possible Jabber environments (e.g., Core, Basic, and Workstation) and each would specify the protocols required for compliance with each environment.

Although this effort is in its infancy, it addresses a fundamental problem facing the formalization of the Jabber standards. I hope we'll see big advances in this area as the Jabber standards mature.

9.1.4 *Today's options for achieving server compliance*

Unfortunately, most of these options for formalization of standards are under development and may not be available for some time. Today, there is no formal method for selecting the right Jabber standards to implement. You are left to your own judgment in determining how much of the Jabber standard to support.

The first option is to implement all existing and proposed standards. There are not that many of them so this can be a reasonable approach for systems that aren't restricted by code size, memory limits, and so forth. The majority of servers and mainstream desktop clients follow this approach.

The other option is to define your own subset depending on your needs. I have chosen this approach with the source code in this book, implementing only the core protocols I consider fundamental to Jabber IM. Specialized clients, like chatbots, will use this approach, as they don't need the full functionality offered by some of the more specialized Jabber protocols. In addition, resource-constrained clients, like PDAs, are often forced to make tradeoffs in capability to minimize the resources consumed by the application.

Specialized applications may find that only a small fraction of the standard Jabber protocols combined with their own specialized protocol extensions are needed. For example, you may have a home automation system that uses Jabber as its underlying framework. You use the basic presence and message protocols for communication, and a set of custom IQ extension protocols for controlling devices. Many commonly supported IM protocols like roster (`jabber:iq:roster`) and groupchat are unnecessary in such a system.

For the present time, selecting what parts of the Jabber standard to implement is a judgment call on the part of the specification, design, and implementation team. The important thing to consider is what you want to use Jabber for. The better your system's Jabber compatibility and the more standard features you implement, the greater your chances of successfully interoperating with other Jabber software. In addition, standards compliance ensures the ability to send your Jabber messages across the rest of the Jabber network to any other Jabber-compliant client. This may not be an issue if your system is closed and proprietary. However, if you want to exploit the Internetwide Jabber network and reach its many users, Jabber standards compliance is a necessity.

9.2   *Server missing pieces*

The Java Jabber server software developed to this point in the book works well as a stand-alone IM server. However, there are a few missing pieces that most Jabber servers should consider implementing to create a finished product. These missing pieces fall into five main categories:

- Server to server communications
- Transports
- Server deployment
- Server maintenance
- Reliability and Availability

Addressing each of these problems will create significant advantages for your Jabber server.

9.2.1 *Server-to-server communications:*
federating Jabber domains

The first and most glaring omission from the book's server is support for S2S communication with other Jabber servers. This results in users on the server only being able to communicate with other users on the same server. This is perfect for isolated workgroups where communication with the wider world may not be possible or desirable.

However, one of the great powers of Jabber systems is their ability to tie together various Jabber servers to create a much larger network. This works just like the email system where users may have accounts on any email server, but can communicate with any other user on any other email server on the Internet.

Jabber supports S2S communication using the protocols defined in the `jabber:server` namespace. Recall that normal client-to-server (C2S) communication uses the `jabber:client` namespace established in the opening `<stream:steam>` tag. The `jabber:server` protocols work almost identically to the equivalent `jabber:client` protocols covered in this book. The connections in a typical Jabber network is shown in figure 9.3.

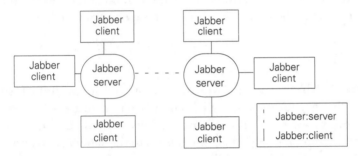

Figure 9.3 **Servers federate Jabber domains using the `jabber:server` protocols.**

There are two critical differences between the protocols. The first is that an S2S connection is considered to be one-way. Although a full bidirectional network socket is created, S2S connections only allow the initiator of the S2S connection to send packets. The receiving server only sends its XML stream packets and error packets back. If the servers need to send packets in both directions, two connections must be made.

The second critical difference is the single `jabber:server` XML stream carries packets for all of the server's users. You can think of the `jabber:server` connection as if it were made of a virtual collection of streams, one for each user on the server.

Since the connection is shared, the receiving server can't make any assumptions about the sender or recipient of a packet. As a consequence, `jabber:server` packets are almost always fully addressed. In other words, both the `to` and `from` attributes of packets are completely specified. The user's server fills in the correct packet addresses before sending them over the S2S connection, protecting the client from these differences. All the client must do is specify the recipient's Jabber server in the recipient server part of their Jabber ID.

For example, suppose Bob on Jabber server A.com wants to send a normal message packet to Sally on Jabber server B.com. The packet Bob's client sends to server A.com would look like:

```
<message to='sally@b.com'>
 <body>howdy</body>
</message>
```

Server A.com receives the message, edits it to add Bob's sender ID from the connection's session, and sends this modified message to server B.com:

```
<message to='sally@b.com' from='bob@a.com/work'>
 <body>howdy</body>
</message>
```

Server B.com receives the message, finds that Sally is online, modifies the message to remove the recipient address, and sends the message to Sally's client:

```
<message from='bob@a.com/work'>
  <body>howdy</body>
</message>
```

It is up to the server whether it removes the recipient address field (as in my example above), changes it to match Sally's client's actual address (for example sally@b.com/meeting), or leaves it unchanged. Sally's client should ignore the recipient part of incoming messages because it is up to the Jabber server to ensure that messages are properly delivered. The incoming message itself implies it was addressed to the client. In most cases, it is best for the server to strip the extra information. This strategy saves the network bandwidth that would be consumed by the unnecessary addressing overhead.

Since a Jabber server acts on behalf of all its users over an S2S connection, securing the connection is an important security problem. Misbehaving or malicious servers can swamp a legitimate Jabber server with packets, send spam messages, and cause mischief and havoc. In addition, if a computer can fool a Jabber server into thinking it is another legitimate Jabber server, it can act as if it were any of that Jabber server's users. This level of access could allow you to send messages that claim to come from these users, change server and client settings, and so on.

There obviously needs to be an authentication protocol to properly identify S2S connection participants. This authentication protocol is known as dialback.

9.2.2 Dialback authentication: S2S security

Authentication for S2S is more complicated than in C2S. In C2S authentication, clients have user accounts on the server with authentication credentials. Only clients with user accounts can access the server. However in the case of S2S, Jabber servers may need to connect to other Jabber servers that they've had no prior contact with. In addition, because the number of Jabber servers can be potentially quite large, it is impractical for servers to create or maintain a server account for each possible server connection.

The dialback protocol is an attempt to create a simple authentication mechanism for ensuring that a server is who it claims to be without any knowledge about the server. It accomplishes this by simply reconnecting (dialing back) to the server using a separate connection and asking for it to verify that it is in fact opening a connection.

An analogy would be authenticating a person's official identity in real life. For example, say a person dressed as a police officer comes up to you and wants to act as a police officer (acting on behalf of the police organization). Using that person's radio to verify the purported officer's identity won't work because they may have an accomplice on the other end of the radio. However, if you use your own phone to call the police station using the phone number in the phone book, you can be relatively assured that the person is a police officer sent from the police station.

In the dialback process shown in figure 9.4, the original connection will contain a randomly generated key sent from the initiator of the connection. The receiving authentication server connects back to the server using that server's host name, and verifies that it is opening a connection using that key. The weakness of the protocol is in the dialback itself.

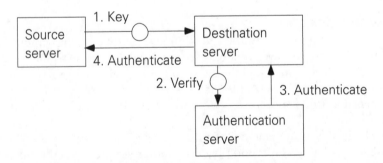

Figure 9.4 Dialback S2S authentication involves three servers. The authentication server assures the destination server that the source server is a legitimate controller for its Jabber domain by dialing back to find the authentication server and verifying the source server's key.

In our earlier analogy of the authenticating a police officer, we rely on the phone book to have a valid phone number for the real police station. If the person posing as a police officer can change the numbers in the phone book, he can cause you to dial the wrong number where their accomplice can falsely verify the person.

In dialback, we rely on the DNS to properly resolve the server's host name to the correct machine. As anyone in computer security will tell you, DNS is not secure and determined hackers can easily overcome authentication schemes based on DNS.

Dialback's reliance on DNS is a known weakness of Jabber's dialback authentication. Unfortunately, there is no standard replacement for dialback at this time. In order for Jabber servers to support S2S connections in a standard manner (and so connect with a maximum number of Jabber servers), they will need to support dialback. I strongly suggest that people with strong S2S security need to get involved in the Jabber Software Foundation's security JIG to help establish a more secure alternative to dialback. For the time being, though, dialback is the best we have.

There are three logical entities involved in the dialback authentication protocol:

- *A source server*—The source server is attempting to create an S2S connection so that it may send packets to the destination server.

- *A destination server*—The destination server is attempting to authenticate the source server so it can decide whether to accept packets from the connection.

- *A source authentication server*—This server will help the destination server authenticate the source server.

DIALBACK AND SERVER FARMS

The dialback source and source authentication servers may be implemented by one server application. However, dialback is designed to support Jabber where multiple server machines work together as a single logical Jabber server. Incoming client connections will look up the Jabber server name to find its network address and special round-robin DNS setups will send the client to one of the machines in the farm.

Unfortunately, if one of the machines in the server wishes to create an S2S connection, dialback probably won't send the destination server to the right source authentication server. To overcome this, dialback makes no assumptions that the source server and the source authentication server are the same server on a single machine. In fact, the only requirement is that both servers must be able to share a secret (the dialback authentication key) and that the source authentication server receives authentication connections.

The basic procedure for dialback begins with the source server forming the primary connection to the destination server. To stress the logically separate entities involved, let's imagine the source server has a domain name of `sender.source.com`. It is sending packets from users in the logical Jabber domain `source.com` to users at the destination server `destination.com`. The destination server sees that the connection is for users in the domain source.com. So the destination server will attempt to connect to a source authentication server at source.com. The source server (sender.source.com) sends the opening stream tag to the destination server (destination.com):

```
<stream:stream xmlns:stream='http://etherx.jabber.org/streams'
  xmlns='jabber:server'
  to='destination.com'
  from='source.com'
  xmlns:db='jabber:server:dialback'>
```

The packet uses the same stream namespace http://etherx.jabber.org/ streams but the default namespace inside of the stream element is set to jabber:server rather than jabber:client. The to and from attributes identify the destination and source server's names. The source server's name (source.com) does not need to match its actual domain name address (sender.source.com). The source server's name is the Jabber domain it will be operating on behalf of. The source server's name is used by the destination server to connect to the source authentication server. Finally, the xmlns:db namespace attributes indicate that the source server hopes to use dialback authentication.

The destination server responds with its opening stream tag:

```
<stream:stream xmlns:stream='http://etherx.jabber.org/streams'
  xmlns='jabber:server'
  to='source.com'
  from='destination.com'
  xmlns:db='jabber:server:dialback'
  id='4208ab093e'>
```

Like the server stream in the C2S protocol, the destination server's opening stream tag contains a session ID. Since the destination server indicates that it also supports dialback, the source server can send its dialback authentication key in a <db:result> packet:

```
<db:result to='destination.com' from='source.com'>0283cd322312</db:result>
```

The key is a disposable authentication credential generated by the source for one-time use with its authentication server. With this key the destination server is ready to authenticate, so it opens an authentication connection with the source authentication server source.com and sends its opening stream tag:

```
<stream:stream xmlns:stream='http://etherx.jabber.org/streams'
  xmlns='jabber:server'
  to='source.com'
  from='destination.com'
  xmlns:db='jabber:server:dialback'>
```

The source authentication server supports dialback so it will respond with its opening stream tag that contains the session ID for the authentication connection:

```
<stream:stream xmlns:stream='http://etherx.jabber.org/streams'
  xmlns='jabber:server'
  to='destination.com'
  from='source.com'
  xmlns:db='jabber:server:dialback'
  id='403a33b093e'>
```

The destination server now sends the key it received from the source server in a `<db:verify>` packet. Notice that a packet ID is set so that destination server can match authentication server responses to the original query.

```
<db:verify to='source.com'
  from='destination.com'
  id='5423ef'>
    0283cd322312
</db:verify>
```

The source authentication server examines the key and determines if there is a primary connection being opened between the source and destination server, and if the dialback key is valid for that connection. It is entirely up to the source and source authentication server how this verification is done. The destination server does not assign any meaning to the key.

The key and its format are not specified by the Jabber specifications. The reference Jabber server uses an SHA-1 digest of parts of the server names to generate and verify the key but the server implementer is free to choose any mechanism they wish.

A valid key will result in the source authentication server sending a valid dialback result to the destination server over the authentication connection:

```
<db:result to='destination.com' from='source.com' type='valid' id='5423ef'/>
```

Upon a successful authentication, the destination server switches back to the primary connection with the source server and sends its own `<db:result>` packet:

```
<db:result to='source.com' from='destination.com' type='valid'/>
```

Packets can now be sent from the source to destination server. Prior to sending the valid `<db:result>` packet, the destination server will drop all packets coming from the source server.

If the authentication fails, the authentication server will send:

```
<db:result to='destination.com' from='source.com' type='invalid' id='5423ef'/>
```

The destination server will switch to the primary connection with the source server and send:

```
<db:result to='source.com' from='destination.com' type='invalid'/>
```

The source server can try again using another `<db:result>` packet and key, or quit.

BIDIRECTIONAL S2S CONNECTIONS

It is very common for servers to need bidirectional S2S connections. If a user is sending messages from one server to another, chances are high that the recipient will be sending messages back. To make sending messages easier, dialback allows the destination server to reuse the authentication connection as its own primary S2S connection with the source server.

The protocol support for this is trivial. At any time, the destination server (now acting as a source server) is free to send its own `<db:result>` packet over the authentication connection containing a dialback key. The authentication server then acts as the destination server and opens a new authentication connection with the destination server's source authentication server. The bidirectional dialback protocol creates the need for three connections as shown below.

Protocol overview for creating a bidirectional S2S connection.

Source Primary Connection		Source Authentication/ Destination Primary Connection		Destination Authentication Connection	
Source	**Destination**	**Destination**	**Source Authentication**	**Source Authentication**	**Destination Authentication**
<stream: stream>					
	<stream: stream>				
<db:result> skey	Create connection				
		<stream: stream>			
			<stream: stream>		
		<db:verify> skey			
			<db:result> valid		

Continued on next page

Protocol overview for creating a bidirectional S2S connection. (continued)

Source Primary Connection		Source Authentication/ Destination Primary Connection		Destination Authentication Connection	
Source	**Destination**	**Destination**	**Source Authentication**	**Source Authentication**	**Destination Authentication**
	<db:result> valid				
Sends S2S packets		<db:result> dkey		Create connection	
				<stream: stream>	
					<stream: stream>
				<db:verify> dkey	
					<db:result> valid
			<db:result> valid		
		Sends S2S packets		</ stream:stream >	
					</ stream:stream >
				Close connection	

Servers must be careful in implementing S2S support. Beyond the weaknesses of the DNS-based dialback authentication, S2S opens the Jabber server up to many other attacks. Once authenticated, the Jabber server can be granted almost complete access to your Jabber server. Such a policy enables very powerful systems of Jabber servers to be built, but also opens them up to exploitation.

To limit these abuses, servers should be very careful to monitor and control their S2S connections. Reasonable safeguards might include limiting the rate and number of packets that can be sent, limiting the types of packets that can be sent, and filtering packets by their destinations or senders. On advanced servers, it may be prudent to be able to adjust these settings based on the server address. This would allow you create white lists of servers that are highly trusted, and black lists of servers that have severe restrictions placed on them for bad behavior.

Despite these potential problems S2S enables Jabber servers to join together to form a much larger Jabber network. If it is true that the value of a network increases geometrically with the number of users, the motivation for connecting and exchanging packets with other Jabber servers is clear.

Jabber's design does not limit S2S connections to other Jabber servers. One of Jabber's claims to fame is its ability to connect with non-Jabber IM systems.

9.2.3 *Transports: integrating with other IM systems*

Due to Jabber's open, packet-based design, Jabber systems are well-suited for use as a generic transportation system for IM messages. This simple design has been exploited in the Jabber open source server to connect Jabber servers to non-Jabber IM systems such as AIM, MSN Messenger, and Yahoo! Messenger systems.

The Jabber server reference implementation uses server modules called `trans-ports` that provide a bridge between the Jabber and these foreign messaging systems (figure 9.5). Transports treat each proprietary IM system as a Jabber IM domain with its own user names creating unique Jabber IDs. Sending a Jabber message to one of these special Jabber IDs causes it to be handled by a transport module. Transports connect with the foreign message systems and act as a client or server on that system in order to relay the messages and presence updates (if supported) between the two systems.

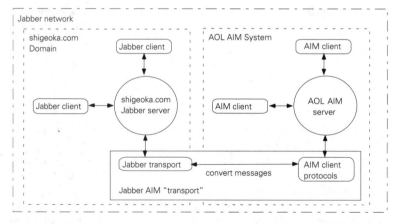

Figure 9.5 Jabber transports act as Jabber server plug-ins, translating packets between two IM systems in order to provide seamless access to both.

For example, if we send a message to screen-name@aol.server.com, the server will recognize that aol.server.com users are really AIM users and let the AIM transport handle the packet. The AIM transport logs into the AIM network and sends the message to the indicated AIM screen name. Each transport must keep track of the mapping between Jabber ID and the third-party IM ID system.[1] All packets that travel between the two systems must be converted between Jabber packets and the native format for messages, presence updates, and so forth in the third-party IM system.

In cases where the IM system is well-documented (such as IRC, creating and maintaining transports is simple and straightforward. On the other hand, many proprietary IM systems (especially AOL) actively change their protocols in order to prevent IM systems such as Jabber from interoperating with them. Supporting these transports becomes an "arms race" between the Jabber transport developers and the proprietary IM system's engineers.[2]

It would be nice to add transports to our Java server. Unfortunately, it is difficult to reuse the existing C language transports to add bridging capabilities to your Java server. In order to do so, you are faced with two options. First, you can use the Java Native Interface (JNI) to access the native C implementations of the existing Jabber transports. Although using JNI is not that difficult, the Jabber transports use some global data structures and a different, C language representation of a Jabber packet that will be hard to emulate. For starters, you'll need to spend a significant amount of time to translate Java `Packet` classes into C versions that the transports will understand.

The other option is to create your own Java server plug-in architecture and port the C transports to Java. Luckily, there is already a standard server plug-in API for Java: the Java Servlet APIs. Java servlets aren't just for web servers. They are actually a generic server extension architecture that is ideal for adding transports to a Java Jabber server.[3]

---

[1] See the `jabber:iq:gateway` protocol in appendix A.

[2] There are also serious legal implications to accessing proprietary IM systems without permission. You should check with legal experts before accessing foreign services without permission.

[3] If you don't want the hassle of supporting the Java `Servlet`, you can also cobble together your own custom interface. Our `PacketListener` interface is the perfect example of this approach. However, following the Java Servlet standard provides the advantage of providing a well-designed, well-documented interface. It should also be easy to find programmers familiar with servlet programming, a serious consideration for commercial implementations. Another alternative is to create a message-driven Enterprise JavaBean container that complies with the J2EE standard. This is more work but offers an even more flexible and robust solution to server extension.

In fact, if you examine our server's packet handler classes, you'll notice that they could easily be rewritten to comply with the `Servlet` interface. The modularization and quick development cycle afforded by using the servlet development model is well-documented for web development. You'll find the same benefits come in using them to customize the behavior of a Jabber server.

The knowledge of other IM systems protocols and how to translate between their data formats and Jabber packets is freely shared in the Jabber development community. Server developers that wish to add transport capabilities to their servers should join the Jabber development community to learn and share transport information.

So let's take a quick trip through the process of creating a Java server transport. First, implement a servlet-compliant server interface. This is simpler than it sounds. First, look at your servlet development kit or your (IDE) JavaDoc for the `javax.servlet` classes. There aren't many integrated development environment's. You'll want to concentrate on the `Servlet`, `ServletConfig`, and `ServletContext` interfaces as well as the `ServletInputStream` and `ServletOutputStream` classes. These are the ones you'll need to override or plug in to your Java server. Many people prefer to start with the `GenericServlet` helper class rather than do the work of overriding the interfaces themselves.

Alternatively, start with an existing servlet engine. There are several free ones that a good web search will reveal.[4] You can use an existing servlet engine as the basis for your Jabber server extension features. You may also find it easier to adapt the Jabber classes developed in this book to become part of the existing servlet engine. The process will involve replacing the servlet engine's existing http-specific code with our Jabber code rather than trying to wedge the servlet engine into the Jabber server.

Second, create a pattern for Jabber IDs that your transport will handle. For example, let's say you are writing an email transport that sends emails using the SMTP (Simple Mail Transfer Protocol) protocol. Jabber addresses for email users might be emailName%mailserver.com@email.jabberserver.com.[5]

---

[4] I'd suggest Tomcat (Jakarta.apache.org) for serious Jabber server efforts. However, Tomcat is a large, high-performance servlet engine and much of its code is complex. If you don't have much Java experience, you may find a smaller servlet engine easier to modify.

[5] This example is typical for existing Jabber transports. However, it violates the standard for Jabber user names because it contains the '%' character. Try to use a different standard compliant pattern for transport Jabber IDs but expect to have to deal with noncompliant Jabber IDs like this one.

Third, modify the QueueThread to detect these Jabber IDs and send them to the appropriate transport-servlet using its service() method.[6] This dispatch process is identical to our existing notification of PacketListener classes.

Finally, create a transport-servlet by creating a subclass of Servlet that overrides the service() method. In the service() method, convert the message from Jabber packet format to a foreign message format and send it using the foreign system's protocols.

In our email example, <message> packets will have their <body> text placed into the email body, and the <subject> text placed in the email's Subject: line. The email's To: address is converted from the special transport Jabber ID into a standard email address (e.g., emailName@mailserver.com). The From: address can use Jabber user's registered email address.[7] The transport then uses SMTP to send the email message through normal email.[8]

At first creating transports can sound like some arcane, magical process. However, you'll find that in most cases, it is almost embarrassingly easy. This is especially true if you have a well-designed plug-in architecture and access to documentation of the foreign messaging system's protocols. The process could be made even simpler if one of the many interoperability standards mentioned in chapter 1 is ever adopted. For now, you'll need to create transports on a case-by-case basis for each foreign messaging system you want to access.

Although communicating with other servers via jabber:server or transports adds valuable features to your Jabber server, there are two other practical issues that are essential to creating a finished server: server deployment and management. I consider these issues more important than S2S communication. If you can't install and administer your server, your users will not care if the server can talk to other systems.

9.2.4 Deployment of Jabber servers and components

Deployment is the first thing that your server's operator will encounter when dealing you're your server. It involves:

- *Provisioning*—Packing up the resources required by the server and installing them in proper locations.

---

[6] It is a good idea to follow the servlet pattern of specifying what servlets handle which URLs in a separate file or through an administration interface. See how the Tomcat servlet engine does for an example.

[7] You might also consider addressing it to the Jabber server using a special email address. The Jabber server can then check for incoming emails to the special address and convert them into Jabber messages.

[8] See the JavaMail standard Java extension (java.sun.com) for an easy to use Java library for accessing email and news systems.

- *Configuring*—Setting up the server's settings, and its environment.
- *Launching*—Getting the server up and running.

In most cases, provisioning and launching server software is a fairly straightforward process. There are many tools that can help you in this process. In the case of Java servers, be sure to remember the Java Runtime Environment (JRE) is part of the resources needed. Not ensuring that a JRE is available, properly installed, and in the correct version can often ruin the best-laid plans.

Configuring the Jabber server is often the most challenging aspect of deploying Jabber servers. In general, configuring the server itself is straightforward and can be done via configuration files. For example, the Jabber open source server uses a simple XML file that works fairly well. The difficulty really begins when trying to configure the server's network environment for maximum performance and security.

In general, the major problems usually center on server names and network security. The simpler is server domain name configuration. As we have seen, clients and servers connect to Jabber servers based on their human-friendly, host domain name. The standard Internet technology for mapping host names to machine addresses is the DNS.

There are a wide variety of tricks you can play with DNS to create pretty much any mapping you like between various host names and machine addresses. For example, I've already mentioned using round-robin DNS to map the same host name to multiple machines in a server farm. This allows multiple machines to share the load of supporting a large number of clients as shown in figure 9.6.

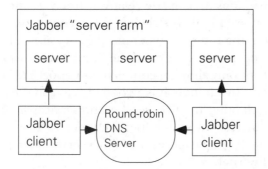

Figure 9.6 A round-robin DNS server directs clients looking up the same domain name to different servers in a Jabber server farm. Redirecting incoming connections allows the DNS server to spread the processing load between servers or "fail-over" to backup servers when primary servers in the farm crash.

In addition, you may wish to have the Jabber server running on a machine with one host name, but have Jabber connections bound for one machine routed to another when connecting to the Jabber port. For example, I may want to run my server on my Jabber machine with the name jabber.shigeoka.com. However, I'd like to have my Jabber IDs use user@shigeoka.com. Logically my Jabber server is shigeoka.com even if it is hosted on jabber.shigeoka.com.

Based on the server name of the Jabber ID, clients will try to connect to shigeoka.com on port 5222 to access my Jabber server. I can configure my router to detect these connections and redirect it to `jabber.shigeoka.com` on port 5222. All other requests (for example, webpage requests on port 80) go to the real shigeoka.com machine, which is my web server.

These are common server configuration issues that are faced by network administrators. It is well worth hiring a network engineering consultant or reading up on networking technologies and techniques in order to ensure that you have properly set up your Jabber network environment.

Once you have your network configured to create the connections you want, you need to configure the network to protect you from connections you don't want. These issues fall under the broad umbrella of network security.

9.2.5 *Server security: creating protected Jabber services*

Jabber servers are like all other Internet servers when it comes to vulnerability to attack. They provide valuable resource that people will try to exploit or destroy. Network engineers have come up with several standard tools for controlling these security risks. One of the most common is the *firewall*.

Firewalls typically allow connections to be made relatively freely in one direction (out onto the Internet) but are highly restrictive in the connections they allow in the other direction (from the Internet to behind the firewall). A firewall limits the parts of your network that people outside of the firewall can attack.

Firewalls can increase security by only allowing connections to port 5222 of the Jabber server machine (figure 9.7). In addition, it is a good idea to run the Jabber server on a dedicated machine. All other Internet servers and services should be shut down to prevent malicious attacks through telnet, web servers, FTP servers, and so forth. Notice that this firewall setup exposes the Jabber server on port 5222 to direct connections from the Internet.

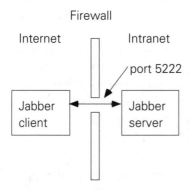

Figure 9.7
A firewall blocks all Internet traffic except through port 5222. This restriction protects the Jabber server while still allowing clients to access it.

This is a necessary risk, as you must allow clients to directly connect to the Jabber server. One of the most valuable services that Jabber servers offer clients is that it allows two clients to exchange messages while both remain safely behind their own firewall. This would be impossible if the clients needed to connect directly with each other. Overcoming firewalls for direct C2C communications is one of the major obstacles to creating practical implementations of the out-of-band protocol in chapter 4.[9]

Firewalls are just the beginning of the tools you can use to protect your Jabber server from electronic attacks. Once again, if you are planning on running a commercial Jabber server, an investment in the services of a network security engineer will be money well spent. There is also a wide variety of excellent books on network security that address the generic issues facing servers on the Internet. A good place to start is *Practical Unix & Internet Security* by Garfinkle and Spafford and *Building Internet Firewalls* by Chapman and Zwicky (both by O'Reilly & Associates).

Deploying a Jabber server tends to get more difficult as the number of users and potential attackers increase. On the one extreme is a server that is connected directly to the Internet and services users from anywhere on the Internet. However, many of these issues are not significant if your network is small and well-protected.

For example, the Java server presented in this book can be deployed as a standard Java application on a protected small-business (20-person) LAN without the need for firewalls, fancy DNS setups, or routers. It is unlikely that your employees will try to hack into your Jabber server, and the number of users on your system will probably never exceed the capabilities of your server's machine. In addition,

---

[9] The jabber:iq:pass (PASS – Proxy Accept Socket Service) is a proposed Jabber standard to allow the server to assist clients in transferring out-of-band data between clients behind firewalls.

the cost of a failure of the Jabber server will probably be minimal. If the server goes down for a few minutes, someone in the office can go over to the machine and restart it.

Large installations face more sources of attack (including from within the organization). In addition, the cost of server failures can become quite large. Any downtime can cost large amounts of money. In such systems, deployment and network security isn't the only important problem facing your server. Managing the server and its users can often loom as a much greater problem.

9.2.6 *Jabber server management*

Like deployment, server management needs often depend on the type of server and the number of users you are supporting. In small networks, simply knowing the server is running rudimentary user management and that is often sufficient. Larger servers will have larger management needs. In general, Jabber servers should consider mechanisms for managing:

- *Users and their accounts*—Creating, removing, reviewing, editing (resetting passwords), and so forth.
- *Resource consumption*—Network "throttling" to control bandwidth usage, database connections, memory usage, and so forth.
- *Software "health" and updates*—Memory leaks, versioning, uptime, and so forth.
- *Audit trails*—Logging, errors, resource accesses, security violations, alerting, reporting, and so forth.
- *Usage policies*—Authorization based on user accounts, time of day, message content, and so forth.
- *Server connections and transports*—Limiting connections, updating connections, closing connections, upgrading/downgrading connections, and so forth.

In addition, in large corporate environments, organizations often have established, standard software and network management tools. Integration with these tools can greatly increase the benefits and appeal of your Jabber server. Java programmers have many excellent options for adding these features. The best is probably using the Java Management Extensions (JMX), a standard Java management extension standard available from java.sun.com.

9.2.7 *Adding reliability and availability*

Servers are often mission-critical parts of businesses. They are expected to offer continuous services without errors. These qualities are usually expressed as the reliability and availability of a server.

Reliability measures the correctness of a server's operation. In other words, how often does the server make mistakes and are the mistakes repairable? Reliability is measured in a percentage with the state of the art server measuring *five nines*, or 99.999-percent reliability.

Availability measures how long the server can provide continuous service. Unlike reliability that indicates errors, availability includes expected service interruptions. For example, servers often must be taken offline in order to upgrade, back up, or maintain them. Availability is typically measured in downtime with state of the art server availability being measured in minutes of downtime over a year.

In order to create high-reliability, high-availability servers, engineers have developed a variety of techniques and tools. The most prominent are:

- *Transactions*—Operations are conducted so they pass the ACID test. This helps to increase the reliability of a server.
  - *[A]tomic*—An operation consisting of multiple steps is carried out as an atomic operation (completely or not at all).
  - *[C]onsistent*—Whether an operation is successful or fails, it will leave the system in a well-defined and consistent state.
  - *[I]solation*—Operations are carried out in isolation. Parallel operations do not affect other operations.
  - *[D]urability*—The results of the operation should become persistent when the transaction completes.
- *Fail-over*—Clusters of servers work together as a single server, or run as mirrors of a master server. When a particular server fails, other servers "instantly" and seamlessly take its place and the service "fails-over" to the other machines. Fail-over helps to increase the availability of the server.
- *Multithreading*—Servers use multiple threads of execution to create more responsive and higher-capability applications. Ensuring that multiple threads of execution are thread-safe can be tricky. The failure to create thread-safe applications is often a large source of server reliability problems.

None of these advanced server features are straightforward or simple to implement. However, Java provides several features and standard extension libraries that can help. Most of these are covered in the Java 2 Enterprise Edition (J2EE) APIs.

In addition, I suggest that users investigate the use of Java Jini (www.jini.org and /java.sun.com/products/jini), another standard Java technology. Jini provides a distributed computing framework complete with transaction support and a simple programming model for creating mission-critical Java servers.

Our Jabber server is half of the Jabber equation. Our Java Jabber client software is also important for creating a Jabber IM system. Like our server, the client code is also missing some useful features that should be considered when using it to build full-featured Jabber clients.

9.3 Client missing pieces

Our Jabber client software provides basic IM functionality and is designed for testing Jabber servers. However, creating simple testing clients is just the beginning of what you can do using the Jabber protocols and custom Java client software. In order to increase the value of the client developed in this book, you may wish to pursue one or more avenues for further client development.

Our client only implements the core Jabber protocols and three IQ extension protocols. There are many other useful Jabber protocols, especially standard IQ extension protocols. Clients will be able to offer users more functionality by completing the implementation of as many Jabber protocols as possible. In addition, our client software does a minimal amount of probing to query a server's capabilities before trying to use them. You can make the client more robust by probing for capabilities and intelligently handling errors and other server responses.

Beyond implementing the Jabber protocols, client developers can extend our client software to address other Jabber client needs. The most interesting is creating graphical user agent clients, enhancing existing applications, and developing innovative chatbots that offer "IM services."

Let's examine these in more detail by discussing the most visible Jabber client software development area: user agent clients.

9.3.1 User agent clients

User agent clients are software applications that act on behalf of the user (hence the name user agent). In order to do this, these client applications must have some way to interact with the user. The most common design is to use a GUI, presenting the client's functionality in windows, buttons, and menus.

The Java development environment makes it simple to create GUI applications using the AWT or Swing libraries. Both are designed to use the MVC design pattern introduced in chapter 3. Our Jabber client software implements the Model of the MVC pattern, leaving you to implement the user interface to provide the View and Controller.[10]

Our `JabberModel` class is especially easy to hook up to Swing GUIs using our event-based packet handling design. In most cases, packet events delivered by the `QueueThread` can be used to trigger GUI changes such as displaying incoming messages or updating the roster with presence updates and roster pushes. The user provides inputs in reaction to these GUI changes.

GUI user agents aren't the only useful design in Jabber. The pervasive nature of IM encourages the development of alternative user interfaces including:

- *Embedded devices*—"Small" IM clients in devices like pagers, mobile phones, and PDAs like the Palm Pilot. The J2ME is becoming increasingly popular among developers because it extends Java into these smaller devices. Unlike desktops, smaller devices require completely different user interface designs, often sacrificing features for ease of use.

- *Command-line clients*—Simple, scriptable clients can often fill a diverse set of needs where a graphical client would be overkill. In addition, there are situations where a simple text-based interface is all that you can access (for example, in a telnet session to a server).

- *Voice-activated applications*—Voice recognition and speech synthesis software is becoming increasingly powerful and accessible. Imagine providing a Jabber IM client you could access over any telephone and control with your voice. Voice-based systems are also useful when the device has a highly constrained user interface or no visual interface at all.

- *3D systems*—The 2D interface provided by the typical desktop GUI is useful. Adding a third dimension allows you to create innovative clients that can display large amounts of complex information.

These are just some examples of user agent Jabber clients. These features can differentiate your client from the crowd and enhance the user experience. I look forward to seeing what you decide to do with your Jabber client software.

In many cases, IM will not be the primary feature of your application. Jabber can provide useful capabilities to your application. Adding Jabber support to your existing application is relatively simple using our client software.

---

[10] I personally like to use IDEs such as Borland's JBuilder (www.Borland.com) to create a GUI. Later, I hook up the GUI to the Model in a normal programming editor.

9.3.2 *Enhancing existing applications*

Many of today's applications would benefit significantly from integrated communication capabilities. We have already seen this trend with email. Most of today's best user applications have facilities to send information using email. For example, most spreadsheet programs allow you to email the spreadsheet you're working on from within the spreadsheet program rather than having to use an external email user agent.[11]

The same is true for IM capabilities. Imagine wanting to ask a simple question of a coworker regarding the spreadsheet. If you had a Jabber client built into the spreadsheet program, you could check your coworker's presence status, and if they're available, start a chat with them.

In addition, IM opens the door for other collaborative features. Imagine that same spreadsheet program except now you can start a group spreadsheet where a single spreadsheet is shared among users. As users make changes to the spreadsheet, the changes are sent as specially formatted IM messages to the other users in the group, perhaps using the groupchat protocol. Collaboration features in such a spreadsheet application allows a group of people to edit the same spreadsheet while chatting using normal Jabber messaging.

Creating our own IM system to support this would be difficult. However, our Jabber client and server are more than adequate for the task. Once again, the JabberModel class provides an easy to use way to access Jabber functionality on the client-side with a minimum amount of work.

The extensibility of the client, server and the IQ protocols opens up the possibility of creating your own IQ extension protocols to provide advanced, application specific features. The possibilities are endless and I expect a large amount of future IM development to be directed in this direction.

Embedded IM in applications is not the only brave new world for IM systems. They also provide a framework for providing the next wave of Internet services using automated chatbots.

9.3.3 *Chatbots: creating IM services*

The chatbot is an application that autonomously behaves like another IM user on the Jabber system. When you send messages to the chatbot, the chatbot application automatically generates its own responses. People develop chatbots to fill a variety of needs. Some are purely whimsical, like automatic poetry generators, or chatbots that tell you jokes.

---

[11] Java developers can use the JavaMail standard Java extension.

However, chatbots can provide useful services. For example, they can provide weather reports when you ask it and automatically send you an IM to alert you of dangerous weather advisories for your area. Another useful chatbot service is machine translations of foreign languages. Imagine chatting with someone who speaks a language like Japanese, you don't understand. You could send their messages to a Japanese-to-English interpret chatbot to translate it.

Chatbot applications of Jabber IM technology can greatly enhance the value of a Jabber system without having to make changes to Jabber servers or other Jabber clients. All you need to do is write a separate Jabber chatbot client application that understands incoming IM messages and responds to them.

Chatbots most closely resemble the test client code we've been using throughout this book. In general, they have no user interface and they communicate exclusively via Jabber packets. The possible applications for chatbots are virtually unlimited. A few examples:

- *Customer support*—Chatbots can answer frequently asked questions and intelligently route more difficult problems to the appropriate support personnel. Many Jabber servers will run a chatbot specifically to provide online help for users.

- *Information services*—Chatbots can provide information on demand, or as Internet updates occur. Possible information services include weather reports/alerts, stock prices, sport scores, advertising alerts, security alerts, news services, and time updates.

- *Lookup services*—Unlike information services that push information to a user, lookup services allow the user to search for information. These go beyond the capabilities that would be provided by a typical web search engine. Phone books, corporate databases, dictionaries, translators, library card catalogs, article searches, and so forth are excellent candidates for chatbot lookup services.

- *Companion/Guides*—The Internet is a big place and sometimes it is nice to have a companion or guide with you. Chatbots can monitor your actions and send suggestions and guidance. Artificial intelligence (AI) techniques will be extremely useful in developing these chatbots. In general, initial systems will probably be highly targeted. For example, a retirement guide chatbot could help employees discover their company's retirement programs, research which option is best for them, and step them through the application process.

In many ways, creating chatbots is a new frontier where creatively meeting customer needs can provide huge rewards for users and developers. The idea behind chatbots as Internet services is a key part of many advanced Jabber-based systems. We'll take a look at these advanced Jabber applications in the next chapter.

9.4 Conclusions

Although we've created a fully functional Jabber IM system, there remain many finishing touches that can be added to our Jabber client and server software. In particular, you should consider the many additional error checking, usability, and robustness improvements that will take the software from an educational toy to a production-ready tool.

In many cases, these changes can result in significantly extending the Jabber system beyond simple IM. This is especially true in the case of specialized Jabber clients such as embedded application clients and chatbots. One of the most exciting aspects of Jabber is the ability to either extend the basic protocols, or to build systems on top of Jabber to tackle a wide variety of important serious problems facing enterprises today.

In the next chapter, we'll take a look at these potential enterprise Jabber systems and the tools we have available to build them.

Enterprise Jabber

10

There is more to instant messaging systems than instant messaging. To explain this seemingly contradictory statement, we need to take a step back from our discussions of Java IM and Jabber to look at the big picture:

- *IM does not exist in a vacuum*—there is a lot of Internet infrastructure and IM systems will need to "play nicely" in order to find its place in the mainstream. Deploying into existing networked systems requires consideration for concerns outside of IM such as working with standard system management tools, integrating with auditing systems, and accessing existing services such as directory servers.

- *IM can do more than messaging*—If IM is only useful for simple text messaging, it's an interesting technology. However, IM systems are being used for more than simple messaging. Microsoft is betting its future on systems that rely heavily on IM technologies and dragging the rest of the computing industry along for the ride. AOL is creating IM-based consumer systems that may transform how a large percentage of online users interact on the Internet. This future market environment makes IM an essential technology for tomorrow's developer. It is vital to keep our eyes on a prize greater than messaging. IM could become a new standard layer of network abstraction on top of TCP/IP.

Chapter 9 covered an alphabet soup of standard Java technologies such as JMX and others that can be used to create a complete Java Jabber server that fits into existing enterprise Java infrastructures. In fact, simply creating Jabber systems in Java is the foot in the door that we need for getting IM into serious deployments.

In this chapter, we'll examine enterprise messaging features that corporate developers will expect, but which are missing from the standard Jabber IM system. Overcoming these shortfalls will enable Jabber to serve in capacities far exceeding normal IM.

One of the most interesting enterprise uses of Jabber is MOM, where messaging systems are used as frameworks for building larger enterprise applications. We'll take a look at how Jabber can serve in these systems.

We'll also spend a good amount of time on the JMS API. It is the closest Java standard to Jabber IM and provides several interesting options to the Java Jabber developer. We'll examine the differences and similarities between the two technologies that would be important in either creating Jabber functionality in JMS servers or building JMS compatibility into Jabber servers.

Once we have grounded ourselves in the details of enterprise Jabber, we can let our imaginations run free to explore the possibilities offered by enterprise-ready IM technology.

Finally, we'll examine alternatives to Jabber and how Jabber stacks up to them. As with most software paradigms, Jabber is not a silver bullet that will solve all of your problems. It is important to know what the alternatives are. As engineers, we are professionally obligated to use the best technology for the problem at hand and not get stuck in fads and hype. There is a common saying, "When all you have is a hammer, everything looks like a nail." We need to make sure our toolboxes contain more than just a hammer so that we can meet tomorrow's challenges effectively. However, we'll also see that Jabber may be one of our most useful tools that we will want to return to time and time again.

Let's kick things off by examining the crucial enterprise messaging features that are missing from the Jabber standard.

10.1 *What is needed to support enterprise messaging*

Jabber was originally designed as an IM system for consumer communication. This had a strong influence on its architecture and protocols. This legacy has had some benefits including an approachable and easily understood design. Unfortunately, Jabber also lacks features that are considered essential for its use in mission-critical applications, thus relegating it to toy or hobbyist status in many enterprise developers' minds.

The Jabber community is aware of this problem and is very interested in extending Jabber to plug these holes. In this section, we'll examine the three major issues I consider the most essential for preparing Jabber for serious enterprise use: security, quality of service, and administration.

10.1.1 *Enhancing Jabber security*

The most unfortunate and understandable shortcoming with the current Jabber system is the lack of industrial-strength security. This is unfortunate because security will likely be the first thing enterprise shops will examine, and is most likely to be the reason for Jabber's immediate elimination as a candidate technology. The lack of heavy-duty security is understandable; Jabber was designed as a consumer IM system where the need for security is limited.

Other than the need for protecting privacy and restricting access to server resources, consumers are typically willing to accept little to no security for communication systems. An excellent example of consumers' indifference to inadequate security is the security of email. Email security is weaker than Jabber's, but is considered adequate for most users and is even used for important business communication.

However, consider how mission-critical enterprise systems are built on top of standard email relatively few, and the problems that arise when it is used in that capacity. Most of the large-scale problems that cause so much damage to businesses are email viruses exploiting flaws in the less than stellar security of enterprise email systems.[1]

Now you may be wondering, "What about the Jabber authentication protocols? Don't they provide Jabber security?" In order to understand the role of Jabber authentication, it is important to first understand what enterprises expect from security and where Jabber authentication fits into that overall picture.

Computer security is concerned with creating and enforcing several important properties:

From table 10.1, it is easy to see that there are several security holes to be plugged to create a secure Jabber system. Fortunately for Jabber, most IM users today are not highly concerned with security as IM is still primarily used for social and entertainment communication. However, as IM is rapidly being adopted in commercial settings, security will become an important part of the IM formula.

Table 10.1 **Computer security properties compared with Jabber's present capabilities.**

Security Property	Description	Existing Technology	Jabber Support
Authentication	Ensures an entity is who it claims to be.	JAAS[a], Kerebos[b], Microsoft Passport	Jabber authentication protocol[c]
Authorization	Determines what an entity has permissions for accessing (data) or controlling (resources).	JAAS, access control lists	Binary authorization. Unauthenticated users are granted certain rights, and authenticated users others.
Integrity	Ensures data has not been tampered with.	Message digests	None
Nonrepudiation	Ensures that the author of data can always be identified.	Digital signatures	None
Confidentiality	Ensures data can be read only by authorized entities.	Encryption	Limited client/server eavesdropping confidentiality using SSL.

a. Java Authentication and Authorization Service (JAAS), a standard Java extension and soon to be a part of the Java Standard Edition (anticipated in Sun's upcoming JDK 1.4).

b. Kerebos is a widely supported authentication service built into many operating systems including most Unix OS's and Microsoft Windows 2000 and later. It is supported by JAAS and Microsoft Passport.

c. The Jabber authentication protocol does not use an existing authentication technology.

---

[1] This is especially true of the enterprise email system implementation of a particular Redmond vendor (that shall remain nameless).

There are a few ways to beef up Jabber security, including conducting communications over SSL and implementing your own, ad hoc security system on top of Jabber. We'll examine these options next.

Security through SSL

As we saw in chapter 3, the most common technique for communicating with a Jabber server is to connect a network socket to port 5222 of the Jabber server. Unfortunately the connection is vulnerable to eavesdropping (not confidential) and the connection itself relies on the client locating and connecting to the correct Jabber server. The former is a weakness of sending unencrypted data across the network, and the latter is a consequence of the insecure nature of DNS and the lack of any server authentication with a client.

You can overcome both of these problems in one step by using SSL.[2] Part of the SSL connection negotiation process requires the server to present its SSL credentials (typically a certificate signed by a well-known certificate authority service). The client can check to make sure the certificate is valid and matches the server to which it is connected. SSL also encrypts all information sent over the SSL socket so eavesdroppers on the network cannot read any of the data passing between client and server. Jabber servers that support SSL connections should listen on the standard Jabber SSL port 5223.

Although the information between client and server is encrypted by SSL, and therefore confidential, the data loses its confidentiality and integrity once it reaches the server. Clients may not be able to trust the server with their messages or with how the server delivers the messages to recipients.

For example, imagine you want to send a nasty message about the Jabber server administrator Bob to his supervisor. Bob could set up the Jabber server so any messages sent to his supervisor containing his name will be held for his approval. He can then edit the message or erase it before it reaches his supervisor.

Unfortunately, Jabber clients and servers do not commonly use SSL because SSL is computationally expensive. Both sender and receiver must encrypt and decrypt all of the information passing over the connection. This is fine for a limited information exchange such as sending small amounts of financial or other sensitive information to a web server (SSL's intended use). However, this much overhead is not practical for the vast majority of IM traffic.

Ideally, clients should be able to create messages and send them through insecure servers while always maintaining the message's confidentiality. There are no

---

[2] Secure socket connections are supported natively in the 1.4 version of the Java Standard Edition and can be added as a standard extension library to previous Java runtime environments.

standard ways to accomplish this using the existing Jabber standards. However, you can add these features on top of the existing Jabber system using your own ad hoc security system.

Ad hoc security

You can easily add a custom security system without requiring changes to the Jabber standards, protocols, or the Jabber server. All you have to do is add the support for your security extensions to your "secure messaging" Jabber clients. Recall from chapter 4, Jabber provides the <x> extension protocol to allow you to extend any of the core Jabber protocols. For example, an <x> packet in a <message> packet can enclose a standard encrypted XML subdocument containing encrypted data. Such a message packet might look something like the following:

```
<message from='senderJID' to='recipientJID'>
  <x xmlns='custom:security'>
    xml encrypted document here
  </x>
</message>
```

In this case, you are using the <message> packet as a simple envelope to send the encrypted data through the Jabber system. Your custom encryption system's separate algorithms and protocols, not Jabber, ensure the security of the message. Notice that the encrypted document can be anything you wish as long as it is valid XML. This gives you the freedom to design your own security system or use an existing standard encryption system such as W3C's proposed XML encryption standard (www.w3c.org).

In addition, you are free to add new IQ extensions in your own <query> namespaces to facilitate things like key exchange and other security support features. Obviously, if you want the server to help support any of the custom extensions, you will have to modify the server.

However the beauty of the Jabber's easily extensible design is that you can work entirely within the Jabber standards while still making these modifications. Sticking with the Jabber standards is a huge advantage. For example, this gives you the option of using off-the-shelf Jabber servers or your own customized servers depending on your needs. In addition, standard Jabber packets will be routed over standard Jabber servers allowing you to only customize the parts of the Jabber network that best suit your needs.

The future of Jabber security

The Jabber community is well aware of the security shortcomings of the current Jabber system. In many ways these security holes have resulted from the evolution of Jabber from its simple IM roots. In addition, one of Jabber's primary goals is to make the creation of Jabber clients simple. Security tends to be difficult to implement well. Making a robust security system a required core part of the Jabber standard may not meet with Jabber's design goals.

To address these concerns and perhaps establish a new security framework for Jabber, the Jabber Software Foundation has formed a security JIG. If you have serious security needs, you should monitor this JIG closely or join in to help shape the future of Jabber security.

Jabber security will need to address all five aspects of computer security discussed earlier:

- Authentication
- Authorization
- Confidentiality
- Integrity
- Nonrepudiation

In addition, there should be standard ways to integrate Jabber security with existing systems.

The design of Java's inherent security mechanisms and the additional security standards that are part of the Java 2 Enterprise Edition is a good example of how the security of an environment like J2EE can be integrated with the security systems of existing applications like databases and messaging servers. Java security standards provide standard mechanisms for connecting to and accessing existing security systems such as authentication services. For example, single sign-on features are possible using existing Kerebos[3] authentication systems through the Java Authentication and Authorization Services(JAAS). A user signs onto her computer using Kerebos and that sign-on automatically authenticates her with any other JAAS enabled system.

Single sign-on authentication is a hot topic with Microsoft pushing its Passport .NET single sign-on service (www.microsoft.com). Many other vendors have banded together to form an open alternative called the Liberty Alliance(www.libertyalliance.com).[4] The Microsoft Passport system is proprietary, available now,

---

[3] Kerebos is a standard Unix authentication service also found (in a mutated form) in Windows NT/2000/XP.

[4] Sun Microsystems, creator of Java, is a key founder of the group.

and easy to use,[5] but it has suffered from the typical problems Microsoft seems to have with security.

The Liberty Alliance, on the other hand, has not yet produced any standards or software. It is beginning to look more and more like a purely defensive marketing move. The resulting uncertainty is confusing and has most developers taking a wait-and-see strategy. The Jabber community is closely monitoring both systems and promises support for both if possible.

Next, let's take a look at the quality of service issues facing advanced Jabber systems.

10.1.2 Guaranteed quality of service

Quality of service (QoS) describes traits of a system that guarantee a certain level of performance. The Jabber standards do not specify any QoS requirements on Jabber clients or servers, leaving it up to implementers to create their own QoS guarantees and marketing language.[6] Typical messaging QoS guarantees cover:

- *Delivery timing*—In some applications, the time between a message being sent and received can greatly affect the application's behavior. For example, a nuclear power plant controller must control the amount of coolant going into the reactor to prevent a meltdown. A command must be sent from the controller to the coolant valves within one second or the reactor could melt down. Being able to guarantee that messages will be received within one second is vital. This certainty is required for real-time behavior. A less dramatic and more common example is multimedia where broadcasts must be sent at a certain rate to avoid transmissions from breaking up.

- *Delivery ordering*—If you can guarantee the ordering of message delivery, your application can display certain behaviors that are difficult to produce otherwise.

- *Delivery priorities*—Some messages are more important than others. For example, nuclear reactor control messages should be sent through the system as quickly as possible while worker's chat messages can be delayed for half a second without causing any problems. This is especially important in systems experiencing heavy loads.

---

[5] Easy using Microsoft tools on Windows... It remains to be seen how easy the system is to access from non-Microsoft platforms.

[6] In my opinion, it is just as important for a standard to establish standardized marketing language as it is to provide technical standards. By enforcing a uniform marketing nomenclature, end users can make informed purchasing decisions by comparing "oranges to oranges" rather than the all-too-typical "apples to oranges" comparisons that confuse and frustrate buyers.

- *Delivery transaction*—It is essential to ensure that a message is delivered to a recipient once and only once. For example, a message may represent an order for parts. When the order is sent the sender must be able to rely on the system to deliver the message. In addition, the system can't accidentally deliver the same message twice as it would cause a double order to be placed. Transactions also strictly define who is responsible for ensuring the delivery of the message, the states of the system before and after the transaction, and the precise behavior of the system in the event of success or failure.

There are no standard ways of specifying these QoS constraints or requirements within the Jabber protocols. Servers and clients are free to extend the basic Jabber protocols using <x> or <iq> extensions to add these features. However, since they are not standard, you cannot rely on them to be enforced or supported throughout the Jabber network.

This may or may not be a problem depending on your needs. For example, in many situations you must ensure message delivery QoS within your own organization and with other partner companies. Collectively, you can establish a set of standard <x> or <iq> QoS extensions and require their support from all participants. On the other hand, this will prevent you from extending your application beyond this group of Jabber domains. For example, if you must send messages to a new partner company, you can't ensure QoS with them without their supporting your proprietary QoS extensions.

The obvious solution to these issues is to create standard QoS Jabber extensions. This is not as difficult as it may sound. The Jabber Software Foundation is always open to new standards efforts and now provides a structured process for passing new Jabber standards. As Jabber begins to be used in advanced systems, I anticipate standard Jabber QoS extensions to become an area of great interest. The beauty of the Jabber protocols is that you can forge ahead and add features to meet your immediate needs without breaking standards compliance. In addition, when you are ready or see the need, you have clear processes in place for creating new Jabber standards.

The last major problem facing advanced Jabber systems is administration.

10.1.3 *Creating system administration tools an techniques*

Ironically, system administration is often the most overlooked component of a server-based system. This can be a showstopper in advanced systems where the capability to integrate management features with other systems is critical. For example, many large IT shops rely on centralized directory services to store and manage all user account information. Systems that can't be integrated with directory services are simply not worth the trouble to support.

The Jabber standards do not support any management or administration-related protocols. It is left to the implementer to create these as they see fit. Java provides many libraries and other tools to ensure that our software is administrable and manageable. These include:

- *JMX (Java Management Extensions)*—Exposes standard administration interfaces that allow existing system management tools to monitor and manage the application.

- *JAAS (Java Authentication and Authorization Service)*—Integrates Java security with existing authentication and authorization services.

- JNDI *(Java Naming and Directory Interface)*—Allows Java applications to generically search and manipulate naming and directory services.

It is understandable that Jabber does not specify administration or management interfaces to Jabber systems. This gives implementers the largest degree of flexibility in creating best of breed clients and servers that differentiate themselves from others. Java developers have a distinct advantage in creating administrable and manageable Jabber systems. I hope to see second-generation Jabber servers written in Java that will take Jabber to the next level of power and performance.

There are strong reasons for elevating Jabber to such high levels of performance and reliability. The most prominent is the possibility of using Jabber in MOM.

10.2 *The promise of MOM*

As mentioned in chapter 1, MOM has long been a fundamental part of enterprise systems. Like databases and other enterprise information systems, MOMs serve as generic tools that intelligent middleware uses to create applications. In the case of databases, they provide basic storage and retrieval services for middleware. In the case of Jabber and other MOMs, they provide reliable delivery of messages between applications.

There are many advantages in large, distributed systems for reliable message delivery. These include:

- *Loose coupling*—The messages in the MOM allows a very loose coupling between applications. Rather than directly calling methods or remote objects, or relying on tight coordination between distributed processes, messages break applications into distinct and independent parts. Messages also link those separate applications allowing them to carry out complex tasks. Loose coupling eases the integration of disparate systems and prevents failures in one application from bringing the entire system down.

- *Communication over space and time*—Messages can travel over space and time. We know how Jabber transports messages over space using its network protocols and standard Internet networking connections. Less obvious is Jabber's ability to deliver messages over time. Senders can dispatch messages to recipients that aren't available. The message will automatically be delivered at a later time when the recipient becomes available. The sender and recipient are essentially communicating across time with the aid of MOM.

- *Scalable*—The loose coupling of MOM systems provides many opportunities for creating scalable systems including load balancing across multiple machines in server farms.

- *Flexibility through an extra layer of abstraction*—The message represents a layer of abstraction between the sender and receiver. As long as the message stays the same, the sender and recipient can change in dramatic ways without affecting each other. This flexibility reduces interdependence between parts of the system making development, upgrades, and code maintenance easier.

The benefits of MOM systems were strong enough to have Sun make the means to access them a standard J2EE API under the JMS standard. The standard is backed by all of the major vendors of MOM systems showing the strong market for MOMs in Java enterprise solutions. Jabber fits well into the MOM landscape as an alternative to the traditional MOMs.

10.2.1 Jabber as middleware

In the midst of giants like IBM and Tibco, Jabber might seem like an unlikely competitor for MOM market share. However, Jabber systems have their own benefits that can provide significant competitive advantages over other large-scale MOM systems. These benefits include:

- *Inexpensive*—Compared with other MOM systems, today's Jabber servers are inexpensive. Cash-strapped enterprises will see Jabber as a possible replacement for the more expensive MOM systems. This is especially true for non-mission-critical applications, proof of concepts, and other systems where the expensive MOM QoS guarantees are unnecessary.

- *XML based*—XML continues to make strides as the common data exchange format for all enterprise systems. Jabber's XML roots make it a perfect part of an XML-based infrastructure. In addition, accessing other enterprise services via XML is simple using Jabber.

- *Open*—The Jabber protocols and a lot of Jabber software is open. The benefits of open software and standards are well-documented. See www.opensource.org for more information.

- *Simple*—Large and small enterprises can easily understand and use Jabber with little training. In addition, developers can implement their own Jabber clients and servers with a minimum of effort.

- *Lightweight*—Jabber's lack of built-in enterprise features such as QoS guarantees makes the protocols extremely lightweight. As a consequence, the software that runs the Jabber network is also compact and efficient. Expensive enterprise features can be added or removed to suit a customer's needs resulting in a much more customizable MOM solution.

The idea of Jabber as MOM is an active area of discussion in the Jabber community. Two user groups have been started at www.jabber.org: JAM and Jabber RPC. Both groups are interested in the application of Jabber technologies as middleware. JAM tends to have a more general discussion on the topic while Jabber RPC concentrates on specific bridges to existing XML RPC efforts such as SOAP.

As Java developers, our interests in JAM probably fall along similar lines. In particular, we're likely to be interested in Jabber and how it relates and integrates with JMS. In addition, Microsoft .NET and XML-based web services initiative will require J2EE Java servers to offer XML access to their services. Jabber may serve as a perfect lightweight bridge between J2EE and XML-based systems. We'll cover both next starting with Jabber and the JMS.

10.2.2   *Jabber and the J2EE Java Messaging Service*

As with other J2EE APIs, the JMS is a standard Java interface to messaging systems.[7] It allows Java developers to access and use messaging systems with a generic Java API, protecting them from the details of any particular one. This gives Java developers the ability to choose best-of-breed messaging systems and switch between them at any time without rewriting any of their own Java code. JMS vendors differentiate themselves by providing JMS-compatible messaging systems with different strengths to match different customer needs.

---

[7] There are many excellent sources of information on JMS including the Sun Java website (java.sun.com) and practically all J2EE books. A good place to start is the book *Java Message Service* by Monson-Haefel, et al (O'Reilly & Associates).

JMS offers two interesting options. First, for organizations that already have JMS servers, developers can modify servers to offer Jabber services. This lets you build upon an existing enterprise server and simply add Jabber functionality. Your JMS Jabber server will also be able to leverage the built-in enterprise features of the JMS server including its security system and quality of service features.

Extending a JMS server to support Jabber is accomplished by writing JMS clients that handle the Jabber connections and parse/produce XML packets. Essentially the JMS system replaces the `PacketQueue` and `QueueThread` classes on our Java server with JMS queues and channels. Jabber groupchat servers and other embedded Jabber services can be built as additional JMS clients. Alternatively, some JMS systems will support the use of message-driven Enterprise JavaBeans (EJB). In those cases, the services can be implemented as EJBs.[8]

JMS offers a second option to existing Jabber servers. JMS provides an API that you can implement to expand your market into the established Java messaging marketplace. The benefits of doing this are numerous. The Jabber server suddenly becomes another standard JMS option that enterprise Java developers can immediately integrate into existing JMS-based systems. In addition, by complying with the JMS standard, the Jabber server will be forced to address most of the missing advanced Jabber features such as security and QoS mentioned earlier.

To become a JMS server, the Jabber server must support JMS clients by creating a JMS driver. The JMS API only specifies the interface between JMS clients and this JMS driver. What goes on behind the scenes between the JMS driver and server is hidden from the JMS client. This gives implementers several standard options when creating a JMS driver including: direct Java Remote Method Invocation (RMI) server access drivers, smart drivers, or protocol adapter drivers.

In a direct RMI server access driver, the driver contains RMI stubs that allow the driver to transparently manipulate remote server objects as if they were local to the client (figure 10.1). The design requires both the driver and server to be written in Java (or have Java access). In those cases where Java is present on both the client and server, a direct RMI connection can be the simplest way of creating a JMS driver.

---

[8] EJBs are often thought of as being synonymous with J2EE. Almost every J2EE book I've read has covered EJBs in depth. Programming both EJBs and JMS clients is beyond the scope of this book and I refer you to the vast library of J2EE programming books.

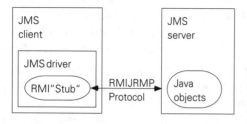

Figure 10.1
A direct RMI server access JMS driver uses RMI to access remote Java objects on the server.

A smart driver implements the JMS system within the driver itself as shown in figure 10.2. This is a common approach in distributed JMS systems that use peer-to-peer technologies to communicate directly between JMS clients. Distributed JMS systems are relatively rare. In addition, this design provides no method for integration with a Jabber server.

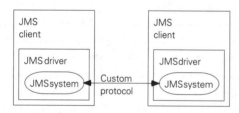

Figure 10.2
A smart driver creates the JMS system within the JMS driver. There is no room for Jabber integration in this design, making it uninteresting for Jabber developers.

Finally, a protocol adapter driver converts JMS calls to the native messaging network format for the MOM (figure 10.3.) In our case, we would convert JMS calls to Jabber packets and send them over a normal Jabber client connection. The advantage of this approach is we don't need to change the server to support the driver and the server does not have to be written in Java.

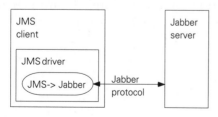

Figure 10.3
A protocol adapter JMS driver converts JMS calls to the messaging system's native protocols. In our case, converting JMS calls to Jabber packets. This type of driver requires no server modifications.

Unfortunately, as we'll see later, the JMS protocols are a superset of the Jabber protocols making it impossible to support a protocol adapter driver using standard Jabber protocols. However, we can always add new Jabber extension protocols to fill in the missing gaps.

There are many challenges to creating a JMS-compliant Java Jabber server. Let's look at the major obstacles facing such a project.

Differences

There are several significant differences between what the JMS standard requires and what the Jabber standards provide. Each of these must be overcome to provide JMS interfaces to Jabber servers:

- *Data typing*—JMS is based on Java with its strong data typing. Jabber, on the other hand, uses XML where text is the only recognized data type. Jabber JMS systems must be able to preserve typing in Jabber messages. There are XML standards being developed as part of the XML RPC efforts to provide XML typing.[9] These may be adapted to provide Jabber message typing.

- *Messaging guarantees*—The JMS standard provides standard methods and expectations for QoS. As we've discussed earlier, Jabber does not provide these QoS features by default.[10]

- *Message expiry*—JMS provides for message expiry as opposed to Jabber where messages are stored indefinitely until forwarded to the proper recipient. There are proposed Jabber standards for adding this feature to Jabber. For now though, there are no guarantees for a compliant Jabber server to honor message expiry.

- *Messaging model separate from architecture*—The JMS messaging model has JMS clients sending messages through the JMS system to other JMS clients. The routing of the messages and guarantee of QoS is handled by the JMS system. However, the architecture of the JMS system is transparent to JMS clients. This means the JMS implementation can be a centralized JMS server, a completely decentralized, peer-to-peer system, or some combination. Jabber defines the messaging model as well as architecture, forming a subset of possible JMS systems.

---

[9] See www.w3c.org for more on XML typing.

[10] Message delivery is assumed to be guaranteed in Jabber. Unfortunately, in the real world, nothing is fail-proof. Jabber does not specify standard behavior in the case of delivery failure and the conditions where failure is possible.

> ■ *Message targets are server entities, not client endpoints*—In JMS, messages are sent to server-managed queues. Clients retrieve messages from these queues or are notified via events when new messages arrive. Jabber on the other hand, delivers messages directly to endpoints identified by a Jabber ID. These endpoints are assumed to be on the client with a point-to-point delivery mechanism. This difference is perhaps the most difficult to overcome.

In addition to these pervasive differences, there are specific differences between the Jabber messaging model and JMS messaging model. Let's look at the major model differences with respect to the two JMS messaging modes: publish-subscribe and point-to-point.

Publish-subscribe

The JMS publish-subscribe messaging mode, often called pub-sub, allows publishers to send a JMS message to a pub-sub queue. The queue's subscribers each get a copy of the messages in the queue. This messaging model closely resembles the behavior of Jabber presence and groupchat.

In both cases, messages are pushed to clients as they are sent by the publisher. Message delivery is a one-to-many model, sending copies of the original message to each subscriber. Additional subscribers can be added at any time, allowing the message's audience to be expanded dynamically.

However, the JMS standard requires additional features that aren't universally supported by the Jabber presence and groupchat protocols. Table 10.2 summarizes the JMS differences with Jabber protocols.

Table 10.2 Differences between JMS requirements for pub-sub messaging and built-in Jabber support for groupchat and presence.

JMS requirement	Groupchat support	Presence support
Multiple publishers to same topic.	Yes, each groupchat participant is automatically a publisher.	No, only one publisher is possible for any particular presence.
Publishers can be added at any time.	Yes, new groupchat group members can be added at any time.	No, only one publisher is possible for any particular presence.
Durable subscriptions	No, users must manually rejoin groupchat groups to receive groupchat messages.	Yes, presence subscriptions persist until canceled.
Delivery of "stored" messages to durable subscriptions (except expired messages)	No, durable subscriptions not possible.	No, presence updates are never stored for later delivery.

These differences create a superset of pub-sub features required by JMS. This makes it easier to build a Jabber system from a JMS system than the other way around. This is especially true when considering the second JMS messaging model: point-to-point messaging.

Point-to-point messaging

JMS's point-to-point(P2P or PTP) messaging model follows the one-to-one message delivery process found in the normal Jabber <message> protocol. In both cases, messages are sent one-way from producer (sender) to consumer (recipient). Messages are stored and forwarded if no consumer is available to accept the message.

JMS's PTP model differs from Jabber's message protocol in several important ways:

- *Delivery targets are queues*—As mentioned before, JMS delivery targets are server-managed queues, not clients or users as in Jabber.

- *One copy of message to a queue consumer rather than an endpoint*—Unlike Jabber, unrelated clients can subscribe to a PTP queue. This is similar to the way multiple Jabber resources can be ready to accept messages sent to a Jabber user. However, in JMS you can specify that messages are distributed to waiting consumers in a variety of ways including strict priority (as with Jabber) or round-robin.[11]

- *Message delivery is strictly ordered*—JMS requires that messages are sent to consumers in the order they are sent by message producers.

- *Message acknowledgement is required*[12]—In order to ensure a message is delivered JMS requires clients acknowledge message receipt. The JMS system will attempt to resend unacknowledged messages. JMS specifies three different types of delivery acknowledgement modes.

- *Multiple producers on each PTP queue*—JMS allows multiple producers to send messages to the same queue. This is similar to the ability of multiple clients

---

[11] *Round-Robin* describes a basic way of evenly distributing messages between consumers. Typically, a round-robin distribution is done by putting the consumers into a circular list and iteratively giving the next message to the next consumer in the list.

[12] JMS acknowledgements are similar to Jabber event messages, part of the proposed Jabber event X extension standard. See the `jabber:x:event` protocol reference in appendix A. In the Jabber model, clients must watch for delivery event packets in order to ensure that a message is delivered. If it is not, the client is responsible for resending the message. Finally, there is a significant difference between the Jabber event indicating the server has successfully sent a message to the recipient, and JMS where the client acknowledges the receipt of the message.

to send messages to the same user or resource in Jabber. However, the delivery target is a queue and not a user changing the model in subtle ways.

- *Messages can be persistent or transient*—JMS messages can be stored indefinitely for later delivery like Jabber. However, you can also specify message expiry times to avoid dead messages from clogging up the server. There is no expiry time limit so messages can be sent that expire immediately eliminating the store and forward feature entirely.

The idea of a JMS server side queue as a messaging target is a subtle difference from Jabber's user/resource delivery system. Server messaging handling has interesting effects on the ease of implementing QoS guarantees and controlling message flow. Once again, these features make it a bit simpler to move from a JMS server implementation to a Jabber server than the other way around simply because JMS is almost a superset of Jabber functionality. In other words, if you were to buy one or the other, purchase a JMS server and customize it to comply with the Jabber specification rather than the other way around.

However, if you are starting from scratch, Jabber is a much smaller and easier to implement specification. You can then expand the Jabber server to meet JMS requirements, as they are needed. In many cases, you will not need all JMS features and can avoid a lot of work by only implementing what you need.

The most difficult part of the JMS specification is advanced MOM features that are completely lacking in the Jabber standard.

Advanced JMS features

JMS requires several advanced messaging features such as message acknowledgement and server resending mentioned earlier. Most of these advanced features are provided in order to ensure that messages are delivered reliably and in a predictable and controllable manner. In general, casual messaging such as provided by Jabber is reliable and you may only experience dropped messages and other delivery failures once per hundred thousand or million messages delivered. However, in mission-critical enterprise systems that dropped message may cost your business millions of dollars!

The most useful advanced JMS feature used to increase reliability are transactions. Transactions help the server to guarantee the ACID properties covered in chapter 9. In JMS, transactions are automatically linked to a transaction session allowing you to specify messages sent in that session to be delivered under standard transaction semantics.[13]

---

[13] JMS transactions follow a basic transaction process where the sending of messages *prepares* the transaction. JMS clients are then free to *commit* or *rollback* the transaction. The traditional *two-phase commit* transaction is also available via the Java Transaction API and the transaction-related interfaces to JMS sessions.

As Java programmers starting with our Java Jabber server we can add transactions in many ways. One of the most straightforward is to implement the Java Transaction APIs, a standard Java extension. In addition, if you use a JDBC database for message storage, you can link your server's message delivery transactions to JDBC transactions. This lets the database do most of the work of implementing transactions.

Transactions are recognition of the fact that in any real-world system there will be errors delivering messages. Although it is not part of the JMS specification, most JMS servers provide other tools for dealing with delivery problems. One of the most common and useful of these are dead message queues for holding messages that have expired or are undeliverable. Dead message queues give you an opportunity to write a special JMS client that handles these dead messages.[14]

Jabber as JMS challenges

Creating a JMS-compliant Jabber server does not stop at simply implementing the JMS specification. JMS is part of the J2EE platform that requires you also to integrate with the entire J2EE environment. This poses additional challenges that have nothing to do with messaging including:

- *Security model*—J2EE requires an interoperable security model. This allows J2EE developers to use one security system across their J2EE infrastructure. This can be a benefit to Java Jabber servers as the J2EE security system is well-documented and designed, filling a gap left in the Jabber standards.

- *Deployment model*—J2EE deployment follows a well-defined process. Your Jabber server will need to support this model. Once again, this fills a gap left in the Jabber standard so may actually help rather than hurt a Jabber server project.

- *JNDI access*—JMS, as with all J2EE technologies, relies on JNDI for customization and implementation-specific tasks (such as finding the JMS driver). Again, this fills a gap in the Jabber standards and fills a critical need for any server.

Although there is a lot of work involved in supporting JMS in a Jabber server, there are just as many benefits as drawbacks. In many ways, JMS provides guidance in the features required of a mission-critical Jabber server. Following the JMS design may feel like "chasing tail lights." However, I like to think of it as avoiding reinventing the wheel. I'd rather innovate in messaging specific areas

---

[14] These clients usually log the dead messages to a file and alert system administrators of possible problems.

or applications built upon the messaging infrastructure instead of recreating yet another server configuration system to replace JNDI.

One of these hot areas of messaging innovation is occurring in the area of XML messaging. This movement has been primarily motivated by the deep interest in XML by the World Wide Web Consortium (SOAP) and Microsoft (.NET).

10.2.3 Jabber, .NET, and SOAP

XML is shaping up to become one of the most fundamental Internet technologies of the future. Not only is it a key W3C standard[15] but also Microsoft, one of the most influential software companies, has decided to make XML the foundation for many of its future technologies. This trend holds interesting possibilities for future uses of Jabber systems, which are f-based.

In this section, we'll look at the Microsoft .NET system and its reliance on XML. We'll then examine the W3C's SOAP standard for sending XML information across the network and what this means for Jabber.

Microsoft .NET platform and Jabber

Microsoft's next-generation computing framework is collectively known as .NET. It is a collection of existing and new Microsoft technologies that replace the somewhat fragmented current generation of Microsoft technologies such as DCOM, back-office servers, ActiveX, and so forth.

For Java developers, it is easiest to understand .NET as the Microsoft version of J2EE. .NET relies on a development environment composed of a virtual machine called the Common Language Runtime (CLR) and libraries similar to Java's JVM, and class libraries. The development environment is programmed by developers through a new version of the venerable Microsoft Visual Studio tools with .NET versions of Visual C++, Visual Basic, and the new Visual C#. The most significant change to Microsoft's strategy is a reliance on open standards XML for information exchange between .NET web services.

The .NET vision is to allow developers to easily create web services that allow both client/server and server-server communication and resource sharing. Users access web services in order to carry out every imaginable task from communication to paying bills to searching databases.

For Jabber developers, one of the most interesting things about .NET is its use of IM technologies for many features. For example, .NET uses a single sign-on system called Passport based on the IM authentication system. In addition, .NET web services will use XML to transport all data between .NET components.

---

[15] The Word Wide Web Consortium (W3C) is the official standards body of WWW technology.

As part of Microsoft's efforts to be a standards advocate, it has submitted many of the .NET technologies to standards bodies. For Jabber, the most interesting is the SOAP standard being developed by the W3C for transporting XML messages.

Jabber as SOAP transport

The SOAP standard establishes a standard method for exchanging information across networks. The SOAP specification describes it as:[16]

> A lightweight protocol for exchange of information in a decentralized, distributed environment. It is an XML-based protocol that consists of four parts: an envelope that defines a framework for describing what is in a message and how to process it, a transport-binding framework for exchanging messages using an underlying protocol, a set of encoding rules for expressing instances of application-defined data types and a convention for representing remote procedure calls and responses.

Its primary design goals are simplicity and extensibility. SOAP avoids common RPC features that are useful but lead to complexity of implementation including:

- Distributed garbage collection
- Boxcarring or batching of messages
- Objects-by-reference (which requires distributed garbage collection)
- Activation (which requires objects-by-reference)

Reading the SOAP specification is almost a repeat of our earlier discussion of issues we need to tackle as part of a JAM effort. In particular, SOAP is already providing standard ways for representing data types and remote procedure calls, two big problems facing a Jabber middleware solution.

SOAP currently defines an HTTP transport binding that provides a standard method for sending SOAP packets via standard web servers. Jabber is already XML-based and contains built-in packet delivery mechanisms. This makes it an excellent SOAP transport candidate. An exciting possibility exists to define a Jabber transport binding and use Jabber networks as SOAP systems.

.NET and web services are still largely hype and potential at this point. However, Microsoft is aggressively pushing forward with .NET components and there is a strong possibility that the future of network computing may rely on SOAP infrastructures. A Jabber entrepreneur is in an excellent position to grab a part of that multibillion dollar market.

---

[16] SOAP specification, version 1.2. (www.w3c.org)

JAM isn't the only exciting application of Jabber technology. There are a wide variety of other Jabber applications that hold a great deal of promise.

10.3 *Examples of Jabber applications*

If Jabber were only useful for basic IM communication, there would be plenty to get excited about. This initial market represents a large part of network usage that will probably rival email in the near future. However, there are many other applications that can be built with or on Jabber that have even more potential! In this section, we'll take a whirlwind tour of these possibilities. I hope one of them will inspire you to create the next generation of Jabber applications.

10.3.1 *Jabber groupware*

One of the biggest advantages of the Internet is the ability to efficiently communicate between people. We can exploit this communication channel to collaborate on projects in exciting new ways. Software that allows network collaboration is often referred to as *groupware*. Jabber provides a new communication channel that can be exploited to create new or improved groupware applications.

These new groupware applications can include:

- *Conferencing*—Meetings can be one of the necessary evils of working in groups. A lot of time is wasted in meetings, not to mention the overhead time spent in traveling to meeting locations (even if it's just down the hall), maintaining meeting rooms, and so forth. Jabber groupchats can provide interesting alternatives to the traditional meeting.

- *Collaborative editing (aka white-boarding)*—There are many situations where a common document must be created, edited, or discussed. The popular IBM Domino system clearly shows the market for such systems. Jabber provides an excellent framework for creating next-generation collaboration tools.

- *Calendaring*—Coordinating people's calendars, setting up meetings, and managing schedules are common problems facing people today. Networked calendaring systems have existed from the beginning of networking including the iCal standard and the ubiquitous (if security-challenged) Microsoft Outlook. Jabber provides interesting possibilities for creating next-generation calendaring systems that can exploit Jabber's concept of presence.

- *File sharing*—Sharing files is an important application that has many uses beyond Napster-like music trading. Advanced file sharing can incorporate data backups, versioning, annotations, and other features.

This is just a short list of possible groupware applications that can benefit from Jabber. I'm sure there are many others waiting to be created. On the other end of the spectrum from large, monolithic applications are lightweight network services.

10.3.2 Jabber network services

There are many small but useful services that can be exposed via Jabber networks. Network services are small network tools for providing specialized information and services. These can either be in the form of chatbots or .NET style web services, depending on whether a user or computer interacts with them. Possible network services include:

- *Time*—Providing the current date time is a valuable service. Jabber's IM features can also add alarms and alerts as well as date sensitive information such as horoscopes.

- *Weather*—Another classic information service. Asynchronous messaging allows you to send severe weather alerts.

- *Movie/show times*—Interesting possibilities exist for advanced features when combined with other Jabber applications such as calendaring groupware.

- *Network storage*—We're already seeing web-based file storage services like Yahoo! Briefcase. It is logical to extend this to Jabber systems, especially when using file sharing systems.

- *Security (authentication)*—Single sign-on IM systems are a key strategy tool for many vendors.

- *Directory services*—There is a classic need for storing and accessing directory information (such as names and phone numbers). XML database access (native or through drivers) is becoming increasingly common. Jabber systems can easily extend these services to the IM world.

As Jabber systems become popular on the Internet, I expect to see a wide variety of network services emerge. Many will likely rely on custom IQ extension protocols. The easy extensibility of the Jabber protocols makes this an exciting area of development.

10.3.3 Applications enhanced by Jabber

Jabber is a perfect network communication infrastructure because it is simple and flexible. As a basic piece of infrastructure Jabber may remain hidden from the end user in many applications. In fact, some of the most practical Jabber projects under development hide much of the IM origins of their Jabber infrastructure.

Possible Jabber applications include:

- *Games*—The computer game industry is rapidly growing to become one of the largest entertainment industries. Online multiplayer features are increasingly becoming required for game success. Jabber provides an excellent, portable, low overhead, free technology for creating online games. Several games under development use Jabber for everything from in-game chat to supporting all game network communication.

- *Home/Factory automation*—Home and factory automation is a nascent market that looks to be finally on the verge of a breakthrough into the mainstream. Automation systems become truly powerful when you can access them via any network. Jabber provides a nice mechanism for interfacing often-proprietary automation networks with the Internet through standard or custom desktop clients.

- *E-commerce*—Both customer-to-business and business-to-business e-commerce are extremely important parts of the Internet economy. It is possible to create secure ordering and fulfillment tracking systems on top of Jabber. Many .NET/SOAP web services are focusing on this market. Jabber is an interesting tool in realizing this vision.

- *Customer service*—Companies spend millions of dollars a year on customer service. Jabber systems offer an interesting way of tackling this difficult problem. Automated chatbots can attempt to help customers without human intervention. If they can't help, they can intelligently route the customer to a human representative. In addition, communicating over IM can be extremely efficient. Unlike a telephone conversation, a single person can carry on several IM chat sessions at the same time, exchange files, and even bring up groupware whiteboards to sketch on (as they say, a picture is often worth a thousand words). If other systems and network services are also Jabber-enabled, the customer service representative could automatically access customer databases, issue refunds, and conduct other business with the customer in real time.

- *B2B exchanges*—Businesses often need to exchange critical information. The information may require special handling including real-time delivery, high security, access to specialized network services, or the capability to handle large amounts of message traffic. Jabber provides an ideal platform for delivering these capabilities in a standardized manner.

- *Process management (aka workflow)*—Business processes often must follow complex business logic. For example, in order to be reimbursed for travel expenses, an employee may need to fill out a specific form and submit it to a superior. The superior can approve the expense, reject it, or send it back for clarification or changes. Once approved, the form must be submitted to the accounting department where it is approved, rejected, or returned for changes by a project account manager. Finally, it goes to the paymaster who issues the reimbursement check. This entire workflow can be managed by Jabber-based applications. In addition, the employee can be automatically informed about where the form is in the approval process and open a Jabber chat with the appropriate person if the form gets stuck somewhere along the way.

- *Expert systems*—Many AI applications such as expert systems are extremely useful tools for businesses. Unfortunately, the difficulty accessing them and integrating them into the rest of the enterprise computing systems has severely hampered their use in the enterprise. Jabber provides an interesting platform for creating developer and user-friendly network service interfaces to these systems bringing them into the mainstream.

- *Training*—Jabber chatbots can serve as automated guides that help users operate and explore complex systems or learn a wide variety of subjects. There are many exciting possibilities for innovative Jabber-based training systems, perhaps with the ability to chat with human instructors when the automated system fails to provide useful results.

As you can see, the potential for Jabber as an enabling technology is quite large. The most compelling applications exploit the communication and instant messaging features of Jabber while extending them in innovative and task specific ways. The value of your Jabber network is greatly influenced by the number of people on the network and the number of network services and applications you can offer. As we've seen, the extensibility of Jabber and the simplicity of creating Jabber clients and servers make a heavily populated Jabber network a likely and fascinating possibility.

Jabber isn't the only communication framework available to developers today. There is a danger when exploring a new and exciting technology to fall into the trap of thinking it can be used to solve every problem out there. The reality is that Jabber and other IM solutions are only one of several useful networking technologies that you should consider when faced with a challenging networked problem. In the next section we'll take a look at some of these alternatives and how Jabber compares.

10.4 *Distributed application alternatives to Jabbers*

Jabber faces several competing technologies for accomplishing the same basic task of allowing users and applications to communicate. Within the IM arena there are many proprietary systems with varying strengths and weaknesses, from small, domain focused IM systems to large hosted systems like AIM.

We discussed Jabber's place in the IM world in chapter 1. Now we'll look at the competing technologies that can fill many of the communication roles that we've been discussing for advanced Jabber applications. These competing distributing computing technologies fall into three main categories: remote procedure call (RPC) systems, peer-to-peer systems, and hybrid systems.

We'll begin with RPC systems.

10.4.1 *RPCs: oldies but goodies*

As long as there have been networks there have been RPC systems designed to allow applications to communicate with each other across them. Microsoft is betting its future on the XML-based .NET RPC system using SOAP. We've already discussed these technologies and how Jabber can be used as a part of the .NET future.

Java offers developers three main RPC alternatives: CORBA, Java Remote Method Invocation (RMI), and Java Jini. CORBA, the common object request broker architecture, is a platform-neutral, language-neutral RPC framework in use in many enterprises. It saw its heyday in the 1990s as a way to bridge new C++ systems to legacy systems built with older technologies.

When Java emerged in the mid-'90s Java CORBA interfaces were quickly added to the core libraries. However, CORBA suffers from a large amount of complexity needed to support a language-neutral RPC system. This includes its own interface definition language (IDL) for describing how RPC is carried out between CORBA systems.

The functionality of CORBA was necessary for Java systems but the complexity made using it expensive and error prone. It is now used only when accessing older applications that already have existing CORBA interfaces.

Java RMI was created as a simplified RPC system.[17] The designers made RMI Java-specific, allowing Java to take care of much of the complexities found in CORBA. For example, RMI uses native Java data types and interfaces, eliminating the need for an IDL.

---

[17] Many CORBA lessons were incorporated into RMI's design. This was natural since many RMI designers were part of the original CORBA effort.

The simplicity and power of RMI has lowered the bar in creating distributed systems. When the J2EE standards were being developed, RMI was designated as the standard RPC technology to be used between all J2EE components. Distributed Java systems are almost always built with RMI.[18]

The core RMI team, after working on distributed systems for so long, noticed several common problems that continued to plague RPC systems. Their solution was the Java Jini system (java.sun.com and www.jini.org). Jini is a lightweight framework built on top of an RPC system (the default is Java RMI). Jini provides lookup services, spontaneous and self-healing networking, mobile objects, distributed transactions, distributed events, and other advanced distributed system features.

RPC systems do not specify a particular architecture for components. However, basic client/server architectures are the most common. In the case of Jini, the line between clients and servers is often blurred producing a distributed server or even peer-to-peer (P2P) architecture.

The key difference between Jabber and RPC systems is the degree of coupling between communicating applications. In RPC, applications communicate directly with each other. A failure in one application will often cause both to fail.[19] In addition, changes to the interface on one application require all other applications to be updated producing maintenance nightmares.

Jabber and other messaging systems provide a much looser coupling between applications.[20] The Jabber server acts as a buffer between the communicating applications preventing failures in one from affecting the other. In addition, messages serve as the interface between applications in Jabber MOM systems. Applications are free to change independently as long as they continue to use the same message format.

The looser coupling does come at a price. Jabber systems have higher communication overheads than RPC based ones. The Jabber server, and the steps required to create, send, and read Jabber messages can often be eliminated in RPC systems. In most cases, developers will sacrifice some performance for the development benefits of looser coupling. This will tip the scales in the favor of Jabber for many systems.

If the overhead of the server is significant, P2P often provide an interesting alternative.

---

[18] CORBA is still widely used to connect to legacy systems.

[19] Jini systems expect this failure and are designed to automatically recover from them.

[20] The Jini standard includes the JavaSpace Service. It serves as a shared object repository and helps Jini systems achieve the same degree of loose coupling found in MOM systems.

10.4.2 P2P systems: the new challenger

P2P systems are designed to allow communication directly between clients or applications without a server. Two of the most interesting P2P systems are JXTA (www.jxta.org) and Gnutella (www.gnutella.co.uk). These systems offer many benefits over traditional server-based systems like Jabber:

- *No server*—There is no server to install, manage or maintain. This also eliminates the server as a weak link in the architecture. In addition, removing the server distributes the control over the network to the clients and removes the server as a target for attack (legal or otherwise).

- *Anonymous*—Most P2P systems are designed to allow anonymous use of the network, although it is usually easy to add the ability to identify yourself if needed. Anonymity has been a traditionally important feature of P2P systems as many began as file-sharing systems.[21]

- *Efficient/scalable network*—The Jabber network is limited by the number of sessions the Jabber server can handle. A P2P system moves computing to the edges of the network, thus helping to distribute the load.[22]

- *Faster/direct transfers*—Since communication is conducted directly between the sender and receiver, information is transferred without overhead from intermediate components. Some P2P systems distribute data across the network in an attempt to cache it close to consumers in order to further increase transfer speed and efficiency.

Unfortunately, P2P systems are not a panacea. There are many dangers and pitfalls associated with P2P. These include:

- *Security and privacy*—P2P clients must communicate directly with other clients. This results in their being exposed to the same security and privacy concerns that face a server operator. For example, it is difficult to operate P2P clients behind firewalls, as other clients must be able to open connections to them. In addition, it is possible for someone to trace who you are by watching your P2P packets. The Jabber server serves as a trusted intermediary that can hide your true identity and protect you from direct attacks.

- *No centralized control*—Without a central server controlling the network, there is no way to exert centralized control over a P2P system. This is an

---

[21] File-sharing systems are often used to share copyrighted material illegally and both server operators and users have been pursued through the legal system.

[22] Several prominent P2P systems have failed to scale as anticipated creating some doubt as to the limits of this claim.

important feature for some applications such as anonymous file sharing. However, businesses must often exert centralized control to enforce policies and control usage. The Jabber server serves as a central administration point for a Jabber system.

- *Quality of service*—P2P systems rely on clients for all communication tasks. This makes it difficult to consistently provide QoS guarantees to users.

- *Anonymous*—Businesses often want (or are required) to audit all their activities. The anonymous nature of many P2P systems can make this difficult or impossible.

P2P systems are well-suited to many applications where the overhead or vulnerability of a server is not desired. However, most enterprise systems will find the lack of security and control major obstacles to using P2P. Jabber systems allow users to balance the need for distributed yet centralized communication systems.

Of course, as engineers we know that sometimes a compromise between extremes is the best solution. Hybrid systems often provide that needed balance.

10.4.3 Hybrid systems: a better compromise

Hybrid systems combine techniques and technologies from P2P systems with classic client/server designs. The most famous hybrid system is Napster (www.napster.com). Napster uses a classic client/server IM infrastructure for chat and file searching. File transfers were handled using direct P2P connections. This balances the need for centralized control and fast, comprehensive file searches, with the efficiencies of using P2P to transfer large amounts of data.

The hybrid system approach is often used as a fallback alternative in otherwise pure client/server or P2P systems. For example, the JXTA P2P system first attempts to use a multicast protocol to discover other JXTA peers. However it will fall back to using well-known rendezvous servers that operate as pseudocentralized lookup services to help bootstrap the P2P network.

Jabber is designed to be a hybrid system. Its distributed server design allows you to break down the Jabber network into arbitrarily sized Jabber domains. These domains can be as small as a single Jabber client forming a P2P-like network. On the other end of the spectrum, a single, isolated Jabber server can handle thousands of users forming a classic, client/server architecture. In addition, the out-of-band protocol we briefly covered in chapter 4 can provide a simple method of adding Napster-like P2P file transfers in an otherwise Jabber client/server IM network.

10.5 Conclusions

We have seen where Java IM systems like Jabber can take us given the proper enterprise enhancements. These possibilities include MOM systems, groupware, network services and distributed applications. In addition, exciting new developments like SOAP and web services opens up whole new domains for IM developers to explore.

The Jabber design proves to have a nice balance of power, simplicity and flexibility. It can be easily adapted to large client/server systems as well as P2P systems and all points in between. Exactly where Jabber will find its best application remains to be seen. Get excited. Get involved. Join us in the messaging revolution!

Jabber reference

This appendix is meant to serve as a quick reference. It provides rapid access to the most significant aspects of each Jabber protocol and packet. Once you understand the basics of each protocol, this reference will provide relevant details for later review.

Core standards

Core standards	Namespace	Standard	Page
Jabber Identifiers	n/a	Yes	R-1
Jabber Addressing and Implicit Addresses	n/a	Yes	R-2
<stream:stream>, <stream:error>	http://etherx.jabber.org/streams	Yes	R-3
<error>	n/a	Yes	R-4
<message>	jabber:client, jabber:server	Yes	R-5
Groupchat Protocol	n/a	Yes	R-6
<presence>	jabber:client, jabber:server	Yes	R-7
<iq>	jabber:client, jabber:server	Yes	R-8
<vCard>	jabber:client, jabber:server	Yes	R-9
<xhtml>	jabber:client, jabber:server	No	R-10
Server-to-Server Authentication: Dialback Protocol	jabber:server, jabber:server:dialback	No	R-11

Info/Query extensions

Info/Query extensions	Description	Namcspace	Standard	Page
agent	Obtain information on server services	jabber:iq:agent	Yes	
agents	Obtain list of service services	jabber:iq:agents	Yes	
auth	User authentication (client-to-server)	jabber:iq:auth	Yes	
autoupdate	Automatic software update notification	jabber:iq:autoupdate	Yes	
oob	Out of band data transfer initiation protocol	jabber:iq:oob	Yes	
register	User account registration and update protocol	jabber:iq:register	Yes	
roster	Roster management protocol	jabber:iq:roster	Yes	

(continued on next page)

Info/Query extensions (continued)

Info/Query extensions	Description	Namcspace	Standard	Page
search	Search the server-managed Jabber User Directory	jabber:iq:search	Yes	
time	Obtain local time on query handler	jabber:iq:time	Yes	
version	Obtain version of query handler	jabber:iq:version	Yes	
browse	Advanced service browsing (replace agent/agents)	jabber:iq:browse	No	
conference	Advanced groupchat conferencing (replace groupchat)	jabber:iq:conference	No	
gateway	Creating and resolution of gateway user addresses	jabber:iq:gateway	No	
last	Obtain "last time" of query handler	jabber:iq:last	No	
pass	Proxy Accept Socket Service (oob helper protocol)	jabber:iq:pass	No	
private	Server-side storage of arbitrary XML data	jabber:iq:private	No	
rpc	Jabber transport binding for XML-RPC packets	jabber:iq:rpc	No	

X extensions

X extensions	Description	Namespace	Standard	Page
autoupdate	Automatic software update notification	jabber:x:autoupdate	Yes	
delay	Annotations of message delivery delays	jabber:x:delay	Yes	
oob	Out of band data transfer information	jabber:x:oob	Yes	
roster	Exchanging roster items	jabber:x:roster	Yes	
conference	Invite users to advanced Jabber groupchat conferences	jabber:x:conference	No	
envelope	Advanced <message> delivery information	jabber:x:envelope	No	
event	<message> delivery event protocol	jabber:x:event	No	

(continued on next page)

X extensions (continued)

X extensions	Description	Namespace	Standard	Page
expire	<message> expiry annotation	jabber:x:expire	No	
signed	<message> signature (Public Key Infrastructure support)	jabber:x:signed	No	
encrypted	<message> encryption (Public Key Infrastructure support)	jabber:x:encrypted	No	
sxpm	Streaming XPM (collaborative whiteboarding)	jabber:x:sxpm	No	

Note

This appendix uses information from a wide variety of sources. I have tried to indicate what documents were used for each entry so that you can look for further details there. However, there are plans to make changes to the website (www.jabber.org) where Jabber documents are stored. Due to these changes, any specific links to these documents will probably be broken by the time you read this. To overcome this, I will be keeping an up to date list of links to Jabber standards documentation at this book's website: www.manning.com/shigeoka.

Jabber Identifier Standard

Type Platform
Namespace All
Summary Jabber addresses identifying a Jabber entity or delivery end point

```
[user@]jabberDomain[/resource]
```

Component	Optional	Format	Description
User	yes	Valid email user name	A particular "user" or "node" in the Jabber network.
jabberDomain	no	Internet domain name	A Jabber domain controlled by a Jabber server.
Resource	yes	Valid URI path name	A particular delivery end point for a user/node.

Example

iain@shigeoka.com User "iain" within jabber domain shigeoka.com
iain@shigeoka.com/work User iain@shigeoka.com with resource "work"

Notes

None

Source

Jabber Identifiers, www.jabber.org.

Jabber Addressing and Implicit Address Standard

Type Platform
Namespace All
Summary The automatic creation and assignment of addresses to packets

In general, all top-level packets sent through the Jabber system will have four standard attributes (or omit them for default values). These attributes will often need to be assigned values by different entities along the delivery path as described in the table below.

Attributes	Sender	Sender Server	Recipient Server	Recipient
from	OPTIONAL	MUST [a]	MUST	MUST
to	MUST	MUST	OPTIONAL [b]	OPTIONAL
id	OPTIONAL	SHOULD COPY	SHOULD COPY	COPY
type	OPTIONAL [c]	MUST COPY	MUST COPY	COPY

a. Servers should override from value to avoid spoofing. Exception: some protocols use the from value and server MUST COPY .
b. Servers may omit recipient address.
c. Omitting the type attribute is common and will have different default values depending on the protocol/packet.

An example `<message>` packet traveling through the system would result in the following address behavior.

Scenario: Users "al@a.com" and "bob@b.org" chat

"al" client	a.com server	b.org server	"bob" client
→	→	→	→
`<message type='chat' to='bob@b.org'>` `<thread>cid_01</thread>` `<body>Howdy</body>` `</message>`	`<message type='chat' to='bob@b.org' from='al@a.org'>` `<thread>cid_01</thread>` `<body>Howdy</body>` `</message>`	`<message type='chat' from='al@a.org'>` `<thread>cid_01</thread>` `<body>Howdy</body>` `</message>`	`<message type='chat' from='al@a.org'>` `<thread>cid_01</thread>` `<body>Howdy</body>` `</message>`
←	←	←	←
`<message type='chat' from='bob@b.org'>` `<thread>cid_01</thread>` `<body>What's up?</body>` `</message>`	`<message type='chat' from='bob@b.org'>` `<thread>cid_01</thread>` `<body>What's up?</body>` `</message>`	`<message type='chat' from='bob@b.org' to='al@a.com'>` `<thread>cid_01</thread>` `<body>What's up?</body>` `</message>`	`<message type='chat' to='al@a.com'>` `<thread>cid_01</thread>` `<body>What's up?</body>` `</message>`
→	→	→	→
`<message type='chat' to='bob@b.org'>` `<thread>cid_01</thread>` `<body>Not much.</body>` `</message>`	`<message type='chat' to='bob@b.org' from='al@a.org'>` `<thread>cid_01</thread>` `<body>Not much.</body>` `</message>`	`<message type='chat' from='al@a.org'>` `<thread>cid_01</thread>` `<body>Not much.</body>` `</message>`	`<message type='chat' from='al@a.org'>` `<thread>cid_01</thread>` `<body>Not mch.</body>` `</message>`

Stream Protocol

Type Platform
Namespace `http://etherx.jabber.org/streams`
Summary The underlying Jabber XML stream (root element of Jabber XML "document")

Packet <stream:stream>

Attributes	Client-to-Server	Server-to-Client	Server-to-Server
to	Server name	MAY	Server name
from	MAY	Server name	Server name
id	MAY	Stream ID	Stream ID
xmlns	jabber:client	jabber:client	jabber:server
xmlns:stream	http://etherx.jabber.org/streams	http://etherx.jabber.org/streams	http://etherx.jabber.org/streams

Packet <stream:error>

- Identical to the standard Jabber `<error>` packet but defined in the `http://etherx.jabber.org/streams` namespace. (See `<error>` reference page.)
- Indicates a failure in the streams protocol (and imminent closing of the stream).

Example
Client-server:

```
<stream:stream to='jabber.org'
          xmlns='jabber:client'
          xmlns:stream='http://etherx.jabber.org/streams'>
```

Server-client:

```
<stream:stream from='jabber.org'
          xmlns='jabber:client'
          xmlns:stream='http://etherx.jabber.org/streams'
          id='23AC323'>
```

Notes
See `<error>` reference for format of `<stream:error>`.

Source
Jabber Protocol Overview v. 1.4, Peter Saint-Andre, www.jabber.org.

Error Packet

Type Platform
Namespace `jabber:client, jabber:server`
Summary Standard Jabber <error> subpacket and codes. Can appear within any core protocol packet.

Packet `<error>`

MUST contain a single `code` attribute indicating error type. Optional text within the <error> packet contains a freeform text error message.

Code	Description
302	Redirect
400	Bad Request
401	Unauthorized
402	Payment Required
403	Forbidden
404	Not Found
405	Not Allowed
406	Not Acceptable
407	Registration Required
408	Request Timeout
409	Conflict [a]
500	Internal Server Error
501	Not Implemented
502	Remote Server Error
503	Service Unavailable
504	Remote Server Timeout

a. Not found in the Info/Query protocol documentation.

Example

```
<message type='error' from='jabber.org'>
  <error code='503'>Nobody is home, go away</error>
</message>
```

Notes

None

Source

Jabber Protocol Overview v. 1.4, Peter Saint-Andre, www.jabber.org.

Info/Query (Protocol Document), Jabber Software Foundation, www.jabber.org

Jabber 1.2 Technical White Paper, Peter Saint-Andre, www.jabber.com.

Message Protocol

Type CORE
Namespace `jabber:client, jabber:server`
Summary Sends XML data between users (typically text messages).

Packet <message>

Type	Description
normal	(Default) A normal text message used in email like interfaces
chat	A typically short text message used in line-by-line chat interfaces
groupchat	A chat message sent to a groupchat server for group chats
headline	A text message to be displayed in scrolling marquee displays
error	Standard Jabber error packet indicating messaging error

Subpacket

Subpackets	Description
<subject>	Short description of message contents
<thread>	A unique identifier for a sequence of messages (used in chat protocol)
<body>	The main message contents
<x>	Any Jabber X extension (see X extensions)
<error>	The standard Jabber error code and descriptive message (see <error> documentation)
<html>	Rich text markup (styled messages). Proposed standard.

Recommended subpacket usage

Subpacket	Message packet type				
	normal	chat	groupchat	headline	error
<subject>	SHOULD	SHOULD NOT	SHOULD NOT	SHOULD NOT	SHOULD NOT
<thread>	OPTIONAL	SHOULD	OPTIONAL	OPTIONAL	SHOULD NOT
<body>	SHOULD	SHOULD	SHOULD	SHOULD	SHOULD NOT
<x>	OPTIONAL	OPTIONAL	OPTIONAL	OPTIONAL	SHOULD NOT
<error>	MUST NOT	MUST NOT	MUST NOT	MUST NOT	MUST

Example

```
<message to='recipientJID@jabber.org'>
  <subject>How are you?</subject>
  <body>Hey there, just wondering how you were doing today.</body>
</message>
```

Notes

- For groupchat messages, see the groupchat protocol.
- For HTML-formatted messages, see the XHTML proposed packet standard.

Source

Message (Protocol Document), www.jabber.org.

Groupchat Protocol

Type   Message subprotocol

Namespace   `jabber:client`, `jabber:server`

Summary   Multiparticipant chat protocol supported by a groupchat server

Groupchat Jabber ID

The groupchat protocol uses a specially formatted Jabber ID of the form:

`groupName@ServerName[/NickName]`

Component	Description
groupName	The name of the groupchat group you wish to participate in
ServerName	The Jabber Domain for the groupchat server (valid Internet domain name)
NickName	The nickname for participants in a particular group.

Participation

Groupchat participation is managed by the groupchat server. Clients join and leave groups using <presence>. Join/Leave a groupchat group using the empty <presence> packet with following attributes:

Attribute	Value	Description
type	available/unavailable	Indicates you wish to join/leave the group
to	Groupchat Jabber ID	Group you wish to join/leave and requested nickname

Messaging

- All messages are sent to the groupchat server. The server resends the message to groupchat participants.

- Jabber IDs are manipulated by the groupchat server to maintain the illusion of groupchat users sending messages.

- Broadcast message—messages sent to the group will be sent to all participants

- Private message—messages sent to a particular groupchat nickname will only be sent to that participant

This table shows the groupchat participants' effects on the value of groupchat <message> packets to and from attributes.

Jabber ID	Sender	Sender's server	groupchat server	group member
to	groupchat JID	groupchat JID	groupchat JID	groupchat JID
from	SHOULD NOT	user JID	groupchat JID	groupchat JID

Notes

Advanced groupchat management and participation is provided by the jabber:iq:conference protocol.

Source

Message (Protocol Document), www.jabber.org.

The Jabber Programmer's Guide (1.0.3 2000), Thomas "temas" Muldowney, Eliot "e-t" Landrum, Peter Millard, and Max "Fingolfin" Horn, www.jabber.org.

Presence Protocol

Type CORE
Namespace `jabber:client, jabber:server`
Summary Update user presence or manage presence subscriptions

Packet `<presence>`

Type	Category	Description
available	Update	(Default) Indicates the user is available to receive messages
unavailable	Update	The user is unavailable to receive messages
subscribe	Subscribe	Request subscription to recipient's presence
subscribed	Subscribe	Grant subscription to sender's presence
unsubscribe	Subscribe	Request removal of subscription to recipient's presence
unsubscribed	Subscribe	Grant removal of subscription to sender's presence
probe	server only	Allows servers to request presence information from other servers
error	Any	This presence packet contains an error message

Subpackets

Subpacket	Description
<status>	Free-form text describing user's presence (i.e., gone fishing)
<priority>	Numerical priority of the sender's resource. Highest resource priority is default recipient of user packets.
<show>	Contains one of four presence "modes": chat, away, xa (extended away), dnd (do not disturb).
<x>	Any Jabber X extension (see X extensions)
<error>	The standard Jabber error code and descriptive message (see <error> documentation)

Recommended subelements for each `<presence>` type

Subpacket	Presence packet type			
	update	subscribe	probe	error
`<status>`	OPTIONAL	OPTIONAL	MUST NOT	SHOULD NOT
`<priority>`	OPTIONAL	MUST NOT	MUST NOT	SHOULD NOT
`<show>`	OPTIONAL	MUST NOT	MUST NOT	SHOULD NOT
`<x>`	OPTIONAL	MUST NOT	OPTIONAL	SHOULD NOT
`<error>`	MUST NOT	MUST NOT	MUST NOT	MUST

Example

Send presence update notifying subscribers that user is available

```
<presence>
```

An unavailable presence update with status message

```
<presence type='unavailable'>
  <status>Gone on Vacation</status>
</presence>
```

Notes

None

Source

Presence (Protocol Document), www.jabber.org.

Info/Query (IQ) Protocol

Type CORE
Namespace `jabber:client, jabber:server`
Summary Exchange information and perform queries using a request-response protocol.

Packet <iq>

Type	Description
get	(Default) Request information from recipient
set	Override information/setting on recipient
result	Results of a query (query information or empty to indicate success).
error	Standard Jabber error packet indicating IQ error

Subpackets

Subpacket	Description
<query>	The envelope for IQ extension protocols (see IQ extensions)
<vcard>	A vCard XML document (temporary draft standard)
<x>	Any Jabber X extension (see X extensions)
<error>	The standard Jabber error code and descriptive message (see <error> documentation)

Notes

vCard follows the temporary vCard protocol (see vCard protocol).

Source

Info/Query (Protocol Document), www.jabber.org.

Temporary vCard Protocol

Type IQ subpacket
Namespace `jabber:client, jabber:server`
Summary Support for the exchange of XML vCards electronic business cards

Packet <vCard>

Attributes	Value	Description
version	"3.0"	Temporary vCard version
prodid	"-//HandGen//NONSGML vGen v1.0//EN"	The generator product id
xmlns	vcard-temp	The temporary namespace for Jabber vCard

Subpackets

Jabber vCard subpackets must comply with v2.0 (March 21, 2000) of the vCard specification.

Notes

- You can obtain a copy of the vCard DTD at: http://protocol.jabber.org/vcard-temp/vCard-XML-DTD-v2-20000321.txt
- Proposed Jabber Profiles standard (Jabber Enhancement Proposal JEP-0006) presents a replacement for vCard. See http://foundation.jabber.org for more.

Source

vCard (protocol document), www.jabber.org.

Profiles, Adam Theo; Michael Hearn; and Eric Murphy, foundation.jabber.org (JEP-0006).

XHTML-Basic Packet [PROPOSED STANDARD]

Type   Message subpacket
Namespace   `http://www.w3.org/1999/xhtml`
Summary   An optional rich-text presentation of message information

Packet <html>

Attribute	Value	Description
xmlns	http://www.w3.org/1999/xhtml	The packet namespace

Subpackets

Subpackets follow the XHTML W3C standard.

Required	<body>,<blockquote>, ,<div>,<em>,<h1>-<h6>,<p>,<q>,<strong>,<a>,<img>,<code>,<ul>,<ol>
Optional	<address>,<abbr>,<acronym>,<cite>,<dfn>,<kbd>,<pre>,<samp>,<var>,<dl>,<dt>,<dd>
Not supported	<table> (all table elements), <form> (all form elements), <title>,<head>,<span>,<meta>,<link>,<base>

Styles

Required	font-size, color, background-color
Recommended	text-decoration, font-family
Optional	text-align, background-image

Example

```
<message to='recipientJID@jabber.org'>
  <body>hi</body>
  <html xmlns='http://www.w3.org/1999/xhtml'>
    <body style='color:red;background-color:green;font-size:large'>
      <p>hi</p>
    </body>
  </html>
</message>
```

Notes

See the XHTML-Basic standard for specific information on element markup (http://www.w3.org/1999/xhtml).

Source

Message Formatting (XHTML-Basic), Julian Missig and Jeremie Miller, www.jabber.org.

Server-to-Server Dialback Protocol [PROPOSED STANDARD]

Type Platform
Namespace jabber:server
Summary Lightweight server-to-server authentication protocol

Packet <stream:stream>

Attributes	Value	Description
to	JID	The name of the server connecting to
from	JID	The name of the server connecting from
id	Random Value	Stream ID sent only by receiving server (see Participants)
xmlns	jabber:server	Server-to-server connections follow the jabber:server protocols
xmlns:stream	http://etherx.jabber.org/ streams	The stream namespace
xmlns:db	jabber:server:dialback	Dialback will be used to authenticate this s2s connection

Subpackets

Subpacket	Description
<db:result>	Contains the result of a verification attempt (see type attribute) or used to exchange keys
<db:verify>	Requests that the recipient verify the contained key

Subpacket <db:result>

Type	Description
valid	The key was valid, the s2s connection is authenticated
invalid	There was a problem verify the key, the s2s connection should be closed as soon as possible.

Participants

Abbreviation	Role	Description
[O]	Originating server	Attempting to establish connection
[R]	Receiving server	Server that will service the orig- inating server's connection
[O Auth]	Originator authoritative server	Server that authenticates origi- nating server (can be the same as the originating server)
[R Auth]	Receiving authoritative server	Server that authenticates receiving server (only used if bi- directional connection needed)

Protocol

Action	Packet
[O] connects to [R] and both establish Jabber streams.	<stream:stream id='stream01'>
[O] sends <db:result> to [R] containing "key"	<db:result to='R' from='O'>key3233</ db:result>
[R] connects to [O Auth] and both establish Jab- ber streams.	<stream:stream id='stream02'>
[R] sends "key" and stream ID to [O Auth] for verification	<db:verify to='O' from='R' id='stream01'>key3233</db:verify>
[O Auth] sends success/failure to [R]	<db:result to='R' from='O' type='valid' id='stream01'/>
[R] sends success/failure to [O]	<db:result to='O' from='R' type='valid'/>

If a bi-directional connection needed:

[R] sends <db:result> to [O Auth] containing "key2"	<db:result to='O' from='R'>key0942</ db:result>
[O Auth] connects to [R Auth] and both establish Jabber streams	<stream:stream id='stream03'>
[O Auth] sends "key2" and stream ID to [R Auth] for verification	<db:verify to='R' from='O' id='stream03'>key0942</db:verify>
[R Auth] sends success/failure to [O Auth]	<db:result to='O' from='R' type='valid' id='stream03'/>
[O Auth] sends success/failure to [R]	<db:result to='R' from='O' type='valid'/>

Notes

- S2S connections are unidirectional (packets travel from originating to receiving server).
- You must use two S2S connections to send information both ways.
- Introduced in the 1.2 version of the Jabberd reference server but not enforced.
- Relies on DNS for security (relatively weak).
- `<stream:error>` supported in S2S connections (see the Stream Protocol reference page.).
- Authentication keys are best if generated randomly and never reused.
- Jabberd reference server (1.2 and 1.4) uses a SHA-1 hash of the server names and session ID to generate key.

Source

Server Dialback, Jeremie Miller and David Waite, www.jabber.org.

Agent Protocol

Type IQ Extension
Namespace `jabber:iq:agent`
Summary Probe/set the properties of a particular "server agent" (typically a transport).

Packet <agent>

Attribute	Description
jid	The Jabber ID that can be used to communicate with the agent.

Subpackets

Subpacket	Description
<name>	Free-form text name of the agent (for display in user agent clients)
<description>	Free-form text description of the agent (for display in user agent clients)
<transport>	Presence of this tag indicates the agent is a Jabber transport. Contains transport ID.
<service>	Presence of this tag indicates the agent is a Jabber service. Contains service type.
<register>	Presence of this tag indicates clients must register using the jabber:iq:register protocol

Standard Jabber <service> types

Service	Description
yahoo	Yahoo! transport
msn	MSN transport
aim	AOL AIM transport
icq	AOL ICQ transport
irc	IRC chat transport
groupchat	Jabber Groupchat service
gc	Jabber Groupchat service
oobproxy	Jabber Out-of-band proxy service (for users behind firewalls)
jud	Jabber User Directory service

Example

```
<iq from='jabber.org' type='result'>
  <query xmlns='jabber:iq:agent'>
    <agent jid='groups@jabber.org'>
      <name>Jabber Groupchat service</name>
      <description>The Jabber Groupchat Server</description>
      <service>groupchat</service>
    </agent>
  </query>
</iq>
```

Notes

None

Source

Agent Properties (protocol document), www.jabber.org.

Agents Protocol

Type IQ Extension
Namespace `jabber:iq:agents`
Summary Probe the properties of all "server agents" (typically transports) on the service.

Packet <agents>

Attribute	Description
jid	The Jabber ID that can be used to communicate with the agent.

Subpackets

Subpacket	Description
<name>	Free-form text name of the agent (for display in user agent clients)
<description>	Free-form text description of the agent (for display in user agent clients)
<transport>	Presence of this tag indicates the agent is a Jabber transport. Contains transport ID.
<service>	Presence of this tag indicates the agent is a Jabber service. Contains service type.
<register>	Presence of this tag indicates clients must register using the jabber:iq: register protocol

Standard Jabber <service> types

Service	Description
yahoo!	Yahoo! transport
msn	MSN transport
aim	AOL AIM transport
icq	AOL ICQ transport
irc	IRC chat transport
groupchat	Jabber Groupchat service
gc	Jabber Groupchat service
oobproxy	Jabber Out-of-band proxy service (for users behind firewalls)
jud	Jabber User Directory service

Example

```
<iq from='jabber.org' type='result'>
  <query xmlns='jabber:iq:agents'>
    <agent jid='groups@jabber.org'>
      <name>Jabber Groupchat service</name>
      <description>The Jabber Groupchat Server</description>
      <service>groupchat</service>
    </agent>
    <agent jid='aim.jabber.org'>
      <name>AIM Transport</name>
      <description>The AOL AIM Transport Service</description>
      <transport>AIM Screen Name</transport>
      <service>aim</service>
      <register/>
    </agent>
  </query>
</iq>
```

Notes

None

Source

Available Agents List (protocol document), www.jabber.org.

Authentication Protocol

Type IQ Extension
Namespace `jabber:iq:auth`
Summary Jabber authentication between clients and servers

Packets

Packet	Description
<username>	The user account name for authentication attempt
<resource>	The resource for the session
<password>	The plain-text password (used in plain and digest authentication algorithm)
<digest>	The SHA-1 message digest (used in digest authentication algorithm)
<hash>	The hash (used in proposed zero-knowledge authentication algorithm)
<token>	The token (used in proposed zero-knowledge authentication algorithm)
<sequence>	The sequence number (used in proposed zero-knowledge auhtentication algorithm)

Plain Authentication Algorithm

Reset

- When authenticated, client sends set IQ query with <username> and <password> containing new values.

Auth

- Client sends set IQ query with <username>, <password>, and <resource>
- Password is any XML-legal character data (case sensitive)

Digest Authentication Algorithm

Reset

- When authenticated, client sends set IQ query with <username> and <password> containing new values

Auth

- Java snippet:
```
java.security.MessageDigest sha = MessageDigest("SHA");
sha.update(SessionID);
String digest = bytes2HexLowerCaseASCII(sha.digest(password));
```

- Client sends set IQ query with <username>, <digest>, and <resource>
- Digest is lower-case hexadecimal representation of the SHA-1 digest of the Session ID and password
- Session ID is the id attribute of the server's <stream:stream> tag.

Zero-Knowledge Authentication Algorithmm [PROPOSED STANDARD]
Reset

- When authenticated, client sends set IQ query with <username>, <hash> containing $hash_N$, <token> and <sequence> (N)

Auth

- Client sends get IQ query with <username> containing user's username.
- Server sends result IQ reply containing <username>, <token>, and <sequence> (N -1)
- Java snippet:
  java.security.MessageDigest sha = MessageDigest("SHA");
  sha.update(token);
  String hash0 = bytes2HexLowerCaseASCII(sha.digest(password));
  String $hash_N$=hash0;
  for (int i = 0; i < sequence; i++){
     $hash_N$ = bytes2HexLowerCaseASCII(sha.digest($hash_N$))
  }
- Client sends set IQ query with <username>, <hash> (containing $hash_{N-1}$, and <resource>
- Server takes $hash_{N-1}$
- Java snippet:
  $hash_N$ = bytes2HexLowerCaseASCII(sha.digest($hash_N$));
- Compare given $hash_N$ with $hash_N$
- On success, server sends empty result IQ reply, store $hash_{N-1}$ as <hash>, and decrement <sequence> (N-1)

Example

```
<iq type='set' id='auth_01'>
  <query xmlns='jabber:iq:auth'>
    <username>iain</username>
    <resource>work</resource>
    <password>mypass</password>
  </query>
</iq>
```

Notes

- A set query without a `<username>` and `<password>` indicates an anonymous login attempt. A successful anonymous login causes the server to send a `result` IQ reply with a `<username>` subpacket containing an anonymous JID (server.com/resource) for use during session

- A get query with only `<username>` specified runs an "authentication probe."

Source

Simple Client Authentication, www.jabber.org.

Zero-Knowledge Authentication, Jeremie Miller, www.jabber.org.

Autoupdate Protocol

Type IQ Extension
Namespace jabber:iq:autoupdate
Summary Automating software updates

Packets

Attribute	Value	Description
xmlns	jabber:iq:autoupdate	Namespace for the packet

Protocol

JID: [client]@[server]/[version]

```
<presence to='winjab@update.server/0.1.0'/>
```

Updates available server sends

```
<message to='user@jabber.org'>
  <body>Update JavaJab now!</body>
  <x xmlns='jabber:x:autoupdate'>javjab@javjab.server</x>
</message>
```

Client requests update information

```
<iq type='get' to='javjab@javjab.server'>
  <query xmlns='jabber:iq:autoupdate'/>
</iq>
```

Server sends update information

```
<iq type='result' from='javjab@javjab.server'>
  <query xmlns='jabber:iq:autoupdate'>
    <release priority='optional'>
      <ver>1.0.1</ver>
      <url>http://javjab.server/javjab/javjab_beta.zip</url>
    </release>
  </query>
  <query xmlns='jabber:iq:autoupdate'>
    <release priority='recommended'>
      <ver>1.0.0</ver>
      <desc>The Final Candidate Release of Java Jabber Client</desc>
      <url>http://javjab.server/javjab/javjab_release.zip</url>
    </release>
  </query>
</iq>
```

Notes

See `jabber:x:autoupdate` reference page.

Update information in `jabber:iq:autoupdate` `<query>` is application specific

Source

The Jabber Programmer's Guide (1.0.3 2000), Thomas "temas" Muldowney, Eliot "e-t" Landrum, Peter Millard, and Max "Fingolfin" Horn, www.jabber.org.

Jabber 1.2 Technical White Paper, Peter Saint-Andre, www.jabber.com.

Out-of-Band File Transfer Protocol

Type IQ Extension
Namespace `jabber:iq:oob`
Summary Coordinates the client-to-client (out-of-band) transfer of data

Packets

Packet	Description
<url>	The URL for the file (typically http:)
<desc>	A free-form text description of the file (for display to the user)

Example

```
<iq to='recipientJID@jabber.org' type='set' id='oob_01'>
  <query xmlns='jabber:iq:oob'>
    <url>http://server.com/file.zip</url>
    <desc>That file you wanted</desc>
  </query>
</iq>
```

Notes

None

Source

Out of Band Data (file transfers, other binary streams/transfers), www.jabber.org.

Registration Protocol

Type   IQ Extension
Namespace   `jabber:iq:register`
Summary   Negotiate user registration with Jabber services

Packets

Packet	Description
<instructions>	Text describing to the user how to fill out the form
<username>	The user account username
<password>	The password (to used with plain and digest authentication (see jabber:iq:auth))
<hash>	The hash (to be used with zero-knowledge authentication (see jabber:iq:auth))
<token>	The token (to be used with zero-knowledge authentication (see jabber:iq:auth))
<sequence>	The sequence (to be used with zero-knowledge authentication (see jabber:iq:auth))
<name>	The user's name
<first>	The user's first name
<last>	The user's last name
<email>	The user's email
<address>	The user's street address
<city>	The user's city
<state>	The user's state
<zip>	The user's ZIP code
<phone>	The user's telephone number
<url>	The user's website
<date>	The date the registration took place
<misc>	Other miscellaneous information to associate with the account
<text>	Textual information to associate with the account
<remove>	Empty flag to remove account

Example

Client requests registration form

```
<iq type='get' id='reg_01'>
  <query xmlns='jabber:iq:register'/>
</iq>
```

Server sends empty form. The server supports plain/digest (<password>) and zero-knowledge (<hash>) authentication.

```
<iq type='result' id='reg_01'>
  <query xmlns='jabber:iq:register'>
    <instructions>Fill out the form carefully</instructions>
    <username/>
    <password/>
    <hash/>
    <email/>
</iq>
```

Client registers using plain/digest password

```
<iq type='set' id='reg_02'>
  <query xmlns='jabber:iq:register'>
    <username>iain</username>
    <password>mypass</password>
    <email>iain@shigeoka.com</email>
</iq>
```

Notes
Client sends an empty get IQ query to obtain a blank registration form.

Source
Registration Requests (protocol document), www.jabber.org.

Roster Protocol

Type IQ Extension
Namespace `jabber:iq:roster`
Summary Send and update the server managed presence subscription roster

Packet <item>

Roster queries can contain zero or more `<item>` packets describing roster items

Attribute	Description
jid	The Jabber ID of the presence subscriber for this item
subscription	The subscription type: none, both, to (user subscribes to item's JID), from (JID subscribes to user)
ask	(Optional) Pending request status: subscribe, unsubscribe
name	(Optional) A nickname for the roster item

Subpackets

Subpackets	Description
<group>	Zero or more groups that the item belongs to (used by clients to organize/present roster items)

Example

```
<iq type='set' id='roster_01'>
  <query xmlns='jabber:iq:roster'>
    <item jid='bob@jabber.org' name='Bob Smith' subscription='both'>
      <group>friends</group>
      <group>Bowling Team</group>
    </item>
    <item jid='bossman@jabber.org' name='Big Cheese' subscription='to'>
      <group>work</group>
    </item>
  </query>
</iq>
```

Notes

- Client sends an empty `get` IQ query to obtain a full copy of the server-managed roster.
- Client sends `set` IQ query to update items. To change `subscription`, `jid`, or `ask` values, you must use the presence protocol.
- Server sends `set` IQ queries asynchronously (server roster pushes) as roster changes.

Source

Roster Management (protocol document), www.jabber.org.

Search Protocol

Type   IQ Extension
Namespace   jabber:iq:search
Summary   **Jabber User database searching**

Packets

Packet	Description
<instructions>	Instructions for filling out the search form
<key>	A randomly generated key to identify this particular search session
<item>	Single jid attribute contains JID for user in result (subelements with other fields filled in)
<name>	The user's name
<first>	The user's first name
<last>	The user's last name
<email>	The user's email
<address>	The user's street address
<city>	The user's city
<state>	The user's state
<zip>	The user's ZIP code
<phone>	The user's telephone number
<url>	The user's website
<date>	The date the registration took place
<misc>	Other miscellaneous information associated with the account
<text>	Textual information associated with the account

Example
Client requests search form

```
<iq type='get' to='users.jabber.org' id='search01'>
  <query xmlns='jabber:iq:search'/>
</iq>
```

Server sends form

```
<iq type='result' from='users.jabber.org' id='search01'>
  <query xmlns='jabber:iq:search'>
    <name/>
    <email/>
  </query>
</iq>
```

Client starts search

```
<iq type='get' to='users.jabber.org' id='search02'>
  <query xmlns='jabber:iq:search'>
    <name>iain</name>
  </query>
</iq>
```

Server sends results

```
<iq type='result' from='users.jabber.org' id='search02'>
  <query xmlns='jabber:iq:search'>
    <item jid='iain@jabber.org'>
      <name>Iain Shigeoka</name>
      <email>iain@shigeoka.com</email>
    </item>
    <item jid='mcdowell@jabber.org'>
      <name>Iain McDowell</name>
      <email>mcdowell@jabber.org</email>
    </item>
  </query>
</iq>
```

Notes

None

Source

Jabber 1.2 Technical White Paper, Nov. 2000, Peter Saint-Andre, www.jabber.com.

Time Protocol

Type   IQ Extension
Namespace   `jabber:iq:time`
Summary   Exchange local time

Packets

Packets	Description
<utc>	The UTC (GMT) time in Jabber time format: YYYYMMDDThh:mm:ss
<tz>	The local time zone
<display>	A human friendly string of the local time

Example

```
<iq type='get' id='time_01' to='iain@jabber.org'>
  <query xmlns='jabber:iq:time'/>
</iq>
<iq type='result' id='time_01' to='requesterJID@jabber.org'>
  <query xmlns='jabber:iq:time'>
    <utc>20020130T15:32:02</utc>
    <tz>Pacific Standard Time</tz>
    <display>01/30/02 3:32:02 PM</display>
  </query>
</iq>
```

Notes
None

Source
Client Time (protocol document), www.jabber.org

Version Protocol

Type IQ Extension
Namespace `jabber:iq:version`
Summary Query the version of a client/server's software

Packets

Packet	Description
`<name>`	The name of the application
`<version>`	A version number (typically dot separate numbers)
`<os>`	The operating system running the application

Example

```
<iq type='get' id='ver_01' to='iain@jabber.org'>
  <query xmlns='jabber:iq:version'/>
</iq>
<iq type='result' id='ver_01' to='requesterJID@jabber.org'>
  <query xmlns='jabber:iq:version'>
    <name>Java Jab Client</name>
    <version>1.0.0</version>
    <os>Mac OS X 10.1.2</os>
  </query>
</iq>
```

Notes

None

Source

Client Version (protocol document), www.jabber.org

Browsing Protocol [PROPOSED STANDARD]

Type IQ Extension
Namespace `jabber:iq:browse`
Summary Advanced service browsing (i.e., directory service).

Packets

Packet element names define the primary JID-type for a browse item. They contain the following attributes:

Attribute	Description
jid	Jabber Identifier for the entity/service
type	(Optional) The subtype for the entity/service. Use type="remove" in set <iq> queries to remove items.
name	(Optional) The user friendly name of the entity/service

Special Packets

Packet	Description
<ns>	Zero or more protocols (namespaces) supported by a particular entity/service
<item>	A placeholder packet used to organize entities/services into an easily browsed hierarchy

Jabber ID Types (JID-Type)

Type	Subtypes
service	jabber, icq, aim, msn, yahoo, irco, smtp, pager, jud (Jabber user directory)
conference	irc, url, list
user	client, forward, device, inbox, voice
application	calender, editor, game, fileserver, bot
headline	rss (RDF site summary), stock, logger, notice
render	en2fr (english to french), jive, tts (text to speech), grammer, spell
keyword	dictionary, thesaurus, faq, web, software, dns, whois

Example

Client requests browse info for user "iain@jabber.org"

```
<iq type='get' id='browse_01'>
  <query xmlns='jabber:iq:browse'>
    <user jid='iain@jabber.org'/>
  </query>
</iq>
```

Server responds with info: Iain has one user account with two clients (Work/ Home Desktop Client) and one online game (Iain's Java Chess).

```
<iq type='result' id='browse_01' to='requesterJID@jabber.org'>
  <query xmlns='jabber:iq:browse'>
    <user jid='iain@jabber.org' name='Iain Shigeoka'>
      <user jid='iain@jabber.org/work'
            type='client' name='Work Desktop Client'/>
      <user jid='iain@jabber.org/home'
            type='client' name='Home Desktop Client'/>
      <application jid='iain@jabber.org/chess'
            type='game' name='Iain's Java Chess'/>
    </user>
  </query>
</iq>
```

Client requests details of client "iain@jabber.org/work"

```
<iq type='get' id='browse_02'>
  <query xmlns='jabber:iq:browse'>
    <user jid='iain@jabber.org/work'/>
  </query>
</iq>
```

Server responds with info: supports out-of-band transfers, time queries, and Jabber events

```
<iq type='result' id='browse_02' to='requesterJID@jabber.org'>
  <query xmlns='jabber:iq:browse'>
    <user jid='iain@jabber.org/work' type='client' name='Work Desktop'/>
      <ns>jabber:iq:oob</ns>
      <ns>jabber:iq:time</ns>
      <ns>jabber:x:event</ns>
    </user>
  </query>
</iq>
```

Notes

- Intended to replace the `jabber:iq:agent` and `jabber:iq:agents` protocols.
- JID-types are like MIME-types and are referred to by "type/subtype" (e.g., service/jabber).
- For efficiency, send only one level of one branch of the browse tree for each request.
- Browsers manually drill-down into the tree by requesting browse information on current leaf nodes.
- True leaf nodes have no browse subpackets and are either empty or contain only `<ns>` subpackets.
- Browser `set` packets can be asynchronously sent from the server to the client as as *browser pushes* in the same manner as roster pushes
- All browser JID entries should be presented with standard GUI options depending on their type:
  - All: message/chat and browse
  - Domains (servers): time, vcard, last, version
  - Users: vcard, last
  - User resources (clients): time, version, oob

Source

Jabber Browsing, Jeremie Miller, www.jabber.org

Conferencing Protocol [PROPOSED STANDARD]

Type   IQ Extension
Namespace   `jabber:iq:conference`
Summary   Advanced groupchat protocol

SubPackets

Subpacket	Description
<nick>	(Optional) A nickname to use in the group (maybe server assigned). Send multiple as alternatives if first is taken.
<secret>	(Optional) Groups may require a password to join/browse.
<name>	(Optional) Name of group (used in browsing)
<privacy/>	(Optional) Flags the server to hide your real JID and only relay <message> packets.
<id>	(server-only) The conference server assigned JID (only send in result <iq> replies to successful join requests)

Protocol

Joining Conferences

1   Use jabber:iq:browse protocol to find conference rooms (JID-type "conference/*").

2   Client sends `available` <presence> to conference JID. This does not cause you to join!

3   Client sends `get` <iq> query, conference server sends `result` <iq> reply containing required fields

4   Client sends `set` <iq> query with required information.

5   Conference server sends `result` <iq> reply containing your conference nickname and a JID for use in the conference.

6   Conference server will push browse packets indicating group participants

7   Conference server interaction follows normal groupchat protocols

Creating Conferences

1   Client sends `get` <iq> query to conference room JID:

   ■ If conference does not exist and:
      –can be created, server replies with "404 Not Found" error
      –cannot be created, server replies with "405 Not Allowed" error

2 Client sends set <iq> query to conference room JID:

- <secret> sets a password for the conference
- <nick> sets your nickname (you're joining and creating at the same time
- <privacy> sending this empty packet allows privacy mode for the conference
- <name> sets the name for the conference.

Example

```
<iq type='get' id='browse_01' to='conferences.jabber.org'>
  <query xmlns='jabber:iq:browse'/>
</iq>
<iq type='result' id='browse_01' to='requesterJID@jabber.org'>
  <query xmlns='jabber:iq:browse'>
    <conference jid='java@conferences.jabber.org'
              type='public' name='Java Users'>
    <conference jid='baking@conferences.jabber.org'
              type='public' name='Bakers Corner'>
    </user>
  </query>
</iq>
<iq type='get' id='conf_01' to='java@conferences.jabber.org'>
  <query xmlns='jabber:iq:conference'/>
</iq>
<iq type='result' id='conf_01' to='requesterJID@jabber.org'>
  <query xmlns='jabber:iq:conference'>
    <nick/><secret/>
  </query>
</iq>
<presence to='java@conferences.jabber.org'/>
<iq type='set' id='conf_02' to='java@conferences.jabber.org'>
  <query xmlns='jabber:iq:conference'>
    <nick>Smirk</nick>
    <nick>BigSmirk</nick>
    <secret>roompass</secret>
  </query>
</iq>
<iq type='result' id='conf_02' to='requesterJID@jabber.org'>
  <query xmlns='jabber:iq:conference'>
    <nick>Smirk</nick>
    <id>java@conferences.jabber.org/3th3</id>
  </query>
</iq>
```

Notes

- Intended to replace basic groupchat messaging.
- Relies on proposed `jabber:iq:browse` protocols (see reference page).
- Use proposed `jabber:x:conference` standard for inviting others within `<message>` packets (see reference page).
- Addresses are rewritten and messages relayed by the conference server in the same manner as groupchat.
- A Jabber Enhancement Proposal (JEP-0007) is underway to improve and expand the conferencing standard.

Source

Generic Conferencing, Jeremie Miller, www.jabber.org.
Conferencing JIG, David Waite, foundation.jabber.org (JEP-0007).

Gateway Standard [PROPOSED STANDARD]

Type IQ Extension

Namespace jabber:iq:gateway

Summary Creating and resolution of gateway (transport) user addresses

Packets

Packet	Description
<desc>	Free form text describing how to fill out the form.
<prompt>	The prompt for user information
<jid>	The Jabber Identifier to use when communicating with the gateway user

Example

Client requests the form

```
<iq type='get' id='gate_01' to='aim.jabber.org'>
  <query xmlns='jabber:iq:gateway'/>
</iq>
```

Server sends form

```
<iq type='result' id='gate_01' to='requesterJID@jabber.org'>
  <query xmlns='jabber:iq:gateway'>
    <desc>Please enter name of the person you wish to contact</desc>
    <prompt>AOL Screen Name</prompt>
  </query>
</iq>
```

Client sends completed form

```
<iq type='set' id='gate_02' to='aim.jabber.org'>
  <query xmlns='jabber:iq:gateway'>
    <prompt>smirk123</prompt>
  </query>
</iq>
```

Server sends Jabber ID for gateway address

```
<iq type='result' id='gate_02' to='requesterJID@jabber.org'>
  <query xmlns='jabber:iq:gateway'>
    <jid>smirk123@aim.jabber.org</jid>
  </query>
</iq>
```

Notes

- Aids in the process of mapping Jabber addresses to gateway addresses.
- Each transport/gateway uses its own address mapping so clients must be able to negotiate these mappings.

Source

Gateway User Address Creation/Resolution, Jeremie Miller, www.jabber.org.

Last Time Protocol *[PROPOSED STANDARD]*

Type   IQ Extension
Namespace   `jabber:iq:last`
Summary   The "last time" for Jabber entities (uptime, last online, and so forth)

Packet <query>

Attributes	Description
seconds	The number of seconds for last time. (time depends on context)

Last Time Measurement

Packet Recipient	Handled By	Last Time Measures	Description
Server	Server	Uptime	Time server has been available.
User	Server	Offline	Time since user last logged out. Text is last unavailable status message.
Client	Client	Idle	The number of seconds since last user activity (as measured by client)

Example

```
<iq type='get' id='last_01' to='iain@jabber.org'>
  <query xmlns='jabber:iq:last'/>
</iq>
<iq type='result' id='last_01' to='requesterJID@jabber.org'>
  <query xmlns='jabber:iq:last' seconds='9398'>
    Gone fishin'
  </query>
</iq>
```

Notes
None

Source
Last Time Request, Jeremie Miller, www.jabber.org.

Proxy Accept Socket Service [PROPOSED STANDARD]

Type IQ Extension

Namespace `jabber:iq:pass`

Summary Allow client-to-client file transfers (oob) with clients behind firewalls

Packets

Packet	Description
<expire>	The number of seconds for the request to last (sent in set <iq> queries).
<server>	The server IP address (with a port attribute) if a PASS is granted (used in result <iq> queries).
<client>	The client end of the proxy. Shows the client's address using the proxy.
<proxy>	The port the PASS requester should connect to and send data to reach the <client>

Protocol

1. A source client requests a PASS proxy on the PASS server.

2. PASS server sends confirmation to source client and listens for connections on a <server> port until time expires or connection made.

3. On connection by consumer client, the PASS server pushes a PASS update to the source client describing both ends of the PASS proxy.

4. The source client connects to the <proxy> port and sends data.

5. PASS server copies data sent to it on the <proxy> port to the <client> connection.

6. Data copy continues until an error occurs or either connection is closed.

Example

Client requests a pass proxy

```
<iq type='set' id='pass_01' to='pass.jabber.org'>
  <query xmlns='jabber:iq:pass'>
    <expire>600</expire>
  </query>
</iq>
```

Server responds with proxy port to use. Client can use this address in Jabber:x: oob messages.

```
<iq type='result' id='pass_01' to='requesterJID@jabber.org'>
  <query xmlns='jabber:iq:pass'>
    <server port='32342'>32.10.38.10</server>
  </query>
</iq>
```

Server push when someone connects to <server> port

```
<iq type='set' to='requesterJID@jabber.org'>
  <query xmlns='jabber:iq:pass'>
    <client port='3233' xmlns='jabber:iq:pass'>42.200.43.3</client>
    <proxy port='32342'>32.10.38.10</proxy>
  </query>
</iq>
```

Notes

Implementations should be very careful about limiting bandwidth and usage to avoid abuse.

Source

PASS—Proxy Accept Socket Service, Jeremie Miller, foundation.jabber.org (JEP-0003).

Private Storage Protocol [PROPOSED STANDARD]

Type IQ Extension
Namespace `jabber:iq:private`
Summary Server-side storage of arbitrary XML data

Packet <query>

- Store/retrieve arbitrary XML data on the server by sending a `set`/`get` IQ query to a user's account.

- All XML data inside of the enclosed `<query>` packet is stored as is.

- A `<query>` packet with a `jabber:iq:private` namespace indicates private storage.

- A `<query>` packet in any other namespace indicates public storage.

Access permissions

Set (write) permission and get (read) permission depends on the storage type and the user accessing the account (owner or others).

Storage type	owner	other users
public	set/get	get
private	set/get	no access

Example

Store data in "iain" private area

```
<iq type='set' id='store_01' to='iain@jabber.org'>
  <query xmlns='jabber:iq:private'>
    <stuff x='200' y='423'>Window title: Iain Rocks!</stuff>
    <stuff x='100' y='323'>
      <toolbox>Drawing tools</toolbox>
    </stuff>
  </query>
</iq>
```

Store data in "iain" public area

```
<iq type='set' id='store_02' to='iain@jabber.org'>
  <query xmlns='links:awesome:programming'>
    <url>http://www.manning.com/</url>
    <url>http://java.sun.com</url>
  </query>
</iq>
```

Notes

Commonly used to store client preferences on the server.

Source

Generic XML Namespace Storage, Jeremie Miller, www.jabber.org.

XML-RPC Protocol *[PROPOSED STANDARD]*

Type IQ Extension
Namespace `jabber:iq:rpc`
Summary Binding XML-RPC to the Jabber transport

Packets `<query>`

- Any packets conform to standard XML-RPC standards (see http://www.xml-rpc.com/spec).

- Requests are made using `set` IQ queries and results sent in `result` IQ replies.

Example

Call a remote procedure on the rpc server

```
<iq type='set' id='rpc_01' to='rpc@jabber.org'>
  <query xmlns='jabber:iq:rpc'>
    <methodCall>
      <methodName>phonebook.getLastName</methodName>
      <params>
        <value><string>iain</string></value>
      </params>
    </methodCall>
  </query>
</iq>
```

Obtain the result

```
<iq type='result' id='rpc_01' to='requesterJID@jabber.org'>
  <query xmlns='jabber:iq:rpc'>
    <methodResponse>
      <params>
        <value><string>Shigeoka</string></value>
      </params>
    </methodCall>
  </query>
  </query>
</iq>
```

Notes

Provides a transport binding to XML-RPC (www.xml-rpc.com).

Source

Transporting XML-RPC over Jabber, D. J. Adams, foundation.jabber.org (JEP-0009).

Autoupdate Packet

Type X Extension
Namespace jabber:x:autoupdate
Summary Allow applications to notify users of updates

Packet <x>

Attribute	Value	Description
xmlns	jabber:x:autoupdate	The namespace for the packet

Usage
Use within:<message>

Example

```
<message to="recipent@jabber.org">
 <x xmlns='jabber:x:autoupdate'>
   A new version of the Java Jabber Client is available,
   see http://www.manning.com
 </x>
</message>
```

Notes

- The packet contains information about available updates (typically link information).
- See the jabber:iq:autoupdate reference page for full documentation.

Source
Jabber 1.2 Technical White Paper, Peter Saint-Andre, www.jabber.com.

Delay Packet

Type X Extension
Namespace `jabber:x:delay`
Summary Tracks/logs packet delivery delays (typically server annotations of presence packets

Packet <x>

Attributes	Value	Description
from	Jabber ID	The entity (usually the server) indicating the delay.
stamp	YYYYMMDDThh:mm:ss	Time stamp in Jabber time format of delay event
xmlns	jabber:x:delay	The protocol namespace

Usage

Use within: <presence>, <message>, <iq> (all core protocol packets)

Example

```
<presence type='unavailable'>
  <x xmlns='jabber:x:delay' from='server.com' stamp='20020129T19:33:02'>
      Temporarily unreachable.
  </x>
</presence>
```

Notes

<x> text content can contain an optional message indicating the reason for delay.

Source

Delay Logging/Tracking (protocol document), www.jabber.org.

Out of Band Packet

Type X Extension
Namespace jabber:x:oob
Summary Facilitates peer-to-peer file exchange by providing a URI where data is available

Packets

Packet	Description
<url>	The URL for the file.
<desc>	Free-form text description of the file (for display in user agent clients)

Usage
Use within:<message>

Example

```
<message to="recipent@jabber.org">
        <x xmlns='jabber:x:oob'>
          <url>http://www.myserver.com/report2001q1.zip</url>
          <desc>2002 Spring Quarterly Report</desc>
        </x>
        <subject>Give me your thoughts...</subject>
        <body>Please comment on my Q1 report before I submit it</body>
      </message>
```

Notes

- You can send multiple jabber:x:oob packets with the same <message>.
- See also IQ extension jabber:iq:oob.

Source
Out of Band Data (File Transfers) (protocol document), www.jabber.org.

Roster Packet

Type X Extension
Namespace `jabber:x:roster`
Summary Sends roster items to another user (exchange contact information)

Packet <item>

Attribute	Description
jid	The Jabber ID for roster item.
name	A nickname for the item.

Subpackets

Subpacket	Description
<group>	Contains a group name used to organize roster items.
<description>	Free-form text description of the agent (for display in user agent clients)

Usage

Use within: <message>

Example

```
<message to="recipent@jabber.org">
  <x xmlns='jabber:x:roster'>
    <item jid='friendJID@jabber.org'>
      <group>friends</group>
      <group>bowling team</group>
    </item>
    <item jid='bossJID@jabber.org'>
      <group>work</group>
    </item>
  </x>
</message>
```

Notes

See also IQ extension `jabber:iq:roster`.

Source

Embedded Roster Items (protocol document), www.jabber.org.

Conference Packet *[PROPOSED STANDARD]*

Type   X Extension
Namespace   `jabber:x:conference`
Summary   Invite users to join a Jabber Conference (advanced groupchat)

Packet <x>

Attributes	Value	Description
jid	Jabber ID	The Jabber ID for the groupchat group to join
xmlns	jabber:x:conference	The protocol namespace

Usage

Use within: <message>

Example

```
<message to='recipientJID@jabber.org'>
  <body>How about joining us for a discussion on Java!</body>
  <x xmlns='jabber:x:conference' jid='java-group@group.server.com'/>
</message>
```

Notes

- See groupchat message core protocol.
- See `jabber:iq:conference` protocol.

Source

Generic Conferencing, Jeremie Miller, www.jabber.org.

Envelope Packet [PROPOSED STANDARD]

Type X Extension
Namespace `jabber:x:envelope`
Summary A client-side tool for advanced message delivery

Packets

Packet	Description
<to>	The primary recipient of the message
<cc>	Recipients to receive carbon copies of the message
<replyto>	The address to send replies to
<from>	The message sender
<forwardedby>	The user (if any) that forwarded this message on behalf of the sender

All envelope packets have a single `jid` attribute specifying the Jabber ID for each address. Their text content is a freeform text description of the address.

Usage

Use within:`<message>`

Example

```
<message to='dilbert@company.com' from='pointyhairedboss@company.com'>
  <body>You're Fired!</body>
  <x xmlns='jabber:x:envelope'>
    <to jid='dilbert@company.com'>Poor Worker</to>
    <cc jid='humanResources@company.com'>Catbert</cc>
    <replyto jid='humanResources@company.com'/>
    <from jid='pointyhairedboss@company.com'>All Mighty Leader</from>
  </x>
</message>
```

Notes

- The server ignores the content of `jabber:x:envelope` packets.
- Enforcing the meaning of `jabber:x:envelope` is entirely up to clients.

Source

Message Envelope Information Extension, Jeremie Miller, www.jabber.org.

Event Protocol *[PROPOSED STANDARD]*

Type X Extension
Namespace `jabber:x:event`
Summary Messaging event framework for tracking message creation and delivery

Packets

Packet	Event Generator	Description
`<offline>`	recipient server	The packet has been stored offline.
`<delivered>`	recipient client	The packet has been received on the client.
`<displayed>`	recipient client	The message has been displayed to the user.
`<composing>`	recipient client	The reply is being composed by the recipient.
`<id>`	n/a	The message ID to which the event refers.

Events are generated by the recipient server and recipient client.

Usage

Use within:`<message>`

Example

Send message requesting events `offline` and `displayed`

```
<message to='recipientJID@jabber.org' id='msg_01'>
  <body>How's it going?</body>
  <x xmlns='jabber:x:event'><offline/><displayed/></x>
</message>
```

Recipient sends code `displayed` events

```
<message to='senderJID@jabber.org' from='recipientJID@jabber.org'>
  <x xmlns='jabber:x:event'><displayed/><id>msg_01</id></x>
</message>
```

Notes

- Events should only be generated for clients that support it.
- Indicate support for events by sending an empty event packet.

- Composing events are generated as the user types.
- If composed messages are not sent or are idle for too long, send an empty event packet to clear composing status.

Source

Message Events, Jeremie Miller, www.jabber.org.

Expire Packet [PROPOSED STANDARD]

Type X Extension
Namespace `jabber:x:expire`
Summary Indicates an expiry time for messages

Packet <x>

Attributes	Value	Description
seconds	Number of seconds	The time for the message to expire (from time message was received)
xmlns	jabber:x:expire	The protocol namespace

Usage
Use within:`<message>`

Example

```
<message to='recipientJID@jabber.org'>
  <body>How about joining us for a discussion on Java!</body>
  <x xmlns='jabber:x:conference' jid='java-group@group.server.com'/>
  <x xmlns='jabber:x:expire' seconds='3600'/>
</message>
```

Notes

- Servers that support the `expire` protocol will time out messages when storing them offline.
- Servers should decrement the `seconds` attribute when delivering messages that were stored offline.
- Clients that support the `expire` protocol should remove messages after timeout if they have been received but not displayed.

Source
Jabber X Expire (protocol document), www.jabber.org.

Signed Packet [PROPOSED STANDARD]

Type X Extension
Namespace `jabber:x:signed`
Summary A cryptographic signature of a packet's contents

Packet <x>

Attributes	Value	Description
xmlns	jabber:x:signed	The protocol namespace

The text of the <x> tag contains the PGP/GPG signature for the contents of:

- <status> for <presence> packets
- <body> for <message> packets

Usage

Use within:<message>, <presence>

Example

```
<message to='recmipientJID@jabber.org'>
   <body>How about joining us for a discussion on Java!</body>
   <x xmlns='jabber:x:signed'>iOen23snthr2THeETHL3093TH30</x>
</message>
```

Notes

- New namespaces will be used for other encryption algorithms.
- <presence> can only be signed when broadcast (server managed presence updates).

Source

PKI/Crypto support for Messaging and Presence, Thomas Muldowney; Peter Millard; and Jeremie Miller, www.jabber.org.

Encrypted Packet [*PROPOSED STANDARD*]

Type X Extension
Namespace `jabber:x:encrypted`
Summary A cryptographic encryption of a packet's contents

Packet <x>

Attributes	Value	Description
xmlns	jabber:x:encrypted	The protocol namespace

The text of the `<x>` tag contains the PGP/GPG encryption of the contents of:

- `<status>` - for `<presence>` packets
- `<body>` - for `<message>` packets

Usage
Use within:`<message>`, `<presence>`

Example

```
<message to='recipientJID@jabber.org'>
  <body>How about joining us for a discussion on Java!</body>
  <x xmlns='jabber:x:encrypted'>iOen23snthr2THeETHL30eou09309anthNETH0390</x>
</message>
```

Notes

- New namespaces will be used for other encryption algorithms.

- `<presence>` can only be encrypted when targeted (presence updates directly addressed to another user).

Source
PKI/Crypto support for Messaging and Presence, Thomas Muldowney; Peter Millard; and Jeremie Miller, www.jabber.org.

SXPM Whiteboarding Protocol [PROPOSED STANDARD]

Type X Extension
Namespace `jabber:x:sxpm`
Summary A cryptographic encryption of a packet's contents

Packets

Packet	Attributes	Description
\<board\>	height, width	Empty packet describing dimensions of the whiteboard.
\<map\>	char, c	Empty packet with character and color value [hexadecimal RGB (#RRGGBB)].
\<data\>	x, y, width	A compressed data bitmap of a region to paint. Uses \<map\> info.
\<cursor\>	x, y	The position of a cursor (used to show where someone is drawing).

Data is compressed and streamed back and forth within a \<message\> packet or set of packets.

Usage

Use within: \<message\>

Example

A 10x10 board with erase character '#' and a 3x3 region of data.

```
<message to='recipientJID@jabber.org'>
  <x xmlns='jabber:x:sxpm'>
    <board height='10' width='10'/>
    <map char='#'/>
    <map char=' ' c='#FFFFFF'/>
    <map char='a' c='#000000'/>
    <map char='b' c='#FF0000'/>
    <data x='2' y='2' width='3'>5a2b2 </data>
    <cursor x='2' y='2'/>
</message>
```

Notes

- Variation on XPM, http://www-sop.inria.fr/koala/lehors/xpm.html.
- Maximum of 17 colors (transparent and 16 user defined pen colors).
- Compression involves simple run length encoding of \<data\> bitmaps.

- Data contains update information for a part of the whole whiteboard by sending a rectangle of information with a given width and (x, y) offset.

- Mapping a char (typically '#') without a 'c' attribute causes it to erase pixels and set to background color (white).

- Server support usually requires streaming `<message>` packet content.

- Work underway in Jabber Software Foundation (http://foundation.jabber.org) to improve sxpm.

Source

Collaborative Imaging (Whiteboarding via Streaming XPM), Ryan Eaton; Thomas Muldowney; and Jeremie Miller, www.jabber.org.

references

This appendix lists additional sources of information about Jabber, related standards, and other related product and programming sites. The Internet sites listed here are valid as of March 1, 2002.

Bibliography

Alhir, Sinan Si. *UML in a Nutshell*. Sebastapol, CA: O'Reilly & Associates, 2001.

Buschmann, Frank et al. *Pattern-oriented Software Architecture: a System of Patterns*. New York: John Wiley & Sons, 1996.

Gamma, Erich et al. *Design Patterns: Elements of Reusable Object-Oriented Software*. Menlo Park: Addison-Wesley, 1994.

Garfinkle, Simson and Gene Spafford. *Practical Unix & Internet Security*. Sebastapol, CA: O'Reilly & Associates, 1996.

McLaughlin, Brett. *Java & XML*. Sebastapol, CA: O'Reilly & Associates, 2001.

Monson-Haefel, Richard et al. *Java Messege Service*. Sebastapol, CA: O'Reilly & Associates, 2001.

Schneier, Bruce. *Applied Cryptography, Second Edition*. New York: John Wiley & Sons, 1996.

Vint, Danny. *XML Family of Specifications*. Greenwich, CT: Manning Publications, 2002.

Zwicky, Elizabeth D. et al. *Building Internet Firewalls, Second Edition*. Sebastapol, CA: O'Reilly & Associates, 2000.

Online resources

Jabber

Instant Messaging in Java: the Jabber protocols—www.manning.com/shigeoka
Jabber Community—www.jabber.org
Jabber Projects—www.jabberstudio.org
Jabber Inc.—www.jabber.com
Jabber Software Foundation—foundation.jabber.org
Jabber Software Foundation announcement—www.jabber.org?oid=1309
Jabber Powered—www.jabberpowered.org

Related Standards

W3C SOAP Specification—www.w3c.org/2002/ws
Liberty Alliance—www.projectliberty.org
Internet Engineering Task Force (IETF)—www.ietf.org
IETF Instant Messaging and Presence Protocol working group—www.ietf.org/
html.charters/impp-charter.html
World Wide Web Consortium (W3C)—www.w3c.org
W3C XML standards—www.w3c.org/xml
Short Message Service (SMS)—www.wheatstone.net/whatwedo/Portal/
Standards/ sms.htm
RSS (RDF Site Summary)—www.purl.org/rss/1.0/spec
SAX (Simple API for XML parsing)—www.saxproject.org

Messaging Products

Microsoft Messenger—messenger.msn.com
AOL Instant Messenger—www.aim.com
Yahoo! Instant Messenger—messenger.yahoo.com
Yahoo! Mail—mail.yahoo.com
Disney (Go) Instant Messenger—im.go.com
AOL ICQ (an instant messenger)—www.icq.com
IBM MQSeries—www.software.ibm.com/ts/mqseries
Microsoft MSMQ—www.microsoft.com/msmq/
TIBCO Rendezvous—www.tibco.com

Java APIs

JavaMail—java.sun.com/products/javamail/

Sun Microsystems Java website—java.sun.com

Java Jini—www.sun.com/jini

JavaSpaces—www.jini.org

Java Software Development Kit (JDK)—java.sun.com

Java 2 Micro Edition (J2ME)—java.sun.com/j2me

Java 2 Enterprise Edition (J2EE)—java.sun.com/j2ee

Java Message Service (JMS)—java.sun.com/products/jms

Java Authentication and Authorization Service (JAAS)—java.sun.com/
products/jaas

Java XML technologies—java.sun.com/products/xml

Java Management Extensions (JMX)—java.sun.com/products/
JavaManagement

Java Naming and Directory Interface (JNDI)—java.sun.com/products/jndi

Java Transactions (JTA)—java.sun.com/products/jta

Java Remote Method Invocation (RMI)—java.sun.com/products/jdk/rmi

Java Security—java.sun.com/security

Java Secure Socket Extension (JSSE)—java.sun.com/products/jsse

Jabber alternatives

Napster—www.napster.com

Common Object Request Broker Architecture (CORBA)—www.corba.org

Java CORBA (RMI over IIOP)—java.sun.com/products/rmi-iiop

Gnutella (P2P, IM, and file sharing)—www.gnutella.co.uk

JXTA (p2p, IM and file sharing)—www.jxta.org

Aimster (file sharing)—See Madster

Madster (file sharing)—www.madster.com

Miscellaneous

Apache Software Foundation—www.apache.org

Apache Java software (Xerces and Ant)—jakarta.apache.org

JUnit testing software—www.junit.org

Manning Publications—www.manning.com

Sun Microsystems—www.sun.com

Slashdot (news for nerds)—www.slashdot.org

Palm Pilot (Personal Digital Assistant)—www.palm.com

Borland (Jbuilder)—www.borland.com
Microsoft (.NET and Passport)—www.microsoft.com
Buffy the Vampire Slayer (used in example)—www.buffyupn.com
Angel (TV, used in example)—www.thewb.com

index